About This Book

D0580329

Why is this topic important?

Staffing assessments such as online personality measures, background checks, and ability tests are used to evaluate millions of job candidates each year. Despite their widespread use, few people fully understand how assessments actually work and their benefits and limitations. This book provides an in-depth, non-technical discussion of staffing assessments, including why they work, the value they provide for improving the accuracy and efficiency of employee selection decisions, strengths and limitations of different assessments, and how to effectively incorporate assessments into a company's hiring process. It is a valuable guide for anyone who wants to understand and possibly use these powerful but potentially risky tools.

What can you achieve with this book?

The book provides a thorough but easy to understand explanation of what staffing assessments are, different kinds of assessments, how they work, and how to use them. It discusses how to evaluate assessments based on their accuracy, fairness, and business value. Readers will gain a basic understanding of staffing assessment science, along with operational guidelines on how to use assessments to guide hiring decisions.

How is this book organized?

The book begins with an explanation of what assessments are and how they work. It then describes different kinds of assessments, their strengths and limitations, and how to choose the best assessments for different hiring situations. Common criticisms of assessments are discussed, followed by a discussion of "best practices" for integrating assessments into a company's hiring process. Every chapter includes case study examples that illustrate key concepts related to designing and using assessments. A glossary is also provided describing common assessment-related terms.

About Pfeiffer

Pfeiffer serves the professional development and hands-on resource needs of training and human resource practitioners and gives them products to do their jobs better. We deliver proven ideas and solutions from experts in HR development and HR management, and we offer effective and customizable tools to improve workplace performance. From novice to seasoned professional, Pfeiffer is the source you can trust to make yourself and your organization more successful.

Essential Knowledge Pfeiffer produces insightful, practical, and comprehensive materials on topics that matter the most to training and HR professionals. Our Essential Knowledge resources translate the expertise of seasoned professionals into practical, how-to guidance on critical workplace issues and problems. These resources are supported by case studies, worksheets, and job aids and are frequently supplemented with CD-ROMs, websites, and other means of making the content easier to read, understand, and use.

Essential Tools Pfeiffer's Essential Tools resources save time and expense by offering proven, ready-to-use materials—including exercises, activities, games, instruments, and assessments—for use during a training or team-learning event. These resources are frequently offered in looseleaf or CD-ROM format to facilitate copying and customization of the material.

Pfeiffer also recognizes the remarkable power of new technologies in expanding the reach and effectiveness of training. While e-hype has often created whizbang solutions in search of a problem, we are dedicated to bringing convenience and enhancements to proven training solutions. All our e-tools comply with rigorous functionality standards. The most appropriate technology wrapped around essential content yields the perfect solution for today's on-the-go trainers and human resource professionals.

www.pfeiffer.com

Essential resources for training and HR professionals

SOCIETY FOR HUMAN RESOURCE MANAGEMENT

About SHRM

The Society for Human Resource Management (SHRM) is the world's largest association devoted to human resource management. Representing more than 210,000 individual members, the Society's mission is both to serve human resource management professionals and to advance the profession. Founded in 1948, SHRM currently has more than 550 affiliated chapters within the United States and members in more than 100 countries. Visit SHRM Online at *www.shrm.org*.

Pfeiffer™

Hiring Success

THE ART AND SCIENCE OF STAFFING ASSESSMENT AND EMPLOYEE SELECTION

Steven T. Hunt, Ph.D., SPHR

BICENTENNIAL
1807
WILEY
2007
BICENTENNIAL

Published by Pfeiffer
An Imprint of Wiley
989 Market Street, San Francisco, CA 94103-1741   www.pfeiffer.com

Wiley Bicentennial logo: Richard J. Pacifico

For additional copies/bulk purchases of this book in the U.S. please contact 800-274-4434.

Pfeiffer books and products are available through most bookstores. To contact Pfeiffer directly call our Customer Care Department within the U.S. at 800-274-4434, outside the U.S. at 317-572-3985, fax 317-572-4002, or visit www.pfeiffer.com.

Pfeiffer also publishes its books in a variety of electronic formats. Some content that appears in print may not be available in electronic books.

Library of Congress Cataloging-in-Publication Data

Hunt, Steven T., 1965-
    Hiring success: the art and science of staffing assessment and employee selection / Steven T. Hunt.
       p.   cm.
    Includes index.
    ISBN 978-0-7879-9648-2 (pbk.)
     1. Employee selection. 2. Employees—Recruiting.   3. Employment interviewing.
    I. Title.
HF5549.5.S38H86   2007
   658.3′11—dc22

   2007007872

Acquiring Editor: Matthew Davis
Director of Development: Kathleen Dolan Davies
Developmental Editor: Susan Rachmeler
Production Editor: Michael Kay
Editor: Rebecca Taff
Manufacturing Supervisor: Becky Carreño

Printed in the United States of America

Printing   10 9 8 7 6 5 4 3 2 1

CONTENTS

LIST OF SIDEBARS, TABLES, AND FIGURES

SIDEBARS

TABLES

FIGURES

AUTHOR'S FOREWORD

Much of my career has been devoted to helping companies improve hiring decisions. Over the years I have participated in a lot of conversations about why one form of hiring method is better or worse than another. Most of these discussions emphasize the return on investment (ROI) or "bottom line" financial impact of different assessment methods used to screen candidates and hire employees. While relevant to business decisions, these financial discussions often fail to address people's fundamental questions about staffing assessments and employee selection.

The choice to give or deny someone a job is not a trivial decision. Concerns about whether to use staffing assessments frequently go much deeper than "How will it make my company money?" Many people want more information than a bunch of numbers on an ROI spreadsheet before they will be comfortable changing the methods they use to evaluate other people. They want to understand how staffing assessments work and why they are better than other methods used to screen and select job candidates. This book addresses fundamental questions about advantages and limitations of various staffing assessment methods. It explains why these tools, although imperfect, are arguably the most accurate and fair way to make hiring decisions that deny or provide people with career opportunities. It is written with the hope that, if people better understand the strengths and limitations of staffing assessments, they will be able to more effectively use these powerful tools.

This book attempts to strike a balance between the accurate yet complex discussions of assessments found in scientific research journals and the more engaging but somewhat simplistic discussions of assessments found in many practitioner journals and assessment vendor white papers. It is written for the person who wants to understand what staffing assessments are, why and how they work, and how to use them for maximum advantage, but who is also not an assessment expert and does not necessarily wish to become one. The contents of this book reflect countless conversations I have had with clients, colleagues, friends, and family members who fit this description. Without those conversations and the interest and support of the people who participated in them, this book would never have been written. It is to those people to whom this book is dedicated.

Steven Hunt

ACKNOWLEDGMENTS

This book was written with direct and indirect assistance from many people. Space does not allow me to list all the people who deserve recognition for their contributions. A few individuals who definitely deserve recognition by name include Charles Handler, Clay Yonce, and Doug Haaland for their professional comments on early versions of material that led to this book. Kristin Charles provided many useful suggestions and caught a lot of mistakes when she reviewed the book near its completion. The support and input I received from my colleagues at Kronos Talent Management Division (formerly Unicru Inc.) was also a critical factor in making this book a reality. My father, Earl Hunt, provided extensive and valuable suggestions on an initial draft of this book that led to a variety of major improvements. This book reflects more than forty years of ideas, support, and inspiration provided by my father and my mother, Mary Lou Hunt, both of whom have done extensive work applying psychological concepts to help people improve themselves and the world around them. Last, but certainly not least, during the time I spent planning, developing, and writing this book I was supported by my wife, Cynthia, and my children, Robert and Antonio, who delightfully and constantly reminded me of the value of the life side of work-life balance.

Introduction

"People are not your most important asset. The right *people are."*

Jim Collins, *Good to Great*[1]

A DISASTROUS HIRE

On August 29 of 2005, Hurricane Katrina struck land a few miles east of New Orleans. The hurricane and the ensuing floods caused over $70 billion in damage, led to the loss of over 1,500 lives, and permanently changed the social and economic structure of the city of New Orleans. People from both U.S. political parties, the press, and the general public stated that much of the havoc created by Hurricane Katrina could have been prevented had the U.S. Federal Emergency Management Association (FEMA) acted more effectively to deal with the storm. Many of these people attributed FEMA's poor reaction directly to flawed leadership by the director of FEMA, Michael Brown.

Criticism of FEMA's disaster response began almost immediately after the hurricane struck. Michael Brown was soon under attack for both the quality of his leadership decisions and his personal behaviors during the critical time following the hurricane's landfall. On September 12, two weeks after Katrina's landfall, Michael Brown resigned his post as FEMA director. Over the subsequent months he was harshly criticized by members of the U.S. government, the media, and the general public as being personally responsible for failing to prevent much of the devastation wrought by the hurricane. On February 10, 2006, Brown testified to a government panel that "he views himself as a scapegoat 'abandoned' by the ... administration" that hired him into the job.[2]

We will never know for certain how much of the damage caused by Hurricane Katrina could have been reduced had Michael Brown been a more effective leader of FEMA. But based on press reports, many people believe that the original decision to hire Michael Brown as FEMA director turned out to be a mistake. The administration that hired him almost certainly wished it had hired someone else, given the political fallout that resulted from the disaster. Even Michael Brown himself, were he able to relive the choice, might choose to turn down the position. He is now likely to be remembered in history primarily for what he failed to accomplish as FEMA director, regardless of what he may achieve in other areas of his life.

So how did Michael Brown end up in a job that he was clearly not well-equipped to perform? Michael Brown's appointment to FEMA director in January 2003 went largely unnoticed by the media. Like many political appointments, the decision to hire Brown as FEMA director was assumed to be based mainly on personal relationships with the current administration. Brown had relatively little prior experience doing work related to disaster management.[3] There appears to be little evidence to suggest that the staffing process used to hire Michael Brown as FEMA director included any rigorous assessment of whether he actually possessed the skills and capabilities needed to lead a disaster relief organization. Although such rigorous staffing assessments are extensively used within many departments of the federal government, they have traditionally not been used for politically appointed hiring decisions such as this one.

One could argue that Michael Brown's poor performance as FEMA director was not due to his shortcomings as a person, but to the shortcomings of the process used to select him into the job. Most people, including Michael Brown, probably lack the skills needed to manage a large organization like FEMA charged with responding to crisis situations similar to Hurricane Katrina. But the selection process used to hire FEMA directors in 2003 apparently did not use methods that rigorously examined whether job candidates possessed the attributes needed to lead a large disaster relief organization. Rather than uncovering his limitations prior to hiring him as FEMA director, Michael Brown's deficiencies only became apparent after he was given the job.

It is probably impossible to determine the degree to which Michael Brown was responsible for the failure of FEMA to prevent more of the devastation caused by Hurricane Katrina. What certainly did fail was the selection process that hired Brown into a critical and highly challenging job that he was ill-suited to perform. This single bad selection decision derailed Brown's career, tarnished the reputation of the administration that hired him, and led to decisions that failed to protect people living in the path of Hurricane Katrina. Much of this might have been prevented had the hiring decision for FEMA director been based more on staffing assessment data designed to evaluate whether Michael Brown had the skills needed to perform the job, and less on the strength of his personal relationships.

The most important decision companies ever make about employees is the decision to hire them. All other decisions are a consequence of this initial choice. Hiring practices have a massive impact on an organization's financial performance.[4] But the impact of hiring decisions extends far beyond the profitability of organizations. Few things cause more stress than being placed into a job you are ill-suited to perform.[5] Bad staffing decisions disrupt the lives of mis-hired employees and the lives of their supervisors, co-workers, customers, and families. Hiring the wrong people also denies career opportunities to other candidates who should have been hired but were not. Hiring the wrong people not only hurts individuals, it undermines the growth and profitability of companies, and ultimately damages the entire economy.

Much of the trauma and financial loss caused by hiring mistakes could be avoided if companies used more accurate staffing assessments to guide selection decisions. Staffing assessments are methods and tools that systematically collect and analyze information from job candidates for the purpose of predicting their future job performance. Assessments include things such as structured interview guides, personality and ability measures, pre-screening and qualifications questionnaires, knowledge tests, background investigations, and work simulations. When properly designed and used, assessments provide an efficient means to measure and evaluate aspects of a candidate's knowledge, skills, personality, experience, and motivation that influence whether he or she is likely to succeed in a particular job.

Extensive research indicates that appropriate use of well-designed assessments greatly improves the accuracy of hiring decisions. The evaluations made by assessments are far more accurate than judgments made by people relying on less structured techniques for evaluating job candidates.[6] Use of well-designed assessments leads to better staffing decisions, which leads to happier and more productive employees, more effective organizations, and ultimately a generally stronger economy and society.

Given the value of staffing assessments, it is reasonable to ask: "If these tools are so good, why isn't everyone using them?" "Why aren't more companies incorporating assessments into their staffing processes?" "Why don't candidates welcome and encourage the use of assessments as a means to ensure they end up in jobs in which they have the greatest chance of success?" The answers to these sorts of questions are varied and complex.

At a general level, there are perhaps two fundamental reasons why assessments are not more widely accepted and used:

1. **Many staffing professionals, hiring managers, and candidates do not understand how assessment tools work and are unaware or skeptical of their value.**

The science that underlies the design of assessment tools is complicated. For example, a well-designed personality assessment that takes less than sixty minutes to complete can accurately predict how an employee will behave months and even years later.[7] Designing assessments with this sort of predictive power is not a simple task. It is unrealistic to expect people outside of the assessment profession to spend the time required to fully understand the intricacies of staffing assessment research. The technical issues that underlie the design of many assessments are not things that can be effectively explained in a ten-minute slide presentation. Because people do not fully comprehend how assessment tools work, they are reluctant to use something that they do not understand. It is also likely that many hiring managers do not realize how poor their current hiring decisions are, and how much better they would be if they used staffing assessments.

2. Not all assessment tools work well and some may not work at all.

Assessments only work if they are well-built and appropriately used. Sadly, this is not always the case. The history of staffing contains many examples of assessments that seem like they might work, but that actually have little relationship to employee performance. For example, an entire graphology industry has been built based on the belief that people's future job behavior can be predicted by analyzing the style of their handwriting, even though empirical research has found no relationship between handwriting and job performance (except for jobs like calligrapher, for which writing is a core part of the job itself).[8] In addition, even the best assessments will fail to work if they are not used appropriately. Before using an assessment to evaluate candidates for a job, it is critical to ensure that the candidate attributes measured by the assessment truly influence performance in that job. Assessments must also be administered using clearly defined and standardized methods that support consistent collection of assessment data and appropriate interpretation of assessment results.

The presence of poor-quality or inappropriately used assessments hurts the entire field of staffing assessment. When someone has a bad experience with these assessments, their negative feelings tend to generalize to all assessments, not just to assessments that perhaps should never have been used in the first place.

The effects these two issues have on the use of assessments can probably never be completely eliminated. However, their impact may be reduced by providing staffing professionals, hiring managers, and job candidates with better explanations of what assessment are, how they work, and how to differentiate between good and bad assessments. This explanation must be straightforward and should not require learning a lot of technical terms and jargon. At the same time, it should not over-simplify the fundamental reasons why assessment tools work or gloss over issues that can undermine their effectiveness. The explanation should clarify the benefits and potential problems associated with different types of assessments, the value companies can realistically expect from these tools, and what resources must be invested to achieve these returns. Providing this sort of explanation is the objective of this book.

This book discusses how staffing assessments work, what is required to use them effectively, and the strengths, limitations, and value of different assessment methods. The book chapters are built around seven basic topics:

1. **Chapter Two. What Staffing Assessments Measure, Why They Work, and When to Use Them.** This chapter discusses what assessments measure and why these things relate to job performance, and clarifies when staffing assessments should be used to guide hiring decisions. The chapter reviews some basic "truths" about people and work that make it possible for assessments to accurately predict employee behavior.

2. **Chapter Three. Different Types of Staffing Assessments.** This chapter describes and categorizes different types of assessment tools available on the market. The chapter also reviews strengths and weaknesses of different assessment methods.

3. **Chapter Four. Evaluating the Effectiveness of Staffing Assessments.** This chapter discusses validity and other concepts related to the effectiveness of assessment tools. The chapter begins with a fairly detailed description of how assessments actually predict job performance. It then reviews issues related to the two basic requirements that lie at the core of any effective assessment: (a) asking candidates the right questions and (b) effectively interpreting their answers.

4. **Chapter Five. Defining Job Performance and Its Relationship to Assessments.** The purpose of assessments is to hire people who will demonstrate more effective job performance. But defining job performance can be a fairly complex undertaking. This chapter discusses the concept of job performance and its relationship to choosing and deploying assessments.

5. **Chapter Six. Common Criticisms of Staffing Assessments.** This chapter discusses several philosophical, operational, and financial concerns often raised regarding the use of staffing assessments.

6. **Chapter Seven. Choosing Among Different Assessment Methods.** This chapter discusses how to determine what types of assessments are likely to provide the most value to a company based on its hiring needs and staffing processes. Emphasis is placed on developing assessment strategies that effectively balance predictive accuracy with operational costs.

7. **Chapter Eight. Incorporating Staffing Assessments into the Hiring Process.** This chapter reviews general principles and guidelines for integrating assessments into a company's staffing process. Examples of assessment-enabled staffing processes are provided for entry-level and professional jobs.

8. **Chapter Nine. Conclusion.** This brief chapter provides summary thoughts regarding the use of assessments within society as a whole.

9. **Glossary of Common Assessment Terms.** Definitions are provided for a variety of assessment-related terms used in the broader human resources market space surrounding assessments.

The goal of this book is to provide a basic understanding of concepts, advantages, and risks associated with different kinds of staffing assessment tools. The book is intended to give you enough knowledge to effectively evaluate and use assessments to guide hiring decisions. It is written to provide a thorough yet easily understood explanation of what staffing assessments are, why they work, their strengths and limitations, and how to use them.

This book does not provide technical information on how to actually build assessments. That would require detailed explanations of statistical methods and psychological theories that could easily fill several thousand pages of text. This book also does not seek to provide highly technical descriptions of different assessment methods. Interested readers can find this sort of more in-depth information in many of the references provided throughout the book.

WHAT INFORMATION IS THE BOOK BASED ON?

Although this book is not written to be a scientific text, the material in the book is based directly on scientific research. Perhaps no other human resource practice has been subject to as much critical evaluation and empirical research as the use of assessments for employee selection.[9] Thousands of carefully designed studies dating back more than seventy-five years have been conducted to investigate the quality and effectiveness of different forms of assessment tools.[10] Countless practitioner case studies and papers have been written discussing the operational strengths and weaknesses of different assessment methods. The popular press also frequently publishes books critically examining the social utility of different kinds of staffing assessments in which authors argue that different kinds of assessments are either over-used or are not used enough.[11]

The information presented in this book is based on a review of this literature, combined with the author's personal experience designing and deploying assessments that have been used with several million applicants applying for thousands of jobs in hundreds of organizations. References are provided throughout the book so readers can look up some of these research sources first-hand. But these references are only a small fraction of all the articles and books that could be cited.*

One of the challenges to writing this book was balancing the desire to provide a good understanding of what are often very complex topics against the concern of overwhelming the reader with too much information and technical discussion. Three techniques are employed to strike this balance. First, extensive use is made of short examples to illustrate concepts in more concrete terms. Second, concepts that are critical to assessment design such as validity and job analysis are revisited several times throughout the book. Rather than trying to exhaustively review an entire concept in one section, these concepts are discussed from the perspective of different issues associated with the operational design, evaluation, and deployment of assessments. Third, text excerpts called "sidebars" are used to share details and facts about assessment that are relevant but not necessarily critical to understanding how assessments work and how to use them. It is not necessary to read these sidebars to follow the flow of the book, but they do contain information providing greater insight into topics discussed in the book. With that in mind, you are invited to read the following sidebar describing some advantages staffing assessments provide for both hiring organizations and job seekers.

HOW ASSESSMENTS CAN BE THE DIFFERENCE BETWEEN STAFFING SUCCESS AND FAILURE

Assessments help place people in jobs in which they will succeed. They also help prevent people from being put into jobs in which they are likely to fail. The following stories illustrate ways that assessments assist both

*Readers who wish to find additional information about the design and use of assessments may also want to visit online sources such as the Society for Industrial and Organizational Psychology (www.siop.org), the Society for Human Resource Management (www.shrm.org), the American Psychological Association (www.apa.org), and the International Test Commission (www.intestcom.org). Additional information about the use of assessments can also be found at sites such as Electronic Recruiting Exchange (www.ere.net), Rocket-Hire (www.rocket-hire.com), and Workforce Management (www.workforce.com).

businesses and individuals through improving the accuracy of hiring decisions. As illustrated in these semi-fictional stories, the use of assessments can often make the difference between staffing success and staffing failure.

A Story of Staffing Failure

Ian Swanson was promoted in April to a senior project manager role in a retail company in Columbus, Ohio. As part of the promotion, Ian was asked to lead a multi-million-dollar project to improve the company's supply chain process. Ian realized that he would need an administrative assistant to handle the logistical details required to successfully coordinate this project. The administrative assistant would need to be adept at using Microsoft Project and Outlook, as these were the primary tools being used for project management, scheduling, and communication.

Ian contacted a recruiter in his company and described the administrative assistant position and its requirements. The recruiter posted the job on several online career sites. The posting included an e-mail address so applicants could send their resumes directly to Ian, but did not utilize any form of online assessment to filter candidates. The job posting was placed on the Internet on May 3. By May 10 Ian had received over one hundred e-mail messages from job applicants. Ian had to scroll through several applicant e-mails simply to find regular work messages from his co-workers. On May 16 Ian asked the recruiter to take down the posting to stop what had become an overwhelming flow of applicants.

Most of the applicant e-mails contained attachments with resumes, cover letters, work samples, and letters of reference. Reviewing the e-mails required opening each e-mail message and the attached documents. It took Ian about two minutes to review each applicant. Given that he had received over one hundred applications, Ian estimated it would take over three hours to simply sort through the applicants.

Ian was also having little luck finding applicants with the mix of administrative experience and knowledge of Microsoft Project and Outlook that he required. Many applications were from people with a project management background instead of administrative assistants. While these people had the technical knowledge needed for the job, they were likely to struggle with the fundamental administrative nature of the position. It seemed unlikely that these people would be satisfied with the salary and long-term career opportunities offered by the job. Applicants who had an administrative background usually had relatively little technical skill with Project and Outlook beyond the most basic experience. When Ian conducted follow-up phone calls with a few applicants whose resumes said they were "highly skilled" with Microsoft Project, he discovered that their definition of highly skilled was more along the lines of what he would call a "passing familiarity." Ian was also frustrated to find that many applicants were from cities hundreds of miles away from Columbus. This posed another problem since the position did not include any budget for relocation.

One e-mail message buried deep in Ian's in-box was from an applicant who had the specific mix of administrative talent and software skills Ian was seeking. For the last three years Mary Jackson had served as administrative coordinator for a large information technology project in a manufacturing company in a suburb of Columbus. To fulfill her role on this project, Mary completed several courses covering advanced applications of Microsoft Project and Outlook. She then demonstrated her ability to use these tools through her work on the job. Mary was recognized in the company for her initiative, positive attitude, and strong organizational and technical skills. However, due to an economic downturn in the manufacturing sector, Mary's job was eliminated in a downsizing.

Mary did not want to leave the Columbus area and was actively searching for local career opportunities on the Internet. She was excited when she saw Ian's job posting and quickly submitted her resume. Unfortunately, Ian never opened Mary's e-mail since it was number 112 in a list of almost 150 messages. Mary never heard any response to her application. She was surprised by this, given the clear match between the job posting and her skills. In talking with her professional colleagues, she commented that the lack of response to her application was because Ian's company is "probably the kind of large, faceless bureaucracy that I wouldn't want to work at anyway."

Ian ended up hiring applicant number 65 from the list of one hundred plus e-mail applications he received. This applicant had a strong administrative background but relatively weak technical skills. Ian was concerned about this and spent almost two hours having an in-depth discussion with the applicant about the job and its demands. Ian did not follow any clear process in this interview, but sought to use his intuition to evaluate whether the applicant "felt right." The applicant expressed enthusiasm about the position and assured Ian that he was highly motivated and could quickly master Microsoft Project and Outlook. He and Ian also found out that they knew many of the same people from a previous company. After the interview, Ian felt he knew the applicant pretty well and thought he had the right attitude to succeed in the position.

The applicant accepted Ian's job offer. But despite two weeks of software training and considerable coaching by Ian, the new assistant was unable to master either Project or Outlook. He ended up quitting less than three months after being hired because the job was "too technical." After this failure, Ian gave up on his efforts to find an administrative assistant and started to wonder whether he should start looking for another job himself.

A Story of Staffing Success

Maggie Anderson is director of training for a firm in Denver that makes software to manage employee records data. Her role is to ensure that the company's clients receive effective training on how to use the software. The people providing this training need a unique blend of knowledge about employee records management, strong technical savvy, and excellent presentation skills. In addition, they must be willing to travel extensively.

On September 22, Maggie put in a requisition to hire a new trainer. A recruiter in her company met with her on September 29 and took her through a structured job analysis process to define the experiences, capabilities, and interests candidates needed to succeed in the job. The recruiter used this information to configure a series of online assessments that would be automatically given to candidates who applied for the job. The recruiter also configured the company's online staffing system to send Maggie an e-mail alerting her to any candidates who met or exceeded the minimum criteria she had outlined as critical for the job. The recruiter then used the system to post the job on a range of career sites and job boards that were likely to be frequented by potentially qualified applicants.

The job was posted on Friday, October 3. By October 10 over fifty people had applied to the job, none of whom had the unique requirements

Maggie was seeking. The company's online staffing system automatically reviewed the applicants' qualifications and generated an electronic response thanking them for their interest in the position. By doing this, the system protected Maggie from spending time reviewing and communicating with unqualified applicants.

At the same time that Maggie was looking for a new trainer, Roy Tarnehan was working in the employee records department of a large corporation in California. Although he was recognized in the company as a technical expert in the area of employee records management, he felt his career was going nowhere. He was bored. He liked the analytical aspects of his job and enjoyed working with the technology used to manage employee records, but wanted to spend more time interacting directly with people. Roy also wanted more variety in his life. He had been with the same company for over five years in the city where he grew up, and he was restless to see more of the country.

Roy arrived home late on Friday, October 10. His day at the office had been particularly frustrating, and on a whim he decided to surf the Internet for alternative job opportunities that might give him the chance to travel. He typed "employee records management, job opportunities, and travel" into an Internet search engine. The result was a list of links to a variety of sites, including one of the national job boards containing Maggie Anderson's job posting. Roy was intrigued by the job description contained in Maggie's job posting and decided to click on the button that said "apply now."

The application process took about twenty-five minutes. It required Roy to answer a series of multiple-choice questions about his experiences, interests, and career expectations. All the questions were easy to understand and struck Roy as being relevant to the kind of work he did. The last thing Roy was asked to do was upload an electronic copy of his resume. After completing the application, Roy clicked on the button "submit application," turned off his computer, and headed off for dinner.

When Maggie started work on Monday morning, October 13, she was pleased to see an e-mail in her in-box with the heading "potentially qualified applicant for your Trainer job posting." The e-mail informed Maggie that a candidate named Roy Tarnehan had applied for the Trainer job posting, and that he appeared to meet all the requirements for the position but one. The e-mail also provided a link to a site containing more information about Mr. Tarnehan. Upon reviewing Roy's resume and application, Maggie felt he was a high-potential candidate except for one concern: he had never actually done work as a trainer. She sent Roy an e-mail asking when they might talk more about his interest in the job.

Roy quickly responded to Maggie's e-mail and they set up a phone call. After interviewing Roy over the phone, Maggie felt he had the knowledge to be a good trainer and was confident that his career goals fit the opportunities provided by the position. But she was concerned about how he would perform when placed in front of a class, because he had never actually worked as a trainer. When Maggie expressed this concern to her recruiter, the recruiter suggested that Maggie invite Roy to complete an online assessment that measured various personality and ability traits associated with different job competencies. Maggie asked Roy to complete this assessment as the next step in the staffing process. Roy accessed the assessment over the Internet from his home computer that evening and completed it in about sixty minutes. When Maggie received the results of the assessment, she was pleased to see that, although Roy had never actually been a trainer, his underlying personality, ability, and motives where similar to those of many high-performing trainers. In some ways he appeared to be a person who was "born to train," but who had never had the opportunity to fully leverage his potential in this area.

After reviewing Roy's assessment results, Maggie arranged to have Roy fly out for an on-site visit and series of interviews. Maggie's company used a technique called "behavioral interviewing" whereby candidates are asked a series of pre-defined questions to determine whether previous things they have done align with the types of things they will need to do on the job. During the interview process, Maggie learned that although Roy had never done training as part of his work, he had spent several years coaching a chess team at the local high school, where he had demonstrated an ability to explain complex concepts in an engaging manner. Although this example did not relate directly to the actual job, the general behaviors Roy displayed as a coach aligned well with the behaviors that some of Maggie's best trainers displayed when working with clients.

A few days after Roy's on-site interviews, Maggie extended him an employment offer to become a trainer. Roy accepted the position and agreed to begin work four weeks later. Thanks to staffing assessment technology, two people living thousands of miles apart with absolutely no awareness of each other in September were able to join forces to support each others' career goals and business objectives by November. The use of more sophisticated online assessment tools helped Maggie see beyond what Roy "had done" based on his past experiences and hire him based on what he "could do" based on his underlying talents, interests, and potential.

ASSESSMENTS: THE DIFFERENCE BETWEEN SUCCESS AND FAILURE

Figures 1.1, 1.2, and 1.3 provide graphical depictions of three different staffing processes, including the processes used by Ian and Maggie that were discussed in the previous sidebar. Each figure depicts the staffing process as a funnel. The individuals in the figures represent applicants. Applicants who possess the characteristics required to succeed in the job have stars on their bellies. The width at the top of the funnel indicates how many applicants are initially included in the staffing process. The narrowing of the funnel reflects how assessments are used to systematically remove less qualified candidates from the hiring process.

Figure 1.1 depicts how staffing processes often looked before the advent of Internet staffing technology. In those days, many companies had no easy way to contact potential applicants. Companies frequently considered only a very small number of people for a given job posting. These people tended to be individuals who had personal relationships with other employees in the company, or people who lived close to the company and happened to apply for a job around the same time a position opened. The main problem with this approach is that it fails to include a large number of applicants who possess the characteristics needed to succeed in the job. You never hire the person who does not apply, no matter how qualified he or she is.

Figure 1.2 depicts the staffing situation in the story about Ian. Ian had the benefit of Internet technology to help him find applicants, but he did not have

Figure 1.1
Staffing Process Without Internet Staffing Technology or Assessments

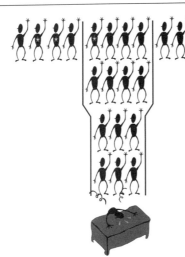

Very few applicants are included in the staffing process

Hiring based on looking at a very limited number of applicants

Figure 1.2
Staffing Process with Internet Staffing Technology But Without Assessments

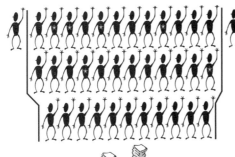

Large number of applicants are included, but not filtered

Hiring managers are overwhelmed by number of candidates

Hiring based on comparing between applicants, all of whom may be unqualified

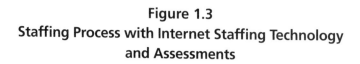

Figure 1.3
Staffing Process with Internet Staffing Technology and Assessments

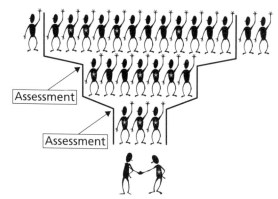

Large number of applicants considered

Hiring managers only see "best of the best"

Hiring based on clear standards

an effective method for sorting through applicants. As a result, Ian was overwhelmed with unqualified applicants. In this scenario, finding good candidates has more to do with when applicants apply, as opposed to their actual qualifications. Rather than hiring the applicants with the best potential for success, the hiring manager simply sorts through long lists of applicants until he or she finds someone who seems "good enough."

Figure 1.3 illustrates the process used in the story about Maggie. Maggie had the benefit of Internet staffing technology to generate applicants, as well as the value of assessments to systematically screen and sort applicants based on their qualifications and capabilities. In this process, the hiring manager only sees candidates with the greatest potential based on assessment data collected earlier in the staffing process. The hiring manager is not the only one who benefits from the process depicted in Figure 1.3. Qualified applicants also benefit, as they are more likely to be recognized as being a good fit for the position, regardless of the order in which they happen to apply for the job.

Notes

1. Collins., J. (2001). *Good to great: Why some companies make the leap ... and others don't.* New York: HarperCollins.
2. CNN. Brown says he's been made Katrina scapegoat. [www.cnn.com/2006/POLITICS/02/10/katrina.brown/index.html]. February 13, 2006.

3. Fonda, D., & Healy, R. How reliable is Brown's resume? [www.time.com/time/nation/article/0,8599,1103003,00.html]. September 8, 2005.

4. Fitz-Enz, J. (2002). *How to measure human resource management*. New York: McGraw-Hill.

5. Tait, M., Padgett, M.Y., & Baldwin, T.T. (1989). Job and life satisfaction: A Reevaluation of the strength of the relationship and gender effects as a function of the date of the study. *Journal of Applied Psychology, 74,* 502–507.

6. Schmidt, F.L., & Hunter, J.E. (1998). The validity and utility of selection methods in personnel psychology: Practical and theoretical implications of 85 years of research findings. *Psychological Bulletin, 124,* 262–274.
   Westen, D., & Weinberger, J. (2004). When clinical description becomes statistical prediction. *American Psychologist,* pp. 595–613.

7. Helmreich, R.L., Sawin, L.L., & Carsrud, A.L. (1986). The honeymoon effect in job performance: Temporal increases in the predictive power of achievement motivation. *Journal of Applied Psychology, 71,* 185–188.

8. Klimoski, R.J., & Rafaeli, A. (1983). Inferring personal qualities through handwriting analysis. *Journal of Occupational Psychology, 56,* 191–202.

9. Austin, J.T., & Villanova, P. (1992). The criterion problem: 1917–1992. *Journal of Applied Psychology, 77,* 836–874.

10. Schmidt, F.L., Ones, D.S., & Hunter, J.E. (1992). Personnel selection. *Annual Review of Psychology, 43,* 627–670.

11. For example, Gould, S.J. (1983). *The mismeasure of man.* New York: Basic Books.
    Herrnstein, R.J., & Murray, C. (1994). *The bell curve: Intelligence and class structure in American life.* New York: The Free Press.
    Paul, A.M. (2004). *The cult of personality.* New York: The Free Press.

What Staffing Assessments Measure, Why They Work, and When to Use Them

When you are deciding whether to offer someone a job, the main question you need to answer is "If I hire this person is he going to do what I want him to do?" In other words, will the person display productive job behaviors and avoid counterproductive behaviors after he is hired. Another important question to consider is "If I hire this person will she remain in the job long enough to justify the costs associated with recruiting and training her?" It is quite costly to hire people only to have them quit shortly after starting the job. Assessments help answer both questions by gathering data from candidates that can be used to accurately predict their future job performance and tenure.

This chapter explains why assessments are such useful tools for helping to make selection decisions. This is done by answering three basic questions:

1. What are the things that assessments actually measure?

2. Why are assessments able to predict job performance and retention?

3. When is it useful to use staffing assessments to guide hiring decisions?

The answers to these questions address some general truths about job performance, candidates, employees, and staffing decisions, and how these things interact to influence a company's profitability. This information provides a foundation for some of the more involved discussions of assessment methods found later in this book.

WHAT DO ASSESSMENTS MEASURE?

Assessments collect data from candidates that can be used to predict their future job performance. They do this by measuring three basic kinds of information: (1) What candidates *have done* in the past based on their previous work experience, job-relevant activities, accomplishments, and education, (2) What candidates *could do* based on their underlying potential and aptitude for different tasks and activities, and (3) What candidates *want to do* in the future based on their work and non-work goals, preferences, and interests. Figure 2.1 indicates how some common staffing assessments relate to these three kinds of information. (Additional information about the design and nature of these assessments is provided in Chapter Three.)

Assessments That Measure What Candidates Have Done

The most common staffing assessments focus on measuring people's past behavior, experiences, and accomplishments. These include interview questions that ask

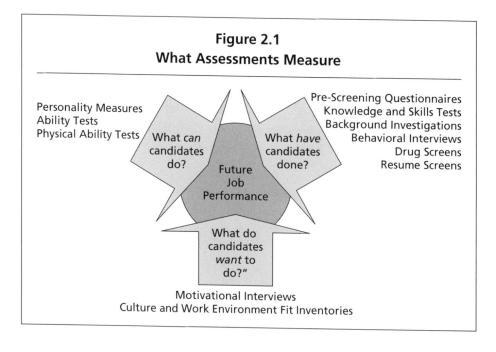

Figure 2.1
What Assessments Measure

Personality Measures
Ability Tests
Physical Ability Tests

What *can* candidates do?

Future Job Performance

What *have* candidates done?

Pre-Screening Questionnaires
Knowledge and Skills Tests
Background Investigations
Behavioral Interviews
Drug Screens
Resume Screens

What do candidates *want* to do?"

Motivational Interviews
Culture and Work Environment Fit Inventories

candidates about past experiences, such as "Tell me about a time when you performed a task similar to ones you will encounter in this job," resume review tools that evaluate candidates based on past work history and experience listed on their resumes, knowledge tests measuring things candidates have learned in the past, and pre-screening questionnaires that ask candidates about prior job-relevant experiences, educational achievements, skills, and credentials.

Assessments that focus on measuring what people have done are based on the principle that the "best predictor of future behavior is past behavior in similar circumstances."[1] This principle is relevant when you are hiring someone to do a job similar to what he or she may have done in the past. But it is less useful when you are hiring people to perform jobs they have never done before, or if you plan to give people all the training they will need to perform the job. Such hiring situations are common when evaluating candidates for promotions, staffing new or rare job types, or hiring employees for entry-level positions.[2] For example, deciding whether to promote someone to a management position requires determining whether he or she can handle the demands associated with being responsible for the work of other people. But unless the person has previously been a manager, he or she may not have had responsibility for managing other people's performance. If companies insisted on only promoting people to management who already had prior management experience, then there would be no way to create new managers. Similar issues occur when hiring people out of school who have little actual job experience, or hiring people to work in an industry that they have never worked in before. What is needed in these situations are assessments that allow companies to predict whether someone can perform tasks or work in environments they have never previously encountered. This brings us to the next category of assessments.

Assessments That Measure What Candidates Can Do

These assessments measure enduring characteristics associated with a candidate's underlying personality and ability.[3] Many of the candidate attributes measured by these assessments are things that are "hard wired" into our physiological makeup (see sidebar "The Genetic Components of Job Performance"). For example, some people have an underlying physical disposition toward risk taking, while other people have a natural disposition to be more cautious.[4] Assessments that focus on measuring what candidates "can do" are able to accurately evaluate things like risk taking and other basic traits that determine who we are in terms of our fundamental psychological characteristics.

When properly designed, assessments that measure what candidates "can do" are among the most valuable tools for predicting job performance.[5] These assessments are also the most difficult to develop. First, they often require measuring intangible attributes that candidates themselves may not even be fully aware of. For example, many people are unable to accurately describe their own personalities and ability levels.[6] Even the most narcissistic individual may see him- or herself as being humble and compassionate. Second, many of the attributes these assessments measure are things that candidates may purposefully try to hide in order to improve their chances of getting a job offer.[7] For example, candidates are unlikely to openly admit to lacking intelligence or being emotionally unstable.[8] Third, assessments may contain questions about things that seem relevant to the job, but that upon closer empirical investigation do not actually predict performance, or predict it in a way you might not expect. No matter how much theoretical rigor is put into the design of an assessment, a significant portion of assessment questions simply do not work as expected. The lesson to be learned is that, just because an assessment is supposed to predict something is no assurance that it does. You need to check the data. For all of these reasons, you need to be very careful when exploring the use of these kinds of assessments. This topic is discussed in much more detail in Chapter Four.

THE GENETIC COMPONENTS OF JOB PERFORMANCE

Whether we like it or not, how we act, think, and feel about our jobs is heavily influenced by genes we inherited from our parents.[9] Even job satisfaction, an attribute that might be expected to depend entirely on a person's current work situation, has been found to be largely predicted by genetics.[10] Some people were simply born to like most of their jobs, while others were born to have a more negative attitude toward work. Similar examples could be provided for a variety of other dispositions and behaviors related to genetically influence personality and ability traits.

While our genetically influenced psychological traits do not fully determine what we can or cannot do with our lives, we must learn to leverage, manage, or compensate for them to be effective in our jobs. People with certain kinds of ability and personality traits find it easier to succeed in certain jobs. People without these traits may have to work much harder to succeed in these same jobs. For example, people who are more outgoing as opposed to shy tend to do better in sales jobs that require a lot of social interaction.[11] This does not mean that shy people are not able to engage others in conversation. However, many shy people find extensive social activity to be tiring and even stressful. As a result, they tend to have more difficulty performing sales jobs that require a lot of social interaction.

Many staffing assessments focus on measuring genetically influenced ability and personality traits that influence various job-relevant behaviors. One thing that often makes people uncomfortable about these assessments is that the candidate attributes they measure are intangible. We can see physical attributes like height and weight. We cannot look at someone and readily see psychological attributes such as self-esteem, extroversion, emotional stability, or reasoning ability. But just because we cannot easily see these attributes does not mean they do not exist. Years of research have shown that people differ on psychological attributes in the same way they differ on physical attributes like strength and height. These differences are stable over time and exert a very real influence on our behaviors. While people are not "held captive" by their psychological makeup, we do have to learn to either capitalize on or compensate for our natural psychological traits in order to succeed in different jobs. Just as a short person may have to find ways to compensate for a lack of height when playing basketball, so must a shy person find ways to compensate for his or her introverted tendencies to succeed at sales jobs that require a lot of socially outgoing behavior. Also, just as athletes tend to do best in sports that complement their natural physical traits (for example, most basketball players are tall), job candidates tend to do best in jobs that complement their natural psychological traits and the behavioral habits these traits create (for example, most sales people are extroverted).

Staffing assessments have been created to measure thousands of different psychological attributes that influence performance in various jobs. These attributes range from very broad traits like "intelligence" to very specific skills such as the ability to distinguish between different words when listening to an unfamiliar, foreign language.*[12] Most of these attributes fall into a few broad categories.[13] In other words, although every person is different, we differ along the same common dimensions. An analogy might be drawn to the differences found between paintings in a museum. While a museum might contain thousands of unique paintings, all of the paintings can be described using mixtures of the same three basic primary colors. So it is with people. We are all different, but our differences tend to fall along the same basic dimensions of personality and ability. One of the most widely used set of these dimensions are the "Big 5" personality traits of conscientiousness, openness to experience, neuroticism, extroversion, and agreeableness.[14] Many of the personality differences found across people can be described using facets and combinations of these five general traits. Although more detailed traits beyond the Big 5 are needed to provide highly accurate and subtle descriptions of personality, the discovery of fundamental dimensions such as the Big 5 has allowed for rapid development of staffing assessment instruments that can be applied across a range of jobs and industries. Similar taxonomies have been developed that describe how people differ in their ability to solve problems and process information.

Somewhat similar to how an artist mixes primary colors to achieve just the right hue for a specific painting, assessment scientists draw on taxonomies that describe basic differences in people's personality and ability that influence job performance. Many of these taxonomies are based in part on genetically influenced attributes that underlie our basic psychological makeup as human beings. Ongoing research investigating the components of these taxonomies has made it possible to efficiently configure assessments that predict how well candidates' natural talents and aptitudes align with the demands associated with different kinds of jobs.

Assessments That Measure What Candidates Want to Do

These assessments measure motives, interests, and goals related to work, for example, interviews that ask candidates "Where do you want to be in five years?"

*This particular attribute predicts performance in jobs that require learning new languages.

or surveys that ask people what kind of tasks they would enjoy doing at work. These types of assessments are often used to predict organizational commitment, retention, and culture fit.[15]

Research indicates that assessments focusing on what people want to do are usually less valuable for predicting job performance, compared with assessments that focus on measuring what people have done or can do. People's interests and goals often show very weak relationships to their actual job performance.[16] Just because you want to do something does not mean you will be good at it. Conversely, most of us have had to do things at work that we did not necessarily want to do. We are often able to do these things effectively, even if we do not enjoy them, at least for a limited amount of time.

Another potential problem with assessments focusing on goals is that many job applicants, particularly those earlier in their careers, have not developed a clear understanding of their employment goals. In other words, many applicants simply do not know what they want to do. Not surprisingly, this can place a limit on the value of assessment tools that focus on asking people about career aspirations. Nevertheless, there are still many situations in which these kinds of assessment tools can provide significant value for predicting job success.

At a fundamental level, all assessments work by measuring one or more of the three categories of what candidates have done, can do, or want to do. The categories also tend to overlap and influence one another. What you can do influences what you want to do, which influences what you have done, which in turn influences what you can do, and so on. No assessment exclusively measures one category. In fact, many of the more effective assessment methods strive to systematically measure candidate attributes across all three categories.

WHY DO ASSESSMENTS WORK?

Companies that use staffing assessments are assuming that information collected from candidates during the application process can be used to accurately predict what these candidates will do weeks, months, or years after they are hired. There are a lot of reasons to doubt this assumption. The influence that the work environment has on employee performance, error in the measurement methods used by assessments, and people's ability to actively control their behavior in response to different situations could undermine the ability of assessments to predict future performance. Accurately predicting employee behavior based on the limited information companies are able to collect from applicants during the hiring process seems likely to be a difficult exercise at best. Nevertheless, extensive research has shown that assessments do predict job performance.[17]

The main reason assessments work is because the behavior of people is remarkably consistent over time. This is true regardless of the jobs they hold and the environments they work in.[18] As self-empowered individuals, we may think that each day we make up our minds about how we want to behave. We might believe that at any given time we could act differently if we really wanted to. However, years of psychological research, as well as countless failed diets, indicate that people do not have as much control over their behavior as they may think or wish. Assessments are able to predict people's behavior because people act in very reliable and predictable ways across both time and situations, whether they want to or not. The consistency of people's behavior over time makes it possible to gather assessment data from candidates during the staffing process that can reliably predict their job performance months or even years after they are hired.

One of the main reasons people act so consistently over time is because much of our behavior is influenced by our basic psychological makeup (see earlier side-bar "The Genetic Components of Job Performance"). Many of the core values, beliefs, and motives that drive our behavior are relatively fixed by the time we reach young adulthood.[19] Although people can and do change over time, the changes tend to be gradual and predictable.[20] They unfold over years, as opposed to occurring in a sudden or unpredictable fashion. For example, if you were loud and boisterous as a child, then you are likely be loud and boisterous as an adult, particularly when compared to other adults who were quiet and reserved when they were children. You may have become more laid back as you have grown older, but this probably occurred gradually over years and not all at once. Even our ability to acquire new knowledge and skills is heavily influenced by the kinds of skills and knowledge we previously acquired. For example, people who have learned many foreign languages in the past are likely to find it easier to learn a new language than individuals who are mono-lingual.[21] In sum, what you are likely to do in the future is largely determined by the biology you were born with and the things you have already done.

The accuracy of staffing assessments does not mean that people are unable to change their behaviors at all. The same research that shows that employee job performance is heavily influenced by stable psychological characteristics that lie outside of the control of companies, and perhaps even the employees themselves, also shows that much of job performance is a result of conscious choices made by employees in response to the work environment companies provide. At best, perhaps 50 percent of job performance can be predicted using staffing assessments. This suggests that 50 percent or more of employee performance depends on things that occur after the hiring decision has been made. How managers treat employees, how the work environment is structured, and how employees choose to react to challenges and opportunities they encounter on the job all have considerable influence on employee performance and retention.

While the use of staffing assessments can greatly improve employee performance, assessments only get at part of the total performance equation. Job performance does not just depend on who you hire. It also depends on how you treat people after they are hired and how employees choose to react to the challenges and opportunities they encounter once on the job. Management practices have a tremendous influence on employee performance and retention. But they work best when you start by hiring people whose attributes already predispose them toward successful job performance.

WHEN IS IT USEFUL TO USE STAFFING ASSESSMENTS?

You should use staffing assessments whenever the value they provide by increasing the accuracy of hiring decisions outweighs the operational costs associated with using them. This might seem simple enough. However, calculating the value of staffing assessments can be fairly complex. This is because it varies based on interactions among three different factors: assessment validity, performance variance, and candidate pools.

Assessment Validity

Validity refers to how well an assessment actually predicts employee job performance and tenure. Assessments that may be very valid for predicting performance in some jobs may show no validity for predicting performance in other jobs. For example, a test measuring how well a person reads Spanish may be very valid when used to predict performance in jobs that require reading Spanish, but may have no validity when used to predict performance in jobs that require reading Chinese.

The most common way to describe assessment validity involves using a statistical variable called a "validity coefficient." Validity coefficients range from 0 to 1**. A validity coefficient of 0 means an assessment does not show any relationship to actual job performance. Such assessments are said to be invalid or lack validity. There is no value in using an invalid assessment.

A validity coefficient of 1 means that an assessment perfectly predicts job performance. No assessment is perfect. It is unrealistic to expect validity coefficients to approach 1. Most well-designed assessments have validity coefficients between .1 and .4. Assessments with validity coefficients in this range are usually valuable for guiding hiring decisions. But their value will also depend on aspects of the next two parameters: the performance variance of the job and the characteristics of the candidate pool.

Performance Variance

This indicates the difference in financial value associated with high- versus low-performing employees. It can be thought of as the difference between the "value of a great hire" and the "cost of a bad hire." Performance variance calls attention to the fact that some hires are more important than others. For example, staffing decisions made for senior executive positions are likely to have a greater impact on the financial performance of a company than staffing decisions made for administrative assistant positions. The higher the performance variance in a job, the more value there is in hiring the best possible candidates for that job.

In jobs with high performance variance, top-performing employees generate substantially more profit for the company than low-performing employees. For example, the revenue generated by high-performing sales employees can be several times the revenue generated by average-sales employees. In jobs with low performance variance, there is little difference between high- versus low-performing employees. These tend to be relatively simple jobs that involve routine tasks that are easy for most people to learn and master. Consider a job like "parking lot attendant" where a person's job is to sit in a booth and collect parking coupons all day. In this job there might be little difference in the revenue generated by average employees

**Technically, validity coefficients range from −1 to 1. A negative validity coefficient means that candidates scoring higher on the assessment tend to do worse on the job. When this occurs, companies usually reverse the scoring of the assessment so that high scores become low scores and vice verse (provided such a change makes theoretical sense). This has the effect of changing the validity coefficient from negative to positive. Chapter Four contains a more detailed discussion of validity coefficients.

versus high-performing employees because there is not much one employee can do that will make him or her more effective than another employee.

Performance variance is a function of both the value of good performance and the cost of bad performance. There are many jobs for which performance variance depends far more on the costs associated with counterproductive behavior than the value of productive behavior. For example, while there may not be much difference in the revenue generated by high-performing versus average-performing parking lot attendants, there may be substantial cost differences between average- and low-performing parking attendants if low-performing employees engage in highly counterproductive acts such as stealing parking fees collected from customers.

The nature of a job's performance variance influences the value of different kinds of assessments. Many assessments focus on predicting positive performance variance in order to help companies select the best candidates. For example, some personality measures can help identify candidates who have attributes associated with being an exceptional sales person. Other assessments are designed to help companies avoid hiring mistakes by screening out unqualified candidates, for example, pre-screening questionnaires that evaluate whether candidates possess specific certifications or educational credentials required for certain jobs. There are also assessments designed to reduce the risk of making what I call "catastrophic hiring mistakes." These assessments include background checks, drug screens, and integrity tests that identify candidates who are likely to engage in extremely counterproductive behaviors such as stealing, breaking machinery, or fighting with co-workers.

Assessments are most valuable when they are used to select candidates for jobs that have high levels of performance variance. In jobs with low performance variance, it does not matter too much which candidates are hired, because every employee basically performs at the same level. If all employees in a job perform at the same level, regardless of who they are, then there may be little value in using assessments to help with choosing among candidates.

Assessments can provide substantial value for jobs with low performance variance if companies hire a lot of employees into these jobs. This is often the case for entry-level jobs such as call center employees or retail clerks. For example, there may be little difference in financial value associated with hiring an average- versus high-performing grocery cashier in terms of a single hire. But if a company hires hundreds of cashiers each year, then small improvements in performance of individual cashiers can quickly add up to provide substantial financial gains.

I have yet to encounter a job for which the level of performance variance is small enough to dismiss the value of using assessments altogether. Virtually every job provides employees with some opportunities to significantly outperform their co-workers through their actions and decisions, as well as circumstances in which they can make catastrophically bad decisions or engage in highly counterproductive activities. Every time a company makes a staffing decision, that company is given an opportunity to hire someone who may contribute substantially to the bottom line and presented with a risk that the employee hired might do something they do not want him or her to do. If either the opportunity or risk could have significant financial consequences for the company, then there is value in using assessments to guide the hiring decision.

Candidate Pools

A candidate pool refers to the number of candidates who are considered to be potentially eligible for the job. A candidate pool is large when the number of eligible applicants who apply for a job is much greater than the number of available job openings. Larger candidate pools mean that more selection decisions must be made for each hire. This is because each hire requires making a selection decision to hire one candidate while also making selection decisions to not hire each of the other candidates in the pool. Because assessments add value by increasing the accuracy of selection decisions, the value of assessments increases with the number of selection decisions made for each hire***. As a result, the value of using assessments increases with the size of the candidate pool.

One often encounters large candidate pools when staffing jobs that have few requirements or that have requirements that are possessed by a large number of people. For example, companies staffing entry-level hourly positions often have candidate pools containing one hundred or more applicants. I once saw a candidate pool for a single administrative assistant position that contained over two thousand applicants. Smaller candidate pools tend to occur when companies are staffing jobs with specialized or rare requirements. Things that commonly limit the size of candidate pools include requiring candidates to possess certain technical expertise, to have very unique types of job experience, or to accept work under very particular conditions. For example, one might imagine the difficulty of finding

***This logic assumes that you are able to evaluate and compare all the candidates in the pool at once. This is possible using staffing technology systems that provide features to rank order candidates based on their assessment scores.

qualified applicants for a job that required that candidates have a Ph.D. in biophysics and be willing to work in Alaska.

There are times when a candidate pool may include a single person, for example, if a company decided it needed to hire the most recent gold medal winner of the men's Olympic downhill ski racing competition to be its spokesperson. Candidate pools containing one candidate also result from companies doing a poor job recruiting and sourcing qualified people for a position. If a candidate pool only has one person, then no selection decision is required since there are no candidates to choose among. In such a situation, an assessment is likely to provide no value to the hiring process, other than possibly being used to gain insight into things about the employee that might help with managing and developing him or her after he or she was hired or deciding that no hire is better than hiring the single applicant found in the candidate pool. For example, if you are told that a requirement of the job includes "that the employee hired also be the CEO's child" and the CEO only has one child, then it is obvious who is going to get the job. Such examples may seem odd, but they do occur from time to time. Assessments only affect these sorts of hiring decisions if they are used to justify delaying filling a job until new candidates can be added to the candidate pool, in other words, deciding that it is better to leave the position unfilled rather than hiring the sole person currently found in the candidate pool. In the previous example, this might mean deciding that, rather than hiring the CEO's current child the company feels that it would be better to wait for the CEO to produce another, more qualified child.

Figure 2.2 indicates how the parameters of assessment validity, performance variance, and candidate pools interact to influence the value of using assessments****. Figure 2.2 represents four different hiring situations: staffing a job that has high performance variance using an assessment with high validity (assessment A1), staffing the same job using an assessment with lower validity (assessment A2), staffing a different job that has lower performance variance using an assessment with high validity (assessment B1), and staffing the same job using an assessment with lower validity (assessment B2). As shown in Figure 2.2, the value of using assessments increases as the size of the candidate pool increases. Figure 2.2 also highlights the fact that assessments provide no value whatsoever when the

****Figure 2.2 presents the interaction between assessment validity, performance variance, and candidate pools as a simple non-linear relationship. The interaction between these three variables is often more complex than is suggested by the simple representation provided in Figure 2.2.

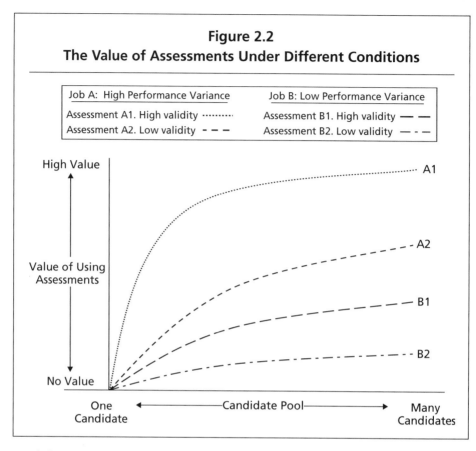

Figure 2.2
The Value of Assessments Under Different Conditions

Job A: High Performance Variance	Job B: Low Performance Variance
Assessment A1. High validity ··········	Assessment B1. High validity — —
Assessment A2. Low validity – – –	Assessment B2. Low validity — · —

candidate pool only contains one person (this assumes that not hiring anyone at all is not considered to be a valid option).

The rate at which the value of assessments increases depends in part on the validity of the assessment. The value of using assessments grows much faster when using more valid assessments. However, even assessments with relatively low validity can add substantial value when they are used to evaluate large numbers of candidates. The value of the assessment is gained each time it is used to help fill a staffing vacancy. Over time, companies filling jobs with high staffing volumes can gain considerable value from using assessments with even marginal levels of validity.

Figure 2.2 also contrasts the value of assessments for jobs with different levels of performance variance. The financial value an assessment provides for staffing a single position can never be greater than the difference calculated by comparing the value of performance for the best possible employee with that of the worst possible employee. For example, imagine you were hiring sales people for a company.

Suppose that the highest performing sales person in the company generated $50,000 more annual revenue then the lowest performing sales person. Now pretend you had a magical assessment that perfectly predicted superior sale performance. Anyone who passed this assessment would perform the job at the highest possible level. Anyone who failed the assessment would perform at the worst possible level. Using this assessment to select candidates, assuming you have more than one candidate in the candidate pool, would provide $50,000 worth of value for each hiring decision. This is the maximum difference in performance between the best- and worst-performing sales person. In reality, assessments never perfectly predict performance like this. But hopefully you get the picture. The maximum financial value assessments can provide is constrained by the level of performance variance found across employees in the job. For a more realistic example of assessment value, see the sidebar "The Financial Value, of Assessments."

Let's now revisit the earlier question "When should staffing assessments be used?" Assessments should be used whenever the value they provide by increasing the accuracy of hiring decisions outweighs the costs associated with using them. This value depends on the accuracy of the assessment, the number of people in the candidate pool, and the performance variance of the job. As each of these increases, the value of using assessments increases.

But what about assessment costs? Assessment costs include things like fees paid to assessment vendors, time spent administering assessments, and time spent training hiring managers to use assessments. Assessment costs depend primarily on market variables and typically have to be calculated on a case-by-case basis. The topics of assessment costs and assessment value are discussed in greater detail in Chapters Five and Seven.

The amount of resources that should be invested into developing and deploying assessments varies considerably across different hiring situations. Having a clear estimate of the financial value of using an assessment to staff a certain job provides you with a good sense of how much you should reasonably expect to pay for an assessment solution. An assessment that makes sense for one job may be far too costly for another. But it is hard to think of a situation in which it does not make sense to use some form of assessment as long as there is more than one person in the candidate pool. This is because of the tremendous value assessments provide for increasing the quality of a company's workforce. These gains in workforce productivity are even more impressive when one considers that they came solely through improving the accuracy of a single decision—the decision of who to hire in the first place.

Many staffing assessments predict about 10 percent of the performance variance across employees. Although 10 percent may not seem like a lot, some simple financial calculations help give a sense of what using these sorts of assessments can mean to a company's bottom line*****.

The largest fixed costs for most companies are associated with employee payroll and benefits. Employing people costs a lot. Companies are willing to pay the cost for employing people because they believe employees generate more revenue than they cost. The amount of revenue employees generate is sometimes referred to as the "Human Value Added" (HVA).[22] Assessments improve a company's HVA by increasing the accuracy of hiring decisions. In other words, people hired based on assessment results tend to perform at higher levels than people hired without the aid of assessments. By increasing companies' HVA, assessments enable companies to receive a higher return on investment from the people they employ.

To illustrate the value of assessments, let's consider what it means financially when a company uses a staffing assessment to hire its workforce. Imagine a company is adding a new department that will be staffed with a workforce of one hundred people. Employees in this department are going to be paid an average annual salary of $40,000. Suppose the company decided to hire these employees using an assessment that predicted 10 percent of the performance variance for the jobs in the department. How will the use of this assessments impact the financial revenue generated by the department's workforce?

To estimate the financial value of using assessments, we need to first calculate the financial value of the workforce itself. In other words, what is the HVA of the workforce? Although there are a lot of ways to calculate HVA, a common "rule of thumb" is to assume that employees

*****Like most of the mathematical formulas provided in this book, the formulas here are intentionally simplified. They are intended to illustrate basic relationships between assessments and financial performance. They are not intended to provide highly accurate estimates of the ROI gained by using assessments or the value of human capital. For more in-depth discussions on calculating the financial value of different human resource strategies, readers are encouraged to review works that discuss human resource metrics, utility analysis, and human capital by authors such as Jac Fitz-Enz, Wayne Cascio, and John Boudreau, among others.

generate revenue equal to roughly twice their salary. Using the "twice their salary" rule, the HVA of this department's workforce would be

$$(2 \times \$40,000/\text{year}) \times 100 = \$8 \text{ million/year}$$

The next step is to calculate the performance variance for this job. Suppose that past financial metrics have shown that the best-performing employees in these types of jobs generate approximately 20 percent more revenue than the worst-performing employees. This means that the best employees generate $16,000 more annual revenue than the worst employees. This is based on the following equation.

$$20\% \text{ of } (2 \times \$40,000) = \$16,000$$

If we assume the company has a reasonably large candidate pool and the quality of candidates is distributed randomly across this pool, then using the assessment will result in hiring a workforce that will perform at a 10 percent higher level than if the employees had been hired without the use of any assessment. Taking into account that the total performance variance in these jobs is $16,000, then on average each employee hired will generate $1,600 more revenue as a result of using the assessment (10 percent of $16,000 is $1,600). Taken across the entire workforce, this equates to an increase in HVA of:

$$\$1600/\text{year} \times 100 = \$160,000/\text{year}$$

This is equivalent to a 2 percent increase in annual HVA across the entire workforce. Whether this increase is worth the cost of the assessment will depend on how much the assessment costs. For the sake of this example, let's assume the assessment costs are equal to $100 per candidate. These costs reflect fees paid to the assessment vendor and time spent by hiring managers to review the assessment results. Let's also assume that there is a 5 to 1 ratio in the candidate pool such that five candidates are considered for every one candidate hired. Since five candidates are assessed in order to make one hire, the total cost of using the assessments is:

$$\$100/\text{candidate} \times (5 \text{ candidates/hire}) \times 100 \text{ hires} = \$50,000$$

$50,000 is substantially less than $160,000. Furthermore, the $160,000 increase in HVA is an annual figure that will be accrued as long as the employees are retained in the workforce. If we assume an average tenure of three years across the workforce, the value of using the assessment increases from $160,000 to $480,000. This would mean that the return on investment associated with using the assessments is 960 percent ($480,000 divided by $50,000). Given the intangible nature of HVA and the simplistic nature of these calculations, this estimate of ROI might be considered an overestimate if it were subjected to detailed financial scrutiny. Even so, there are few business investments for which it is even feasible to consider the potential of having an ROI approaching 1,000 percent.

The numbers and calculations in this example are intentionally simplified for the sake of understanding. But these simple calculations illustrate a key point about staffing assessments: the revenue generated through hiring better-quality employees usually far exceeds any costs associated with using a valid staffing assessment to guide selection decisions.

CONCLUDING REMARKS: WHY ASSESSMENTS WORK

Assessments work by measuring candidate attributes that influence performance in different kinds of jobs. These attributes range from highly specific aspects of a candidate's job history and work experience to relatively broad and intangible personality and ability traits that are influenced by the candidate's genetic makeup. Designing effective assessments is not a simple task. Care is needed to ensure that they are truly measuring things that matter for job performance. Furthermore, the value of assessments does not depend solely on assessments themselves. It also depends on the performance variance found between high- and low-performing employees in the job, as well as the number and quality of applicants found in the candidate pool. All these things come together to determine whether an assessment will work and how well it will work. And they should all be considered when developing staffing assessment processes.

Notes

1. Janz, T., Hellervik, L., & Gilmore, D.C. (1986). *Behavioral description interviewing.* Boston, MA: Allyn & Bacon.
2. Charan, R., Drotter, S., & Noel, J. (2001). *The leadership pipeline: How to build the leadership-powered company.* San Francisco, CA: Jossey-Bass.
3. Ackerman, P.L., & Humphreys, L.G. (1990). Individual differences theory in industrial and organizational psychology. In M.D. Dunnette & L.M. Hough (Eds.), *Handbook of*

industrial and organizational psychology (2nd ed., Vol. 1, pp. 223–282). Palo Alto, CA: Consulting Psychologists Press.

Robert, B.W., & Hogan, R. (2001). *Personality psychology in the workplace.* Washington, DC: APA Press.

4. Zuckerman, M. (1984). Sensation seeking: A comparative approach to a human trait. *Behavioral and Brain Science, 7,* 413–471.

5. Hunter, J.E., & Hunter, R.F. (1984). Validity and utility of alternative predictors of job performance. *Psychological Bulletin, 96,* 72–98.

   Schmidt, F.L., & Hunter, J.E. (1998). The validity and utility of selection methods in personnel psychology: Practical and theoretical implications of 85 years of research findings. *Psychological Bulletin, 124,* 262–274.

6. Kruger, J., & Dunning, D. (1999). Unskilled and unaware of it: How difficulties in recognizing one's own incompetence lead to inflated self-assessments. *Journal of Personality and Social Psychology, 77,* 1121–1134.

7. Merydith, S.P., & Wallbrown, F.H. (1991). Reconsidering response sets, test-taking attitudes, dissimulation, self-deception, and social desirability. *Psychological Reports, 69,* 891–905.

8. Holden, R.R., & Jackson, D.N. (1981). Subtlety, information, and faking effects in personality assessment. *Journal of Clinical Psychology, 37,* 379–386.

9. Bouchard, T.J., Lykken, D.T., McGue, M., Segal, N., & Tellegen, A. (1990). Sources of human psychological differences: The Minnesota study of twins reared apart. *Science, 250,* 223–228.

10. Arvey, R.D., Bouchard, T.J., Segal, N.L., & Abraham, L.M. (1989). Job satisfaction: Environmental and genetic components. *Journal of Applied Psychology, 74,* 187–192.

11. Mount, M.K., Barrick, M.R., & Stewart, G.L. (1998). Five-factor model of personality and performance in jobs involving interpersonal interactions. *Human Performance, 11,* 145–165.

12. Carroll, J.B. (1962). *The prediction of success in intensive foreign language training.* Pittsburgh, PA: University of Pittsburgh Press.

13. Carroll, J.B. (1993). *Human cognitive abilities.* Cambridge, England: Cambridge University Press.

    Digman, J.M. (1990). Emergence of the five factor model. *Annual Review of Psychology, 41,* 417–440.

14. John, O.P. (1990). The "Big Five" factor taxonomy: Dimensions of personality in the natural language and in questionnaires. In L.A. Pervin (Ed.), *Handbook of personality theory and research,* pp. 66–100. New York: The Guilford Press.

15. Van Vianen, A.E.M. (2000). Person-organization fit: The match between newcomers' and recruiters' preferences for organizational cultures. *Personnel Psychology, 53,* 113–149.

16. Kanfer, R. (1992). Work motivation: New directions in theory and research. In C.L. Cooper & I.T. Robertson (Eds.), *International Review of Industrial and Organizational Psychology, 7,* pp. 1–53. London: John Wiley & Sons.

17. Schmidt, F.L., Ones, D.S., & Hunter, J.E. (1992). Personnel selection. *Annual Review of Psychology, 43,* 627–670.

18. Ackerman, P.L., & Humphreys, L.G. (1990). Individual differences theory in industrial and organizational psychology. In M.D. Dunnette & L.M. Hough (Eds.), *Handbook of industrial and organizational psychology* (2nd ed., Vol. 1, pp. 223–282). Palo Alto, CA: Consulting Psychologists Press.

19. Bouchard, T.J., & McGue, M. (1990). Genetic and rearing environmental influences on adult personality: An analysis of adopted twins reared apart. *Journal of Personality, 58,* 263–291.

20. Srivastava, S., John, O.P., Gosling, S.D., & Potter, J. (2003). Development of personality in early and middle adulthood: Set like plaster or persistent change? *Journal of Personality and Social Psychology, 84,* 1041–1053.

21. Hansberry, M.L., Florentine, M., & Buss, S. (1997). Age of second-language acquisition and perception of speech in noise. *Journal of Speech & Hearing Research, 40,* 686–693.

22. Fitz-Enz, J. (2000). *The ROI of human capital: Measuring the economic value of employee performance.* New York: AMACOM.

Different Types of Staffing Assessments

S taffing assessments are designed to predict whether candidates will be successful in a particular job or class of jobs. There are many ways to accomplish this goal. Assessments come in all shapes and sizes, ranging from chemical drug screens to interactive video-based job-simulation exercises. One reason it can be difficult to understand staffing assessments is because there are so many kinds of assessments available.

There is some order to the chaos of staffing assessments available on the market. First, assessments can be categorized based on how they collect candidate information. For example, do they ask candidates to respond to questions about themselves (for example, personality tests) or look up information about candidates using third-party databases (for example, credit reports)? Assessments that collect information using the same basic methods tend to share common strengths and limitations. Categorizing assessments based on how they collect candidate information provides a good framework for thinking about assessments in general.

Assessments can also be categorized based on whether the information they collect is interpreted directly or indirectly to make hiring decisions. For example, drug test results tend to be interpreted directly. Candidates may be denied jobs simply because their drug test results were positive. Failing drug tests is often considered by itself to be adequate grounds for denying someone a job opportunity, regardless of whether candidates who fail drug tests are actually more likely to perform poorly in the job. In contrast, ability and personality tests tend to be interpreted indirectly, based on the strength of the relationships between test scores and other job performance criteria. For example, candidates who score high on an ability test might be given preferential treatment in the hiring process. But this is probably not because they had high test scores, but because prior research suggests that candidates with high test scores are likely to be more successful at the job. It is not the ability test score that matters, but what that test score allows one to infer about the candidate's likely performance on the job. Assessments such as ability and personality tests that are interpreted indirectly based on their value for predicting job-relevant behaviors are often referred to as "behavioral assessments." It is often helpful to classify assessments as being either direct or behavioral because it has implications for how they are used and evaluated.

This chapter discusses eighteen of the most common types of assessments. The first section of the chapter describes these assessments and places them in different categories based on how they collect information from candidates. The second section discusses assessments from the perspective of whether the information they collect is interpreted in a direct or a behavioral manner. By the end of this chapter, you should have a good sense of what kinds of assessments exist to guide hiring decisions, how these assessments relate to one another, and broad strengths and limitations associated with different types of assessments.

CATEGORIZING ASSESSMENTS BASED ON HOW THEY COLLECT CANDIDATE INFORMATION

Most staffing assessments used in the United States can be placed into one of seven categories based on how they collect information from candidates:

Physical Exams

Investigations

Interviews

Resume Screens

Self-Report Measures

Knowledge, Skill, and Ability Tests

Situational Measures

Table 3.1 groups eighteen common assessments into these seven categories. For example, the category "Self-Report Measures" includes pre-screening questions, personality measures, integrity and reliability tests, biodata inventories, and culture and work environment fit inventories. Although these assessments have different characteristics and content, they all collect information from candidates by asking them to respond to multiple-choice questions about their personal beliefs, experiences, or attitudes. In comparison, the category "Investigations" includes criminal record checks, Social Security verifications, reference checking, and credit reports that are similar assessments in the sense that they all collect information about candidates from sources other than the candidate him- or herself. The remainder of this chapter discusses the seven assessment categories in greater detail and describes the types of assessment instruments found in each category.

PHYSICAL EXAMS

Assessments in this category use medical or laboratory techniques to collect and evaluate information about candidates' physical characteristics. Examples of commonly used physical exams include:

- *Drug Screens.* These use medical screening procedures to detect whether candidates have used illegal or controlled substances. Drug screens include things such as urinalysis and analysis of hair samples.

- *Physical Ability Tests.* These require candidates to perform physical tasks that involve things such as lifting weights, completing cardiovascular exercises, or demonstrating flexibility. These are typically only used for jobs that are very physically demanding (for example, police and firefighting jobs).

Because of their highly objective nature, physical exams can be very effective for screening candidates based on specific physical job requirements, for example, determining whether a person applying for a baggage handler job can safely lift a fifty pound item of luggage. However, physical exams also have a variety of fairly major limitations. First, these assessments tend to be relatively expensive to conduct compared to other assessments. Some candidates also find certain types of physical exams such as urinalysis to be invasive or unpleasant. The use of physical exams is also subject to a variety of fairly stringent legislative restrictions. For example,

Table 3.1
Types of Staffing Assessment Tools

Assessment Tool	How Does It Evaluate Candidates?	What people have done	What people want to do	What people can do	What It Does	Common Limitations
Physical Exams						
Drug Screens	Use medical screening procedures to detect whether candidates have used illegal or controlled substances (for example, urinalysis, analysis of hair samples).	X			• Identify people who may work under the influence of controlled substances and engage in other counterproductive behaviors associated with drug use	• Not useful for predicting superior job performance • Will not identify poor hires who do not use drugs • May be relatively costly compared to other assessments
Physical Ability Tests	Require candidates to perform physical tasks such as lifting weights, completing cardiovascular exercises, or demonstrating flexibility.			X	• Determine whether people can handle physical demands associated with a job	• Only relevant for jobs that have a clear and well-defined physical component • May pose legal risks associated with Americans with Disabilities Act (ADA) and/or potential adverse impact against women

The "What It Measures" header spans the three columns: What people have done, What people want to do, What people can do.

Investigations

Method	Description		Benefits	Drawbacks
				• May be relatively costly compared to other assessments
Criminal Record Checks	Searches public records and private databases to determine whether applicants have any prior criminal convictions.	X	• Identify people with known criminal histories who are more likely to engage in counterproductive behavior	• Not useful for predicting superior job performance • Will not identify poor hires who do not have a criminal record • May be relatively costly compared to other assessments
Social Security Verification	Searches online databases to ensure that a candidate's Social Security number is valid.	X	• Verify candidate's identity • Comply with regulations related to U.S. and state hiring laws	• Not useful for predicting actual job performance
Reference Checks	Collect information from former employers or academic institutions to verify previous employment status and educational credentials; may also gather information about candidate performance in previous jobs.	X	• Verify candidate employment and educational history • Additional source of information about a candidate	• Many former employers are reluctant to provide reference information • Reference information is often of questionable quality • May be relatively costly compared to other assessments

(Continued)

Table 3.1 (*continued*)

Assessment Tool	How Does It Evaluate Candidates?	What It Measures			What It Does	Common Limitations
		What people have done	What people want to do	What people can do		
Credit Reports	Contact credit reporting agencies to obtain information about a candidate's financial history.	X			• Provide insight into candidate's fiscal responsibility; may be particularly relevant for jobs in which candidates will have direct access to cash	• Debate exists about appropriateness of using credit information to evaluate candidates; may be perceived as invasive by candidates • May be relatively costly compared to other assessments
Resume Screens						
Electronic Recruiting Agents	Search the web for qualified candidates based on words found in resumes posted on internal or external career boards.	X			• Can uncover candidates who might have gone unnoticed otherwise • Good for finding candidates with unique skills and qualifications	• Effectiveness is limited by quality of resumes posted on the web • May overlook candidates who have incomplete resumes and overly favor candidates with inflated resumes

Method	Description				Benefits	Limitations
Resume Capture and Reviews	Evaluate candidates based on the content of resumes they submit directly to the company or that are posted to web-based job boards.	X			• Good for screening candidates based on unique skills and qualifications	• May overlook candidates who have incomplete resumes and overly favor candidates with inflated resumes • Can be time-consuming and complex to use with large numbers of candidates sharing similar backgrounds
Interviews						
Unstructured Interviews	Evaluate candidates by having a discussion with them about topics that seem relevant to the job.	Depends on the questions used	Depends on the questions used	Depends on the questions used	• Can be used to build relationships with candidates • Build "buy-in" toward selection decisions among hiring process stakeholders	• May not predict job performance
Structured Interviews: Motivational Questions	Evaluate candidates by asking pre-defined questions about interests, career goals, and plans.		X		• All the benefits of unstructured interviews • May be useful for predicting tenure and organizational commitment	• May not predict job performance as well as situational or behavioral interview questions
Structured Interviews: Situational Questions	Evaluate candidates by asking how they would respond to hypothetical situations similar to what they may encounter on the job.			X	• All the benefits of unstructured interviews • May be useful for predicting how candidates will handle situations they have not encountered in the past	• May not predict job performance as well as behavioral interview questions

(Continued)

Table 3.1 (continued)

Assessment Tool	How Does It Evaluate Candidates?	What It Measures			What It Does	Common Limitations
		What people have done	What people want to do	What people can do		
Structured Interviews: Behavioral Questions	Evaluate candidates by asking them to describe experiences and accomplishment that relate to things they will have to do on the job.	X			• All the benefits of unstructured interviews • Considered to be the most effective type of interview	• May be less valuable for predicting how candidates will handle situations they have not previously encountered
Self-Report Measures						
Pre-Screening Questionnaires/ Weighted Application Blanks	Ask very direct questions to candidates to determine whether they possess specific skills, experiences, or credentials needed to perform a job (for example, "Are you willing to work weekends?" "Have you ever used MS Excel?").	X	X		• Can be an efficient method to screen out poorly qualified candidates • Readily available through many applicant tracking and staffing systems	• Provide little value for differentiating among top candidates • Susceptible to candidate faking • Can be difficult to develop effective questions

Method	Description		Strengths	Weaknesses
Personality Questionnaires	Ask candidates a series of self-descriptive questions about their likes, preferences, behaviors, and past experiences that reflect personality traits associated with job performance.	X	• Effective for predicting "soft" aspects of performance related to interpersonal style, emotional stability, attitudes, and motivation	• May be perceived as invasive or non-job-relevant by candidates • Difficult to develop; easy to create measures that do not work well
Integrity and Reliability Tests	Ask candidates about beliefs, preferences, and experiences that reflect a propensity for counter-productive behavior.	X	• Useful for screening out applicants likely to engage in theft, drug use, and other highly deviant behaviors	• Little value for predicting superior job performance • Only relevant for those jobs in which employee counter-productivity is an issue • Some questions may offend or insult applicants • May be subject to legal restrictions in some states
Biodata Inventories	Ask questions about previous life experiences and accomplishments that show statistical relationships to job performance.	X	• Effective for predicting "soft" aspects of performance such as interpersonal style, emotional stability, attitudes, and motivation	• May be perceived as invasive or non-job-relevant by candidates • Difficult to develop; easy to create measures that do not work well

(Continued)

Table 3.1 (continued)

Assessment Tool	How Does It Evaluate Candidates?	What It Measures			What It Does	Common Limitations
		What people have done	What people want to do	What people can do		
Culture and Work Environment Fit Inventories	Ask questions about job preferences, values, beliefs, and desired work environment to predict organizational commitment and job satisfaction with a specific job or company.		X		• Can be effective for predicting job satisfaction and tenure	• Tend to show low relationships to actual job performance • Difficult to develop; easy to create measures that do not work well
Knowledge, Skill, and Ability Tests						
Ability Tests and Measures of Problem-Solving Aptitude	Predict ability to solve problems and interpret information by asking applicants to solve questions that require processing information to arrive at logically based conclusions.	X		X	• Considered to be the single most accurate type of assessment for predicting job performance • Particularly valuable for jobs that require ongoing learning, processing complex information, and solving novel problems	• Show adverse impact against certain EEOC protected groups • Tend to be disliked by applicants

Measure	Description				Strengths	Limitations
Knowledge and Skills Tests and Measures of Past Learning "Achievement"	Assess familiarity and mastery with regard to specific types of information or tasks (for example, knowledge of accounting rules, ability to use certain software programs, typing skills).	X	X	X	• Useful for determining candidates' skill level with regard to critical job functions	• May assess things that could be learned on the job
Situational Measures						
Low-Fidelity Job Simulations/ Situational Judgment Tests	Ask candidates questions about different hypothetical work situations.	X	X	X	• Tap into a broad range of job-relevant interests, experiences, and abilities • Can predict "soft" skills associated with interpersonal behavior and work style • Highly job realistic; tend to be favorably received by applicants	• May only be relevant for a narrow range of jobs • Can require somewhat more time to administer than measures of personality and ability that may predict the same aspects of job performance
High-Fidelity Job Simulations/ Assessment Centers/Work Samples	Use audio, video, computer simulations, and/or human actors to re-create actual job situations and then assess how candidates react to these scenarios.	X	X	X	• Tap into a broad range of job-relevant interests, experiences, and abilities	• Labor-intensive to construct • May only be relevant for a narrow range of jobs

(Continued)

Table 3.1 (continued)

Assessment Tool	How Does It Evaluate Candidates?	What It Measures				What It Does	Common Limitations
		What people have done	What people want to do	What people can do			
						• Can predict "soft" skills associated with inter-personal behavior and work style • Highly job realistic; tend to be favorably received by applicants	• Can require considerably more time to administer than other measures of personality and ability that may predict the same aspects of job performance • Can be very costly to create and support
Cognitive Task Simulations	Candidates perform simple tasks or "video games" that require the use of skills that influ-ence job performance.			X		• Can be very effective for predicting performance of job tasks that involve processing and reacting to information in real time • If designed properly, can be highly engaging for applicants; provide a realistic preview of job activities	• Relatively unexplored type of assessment • Scores on cognitive tasks tend to be related to ability test scores; may show adverse impact

most physical exams can only be used in the United States after a contingent offer of employment has been made to the candidate.

INVESTIGATIONS

Assessments in this category evaluate information about candidates gathered from public records, past employers, and other sources that are outside of the control of the actual candidate. Common types of investigations include:

- *Criminal Record Checks.* These involve searching public records and private databases to determine whether applicants have prior criminal convictions or records. Depending on the cost, these may utilize automated searches of electronic databases and/or physical searches of court records.

- *Social Security Verification.* These are usually done automatically by searching government databases to ensure that a candidate's Social Security number is valid.

- *Reference Checking.* These typically involve contacting former employers or academic institutions to verify previous employment status, prior job performance, and educational credentials. More in-depth reference checking may also include conducting interviews with previous co-workers and/or customers. Research indicates that the value of reference checking can be significantly improved through carefully structuring the questions used to interview previous employers or co-workers.[1]

- *Credit Reports.* These involve contacting credit-reporting agencies to obtain information about a candidate's financial history. The appropriateness of using credit reports as a general source of information to evaluate candidates has been subject to some debate, although arguments can be made for its relevance when staffing positions that involve a high degree of financial responsibility.[2]

Investigations can be highly effective for avoiding "catastrophic" hiring mistakes that may result from employing someone who has a history of engaging in highly counterproductive or criminal behavior or who lacks legally required credentials or qualifications. For example, in 2004 the U.S. government hired a person to oversee the distribution of over $80 million worth of funds to various organizations in Iraq. Less than a year later, the government discovered that tens of millions of dollars had gone "missing." Had the government run a criminal record check on this person prior to hiring him, it would have found that he had been previously convicted for fraud.[3]

Investigations substantially reduce the risk of making bad hires, but have less value for determining whether someone is likely to be an outstanding candidate. Knowing that someone does not have a criminal record or does not use illegal drugs does suggest that the person is less likely to engage in highly counterproductive job behaviors. However, just because someone is not a drug-using criminal does not mean he or she will be a particularly effective employee. Most investigations are more useful for screening out bad candidates than for selecting good ones. An exception to this can be made for certain types of reference checking that focus on gathering detailed information about the quality of a candidate's past on-the-job performance.[4]

INTERVIEWS

Interviews are probably the most common assessment method used to make selection decisions. The idea of interviewing is pretty simple: have people who are familiar with the job ask candidates questions to evaluate the candidates' suitability for the job based on the interviewer's opinion of the candidates' answers. Typical interviewers include hiring managers, recruiters, co-workers who will work with the candidate if he or she is hired, and more senior leaders who may oversee the manager who is doing the hiring. These people are usually presumed to have a fairly good understanding of what the job requires.

I have yet to find a company that does not include some sort of interview in their staffing processes. Most managers will not hire candidates without first interviewing them in person. Candidates also expect to be interviewed during the staffing process. Many candidates react negatively if they are not at least given the opportunity to interview for a job. This is because interviews are often perceived as the most "fair" way to evaluate a person.[5] But despite their popularity and widespread acceptance, many interviews provide little useful information for evaluating candidates. This is because the techniques used by many interviewers to assess candidates are highly misleading and inaccurate.

Interviews can be placed into two basic categories: *structured* and *unstructured*. Unstructured interviews are probably the most common. Unstructured interviews do not follow a clearly defined process for asking candidates questions and evaluating their responses. Although the interviewer may have a few "favorite interview questions" he or she tends to use, for the most part an unstructured interview consists of a loosely structured conversation with the candidate about different topics that may or may not relate directly to the job. Different candidates may be asked to talk about significantly different things, depending on how the conversation during the interview unfolds. At the end of an unstructured interview, the interviewer evaluates the quality of the candidate based on general feelings and attitudes. No clearly defined criteria or guidelines are used to interpret whether candidate answers to questions should be considered to be good or bad.

Unstructured interviews have been shown to have very little validity for predicting job performance.[6] The poor validity of unstructured interviews is due to a variety of factors. Different candidates are often asked completely different questions during the interview, so there is no way to make a direct comparison between candidate responses. Because interviewers do not follow a clear agenda, they may fail to address important topics relevant to determining whether the candidate is suitable for the job. Because the interviewer is not evaluating the candidates against clear criteria, evaluations of candidates are often based on more superficial characteristics such as their physical appearance. In many unstructured interviews, the interviewer actually does most of the talking, leaving the candidate to simply sit and listen. When interviewers do ask questions, the questions are often highly leading, with the correct answer implied in the question itself. For example, "Do you agree with me that it is better to ask others for input before making decisions?" Often the best way to do well in an unstructured interview is to merely refrain from interrupting the interviewer when he or she is talking and nod in agreement with whatever the interviewer may happen to say.

As implied by the name, structured interviews follow a very clearly defined process. In a structured interview, the interviewer is provided with a clear agenda and list of questions to cover during the interview. The interviews are designed so that all applicants for a certain job or class of jobs are asked the same questions during the interview process. Most structured interviews also provide interviewers with well-defined rating scales for evaluating candidate responses to each question. Unlike unstructured interviews, structured interviews often show fairly high levels of validity for predicting job performance.[7]

Conceivably, any type of question could be included in a structured interview. However, most structured interviews use one or more of the following types of questions to evaluate candidates.

Motivational Questions

These ask candidates about goals and motives related to their careers and the job they are applying for. The following are examples of motivational interview questions:

- "How would you describe your ideal job?"
- "Where do you want to be in three years?"

The main limitation of motivational questions is that what people want to do and what they are good at doing are often not the same thing. In addition, many people have difficulty articulating their long-term career goals and may not actually know what truly motivates them.[8]

Situational Questions

These ask candidates how they would react to different hypothetical job-relevant situations. The following are examples of situational interview questions:

- "Describe how you would calm down an irate customer."
- "Imagine a co-worker told your supervisor that he or she thought you were not working hard enough. How would you respond?"

Situational interview questions tend to be more predictive than motivational questions. However, these questions suffer from the problem that what people say they would do in a situation is often different from what they actually will do. For example, it is one thing to respond to an interview question by saying that you would remain calm and collected if asked to deal with an angry, abusive customer, but it is quite another thing to actually remain calm when a customer is screaming in your face.

Behavioral-Based Questions

These ask candidates about their past experiences performing tasks or dealing with situations that are similar to those they will encounter in the job. The following are examples of behavioral-based interview questions:

- "Tell me about a time you had to manage a large project that required coordinating the work of several different groups."
- "Tell me about a time you had to calm down a customer or another person who was upset and emotional."

An advantage of behavioral interview questions is that they ask candidates to provide examples of things they have actually done in the past, as opposed to having them talk about hypothetical actions they might take in the future. There is evidence that behavioral-based interviews can be the most effective type of structured interview.[9] But because behavioral-based questions focus on past experiences, they may be less effective for determining people's ability to do things they have never had an opportunity to do before.

Structured interviews are usually conducted in person or over the phone. They can also be automated by having candidates read interview questions on a computer and then type in their answers electronically. While it is possible to design computer programs to automatically interpret and score candidates' written responses to interview questions, this type of scoring is complex and has questionable accuracy. Consequently, automated interviews usually still require having someone manually read and evaluate candidates' answers to different questions. Because structured interviews are typically conducted and scored by people, their effectiveness depends heavily on providing appropriate training to ensure that interviewers ask the questions in the right way and accurately interpret the candidates' responses.[10]

Interviews play multiple roles in the staffing process that go beyond merely assessing candidates. One should not evaluate the worth of interviews solely on their utility for predicting job performance. They are also used to help recruit candidates, provide hiring managers and other employees with a sense of involvement and ownership around staffing decisions, and give candidates a sense of being fairly evaluated. Even though unstructured interviews have questionable value for making selection decisions, they can still play a useful role in terms of building candidate relationships or giving hiring managers a greater sense of comfort about the staffing process. Nevertheless, it is almost always better to use structured interviews rather than unstructured interviews. When structured interviews are designed to include some time for more informal discussions with candidates, they provide accurate information for making hiring decisions and fulfill all the functions served by unstructured interviews.

RESUME SCREENS

Assessments in this category use key word search engines, text interpretation software, and other methods to screen or rank candidates based on the content of their resumes. Common types of resume screens include:

Resume Capture and Reviews

Resume capture and review systems allow candidates to upload their resumes into a company's career site or onto a job board. Candidates are assessed either by manually reading their resumes or through using automated text-searching software to identify resumes containing certain combinations of key words.

Electronic Recruiting Agents

These are software programs that actively search the web for qualified candidates by finding key words in resumes and biographical summaries posted on the web. They use complex key word searching and matching algorithms to take advantage of the increasing number of resumes that are posted to sites throughout the Internet. These assessments are specifically designed to help companies "source" candidates by finding people who may be qualified for different job opportunities.

Resumes screens are particularly useful for companies that receive large numbers of electronic resumes from candidates applying for jobs over the web. Their primary disadvantage is that they depend solely on using resumes to draw conclusions about candidates. Resumes are often a poor source of insight into a candidate's true experience and potential.[11] On the other hand, resumes are sometimes the only source of information readily available to companies about many candidates. Resumes can also provide useful insight into what candidates perceive to be their greatest strengths and most impressive and job-relevant skills and experiences.

SELF-REPORT MEASURES

The assessments in this category collect information from candidates by asking them to answer multiple-choice questions about their capabilities, attributes, interests, beliefs, or background. The questions used by these assessments are self-descriptive in nature. For example, asking candidates "Do you like to take risks?" "Do you have a lot of experience managing people?" or "Are you willing to work in a job that requires standing on your feet all day?" Self-report measures range from simple pre-screening questionnaires that take a few minutes to answer to in-depth personality inventories that may ask candidates three hundred or more questions about a wide range of interests, beliefs, and experiences.

How candidates answer questions contained in self-report measures depends primarily on their personal views, experiences, beliefs, and self-perceptions. In most cases, the answers to questions on self-report measures cannot be evaluated categorically as being factually or logically "correct" or be assumed to always be the "best" answer for any given job. For example, there are no objectively correct answers to questions like "Do you find it easy to ignore criticism from others?" Nor is there a single best answer to a question like "What is the largest number of employees you have managed at one time?" A company may decide that a certain answer is better in terms of a candidate's qualifications and potential for a specific job, but this answer may not always be the "correct response" for every job. From this perspective, self-report measures can be contrasted with assessments like knowledge, skills, and ability tests that use questions for which the answers are based on logic and facts and the correct response is always the same, regardless of the situation (for example, "What is 21 divided by 3?" or "What are the EEOC guidelines?").

Candidate responses to self-report measures are interpreted using pre-defined scoring algorithms. These scoring algorithms range from simple "pass-fail" scores assigned to individual questions to highly complex non-linear mathematical formulas that look at interactions based on responses to dozens or even hundreds of questions. For example, a candidate's response to a self-report question like "Can you work weekends: yes or no?" might be scored so that any candidate who responds "no" is screened out of the candidate pool. In contrast, a candidate's responses to self-report questions like "Do you like to go to parties?" "Do you like being the center of attention?" and "Do you find it easy to talk with strangers?" might be averaged together to create an overall score that is assumed to reflect an aspect of the candidate's underlying personality. Much of the value of self-report measures is associated with how they are scored, and developing appropriate scoring for self-report measures can be a highly complex undertaking.

Self-report measures represent perhaps the broadest category of assessments. Some common types of self-report measures include:

Pre-Screening Questionnaires

These ask candidates questions to determine whether they possess specific skills, experiences, or credentials relevant to employment eligibility and job performance. Pre-screening questionnaires are also referred to as "qualifications screens" or "qualifications questionnaires." The following are examples of the kinds of questions often found on pre-screening questionnaires:

- "Rate your skill level using Microsoft PowerPoint: none, novice, intermediate, expert."

- "How many years of experience do you have managing people?"
- "Are you legally eligible to work in the United States?"

Weighted Application Blanks

These are a form of a pre-screening questionnaire that give candidates an overall score based on their responses to different pre-screening questions. Candidates receive a certain number of points based on their answers to each question. These points are then added together to create a single score that is used to estimate the overall quality of the candidate.

Pre-screening questionnaires are typically used for "screening out" candidates who do not meet clearly defined, objective minimum requirements such as job-relevant experience, schedule availability, educational degrees, or citizenship status. Some pre-screening questionnaires also highlight candidate responses that should be further investigated during subsequent employment interviews. For example, noting that a candidate responded "yes" to a question asking if he or she had ever been fired from a previous job.

Many staffing technology systems contain tools that allow companies to create their own pre-screening questionnaires. These tools can be used to select or rank order job applicants based on their responses to pre-screening questions. Due to the widespread availability of these tools, pre-screening questionnaires have become one the most widely used types of staffing assessments.[12] But developing effective pre-screening questionnaires is not as simple as it may appear (see sidebar "Pre-Screening Questionnaires and Do-It-Yourself Assessments" below). Consequently, in addition to being one of the most widely used types of assessments, pre-screening question-naires are probably also among the most frequently misused assessments.

PRE-SCREENING QUESTIONNAIRES AND DO-IT-YOURSELF ASSESSMENTS

The concept behind pre-screening questionnaires is very straightforward: ask candidates direct questions about what they can do, have done, or want to do and then use their responses to evaluate whether they appear to be good fits for a certain job or group of jobs. Many staffing technology systems provide tools that allow companies to write and score pre-screening questions on their own. This development approach is markedly different from the methods typically used to create other assessment tools such as ability tests or personality measures in which questions and scoring algorithms are usually designed by assessment professionals.

Developing effective pre-screening questions is not as easy as one might expect. It is easy to create pre-screening questionnaires that hurt more than help in terms of finding the best candidates. The best way to avoid these problems is to work with assessment professionals to create and score pre-screening questions. The following guidelines can also help in managing the risks associated with "do-it-yourself" pre-screening.

- *Recognize the strengths and limitations of pre-screening.* Pre-screening can efficiently screen out applicants who admit to lacking job-relevant skills, experiences, or qualifications. This can reduce applicant pools by 50 percent or more. This provides tremendous value when dealing with large numbers of candidates. Pre-screening can also be effective for identifying whether candidates possess highly specific and unique qualifications (for example, speaking Inuit or having experience using a tunneling microscope). On the other hand, pre-screening questions have limited value for actually predicting job performance. Just because a candidate says he or she has certain skills is little guarantee that the person is truly skilled.[13] Companies that expect pre-screening questions to effectively identify the top 10 percent of candidates are usually setting themselves up for disappointment. Pre-screening questionnaires tend to work best when they are used as tools to remove the bottom half of the applicant pool, not to sort the top half.

- *Write questions about specific, verifiable skills and experiences.* As a rule, assume that candidates will respond positively to a pre-screen question if they feel they can justify or rationalize their answers. Most candidates probably prefer to be eliminated during an interview rather than by a computer, and if this means stretching the truth to pass pre-screening, then so be it. The best way to counter this is to ask very specific questions about things that candidates clearly have or have not done. For example, rather than asking whether someone is an "expert in Excel," ask if he or she has "written Excel macros." Instead of asking if candidates have "managed people," ask whether they have been "responsible for making hiring and promotion decisions."

- *Ensure all questions are legal.* Make sure you can demonstrate direct relationships between the content of pre-screening questions and job requirements. This is especially important if you are using questions to eliminate applicants from the candidate pool. Do not simply put in questions because people want to ask them. Challenge hiring managers to explain why the skills and experiences addressed by the questions are critical to job performance. Make sure that questions do not violate any legal regulations and that they will not seem offensive to applicants. Be wary of letting hiring managers write their own questions, unless they are very familiar with employment hiring laws. If you are using pre-screening to eliminate candidates based on qualifications, periodically review hiring statistics to ensure you are not disproportionately eliminating candidates from certain legally protected groups.

- *Focus on "high-impact" questions.* The goal of pre-screening is to remove the maximum number of unqualified applicants with the minimum number of questions. Avoid questions that are answered the same way by the majority of candidates. These provide little value for distinguishing among candidates. For example, a pre-screening question asking whether candidates are able to use Microsoft Word is not very useful if 99 percent of the candidates respond "yes," even if the ability to use Microsoft Word is a key job requirement.

- *Be consistent.* It is critical that every applicant for a position be asked the same pre-screening questions. Consistency is often important for establishing the legal defensibility of a selection process. Do not allow managers or recruiters to change pre-screening questions after candidates have started to apply for a position. Using screening inconsistently will reduce the effectiveness of your hiring process.

- *The highest scores are not always the best.* Research indicates that candidates who receive the highest pre-screen scores are often overqualified, are more willing to "stretch the truth" in their responses, or have job-relevant skills but non-job-relevant experience (for example, an IT professional applying for a administrative job on the basis of his or her knowledge of MS Office software).[14] Often the best candidates are not the ones who score in the top 10 percent, but the ones between the 50th and 90th percentiles.

- *Emphasize pre-screening as one part of the staffing process.* The purpose of pre-screening is to make high-level decisions about applicants' general qualifications early in the staffing process. While pre-screening questionnaires can be an excellent first step to narrow down the number of applicants, they are not well-suited for determining which applicants are the best fit for a particular job. Nor will they guarantee that the right applicants are applying in the first place. Pre-screening should be seen as one step in a larger staffing process. This process should also include using appropriate candidate sourcing methods prior to pre-screening and using more in-depth assessments such as personality measures, ability tests, and structured interviews to evaluate the knowledge, skills, and competencies of candidates who pass pre-screening.

The above guidelines address the major risks of pre-screening questionnaires while highlighting some of their advantages. While following these guidelines won't guarantee great hires, it will decrease the danger of implementing a pre-screening system that inadvertently eliminates high-potential applicants or puts your company at increased legal risk.

Personality Measures

When people think of self-report measures, what they often think about are personality measures. Personality measures provide insight into an applicant's behavioral tendencies, work habits, and interpersonal style by asking self-descriptive questions about likes, preferences, behaviors, and past experiences. To avoid being confused with clinical tests of personality, many assessment vendors do not refer to their assessments as "personality" measures, and instead use terms such as "work style measures," "talent assessments," or "value indexes." Personality measures can contain a variety of different types of questions, but most involve having candidates make some evaluation of whether they agree or disagree with statements about their beliefs, experiences, or preferences. Examples of common types of personality questions include:

- "Using a scale from 1 to 5, where 1 means strongly agree and 5 means strongly disagree, indicate your agreement with the following statements:

I like taking risks.

I take the lead in group discussions.

Hard work pays off."

- "Mark whether the following statements are generally true or false descriptions of you:

  I enjoyed school: True or False.

  I like going to loud parties: True or False."

- "Mark the adjective that best describes you: creative or outgoing."

- "Which statement better reflects how you behave at work: (a) I take time to gather a lot of input from others before making decisions or (b) I make decisions quickly without worrying too much about others' concerns."

Personality measures are usually untimed. They may contain from as few as thirty to well over three hundred individual questions. The number of questions depends primarily on the number and complexity of the candidate attributes being measured. Accurately measuring the full range of personality traits that influence performance in more complex or specialized jobs often requires using personality measures with two hundred or more questions. On the other hand, it is possible to gain insight into a few specific personality traits or broad personality characteristics using measures with fewer than fifty questions.

When appropriately designed and deployed, personality measures can be very effective for assessing candidate attributes associated with "soft skills" such as leadership, sales, teamwork, reliability, customer service, and work commitment. But they are also among the more difficult types of assessment to build. It is easy to create personality measures that look effective on the surface but that do not actually predict job performance.

Integrity and Reliability Tests

These are a specific type of personality measure designed to predict whether an applicant will engage in highly counterproductive activities such as theft, drug use, violence, or reckless and unsafe behavior. Integrity and reliability tests fall into two general categories: *overt* and *covert*. Overt tests ask candidates direct questions about attitudes, beliefs, and experiences with different types of illegal or counterproductive activity. Covert integrity tests ask candidates about general beliefs, preferences, and experiences that reflect a propensity for counterproductive behavior. The following are examples of the kinds of questions often found on integrity tests:

Overt Integrity Questions

- "How many times have you come to work under the influence of alcohol?"

- "Is the following statement true or false? Most people steal from their employers."

Covert Integrity Questions

- "Using a scale from 1 to 5, where 1 means strongly agree and 5 means strongly disagree, indicate your agreement with the following statements:

  I dislike it when people tell me what to do.

  I consider myself to be something of a 'rebel.'

  It's sometimes necessary to break the rules to get the job done right."

Integrity tests are a type of personality measure and share all the strengths and weaknesses of these measures. They can help companies avoid making catastrophically bad hires by screening out candidates with a propensity for unsafe, illegal, or otherwise highly counterproductive behavior. But like drug screens and criminal records checks, they tend to have much less value for determining whether candidates are likely to be highly productive. Integrity tests, particularly those that use overt questions, may also be perceived as inappropriate and accusatory by some candidates. Some states have even passed legislation that significantly limits the use of certain kinds of integrity tests.[15]

Biodata Inventories

The term "biodata" refers to biographical information about candidates that can be used to predict their job performance. Biodata inventories ask candidates questions about previous life experiences and accomplishments that show a statistical relationship to various job-relevant behaviors, for example, asking candidates applying for a sales job to answer questions about their previous experience working in jobs where their pay is based on sales commissions.

Biodata questions may address topics as varied as distant childhood experiences, high school education, hobbies, previous job experience, and recent social activities.

The following are examples of the kinds of questions one might find on a biodata inventory:

- "How many jobs have you held in the past two years?"
- "Mark whether the following statements are generally true or false descriptions of you:

  I was among the first people chosen for sports teams when I was in school.

  I often play video games in my free time."

Biodata inventories are often criticized for containing questions that do not appear job-relevant. Candidates may perceive certain biodata questions as being overly invasive or inappropriate, for example, asking people about their performance in a high school they graduated from over thirty years ago. Nevertheless, biodata inventories can be highly valid when appropriately designed and scored and are often among the more valuable tools for predicting job performance.

Culture and Work Environment Fit Inventories

These assessments are used to determine how well an applicant will fit into or enjoy a particular work environment or organization. They do this by asking candidates questions about their preferences, values, beliefs, and desired work environments and then mathematically comparing their responses against a profile constructed to reflect the work environment found in a particular organization or job. The following are examples of the type of questions one might find on a culture or work environment fit inventory:

- "Which of the following things do you most want from a job (mark one):

  The opportunity to make a good deal of money.

  A stable source of income and benefits.

  The chance to help those less fortunate than myself.

  Being allowed to work with advanced technology."
- "What type of activities would you most enjoy (mark one):

  Building a table out of wood.

  Designing and painting a mural on a large wall.

Helping teach elementary school students.

Helping patients in a hospital."

There is evidence that culture and work environment fit inventories can reliably predict tenure and organizational commitment.[16] However, these assessments may be less effective for predicting actual job performance.

Most self-report measures can be placed into one of the five subcategories of pre-screening questionnaires, personality measures, integrity tests, biodata inventories, and culture and work environment fit inventories. However, it is not unusual for a single self-report measure to contain a mix of questions from different categories. There is nothing wrong with this sort of mixed design, as long as the measure has been appropriately developed. In fact, there is often value in using measures that purposefully incorporate questions reflecting several subcategories.

Because of their ability to measure underlying aspects of candidate potential related to a wide range of jobs, self-report measures have become a fairly common form of assessment. They are also among the most criticized assessments. Candidates perceive the questions found on some self-report measures to be overly invasive or irrelevant to the job. Some candidates and hiring decision makers are uncomfortable with the fact that the questions usually have no clear "right" or "wrong" answers. Finally, hiring decision makers frequently express concern that applicants will intentionally fake their answers to look good on these assessments. These concerns are discussed in considerable detail in Chapter Six.

KNOWLEDGE, SKILL, AND ABILITY TESTS

This category includes tests, exams, and other assessments that ask candidates to respond to questions that have objectively correct answers based on facts and/or logic. Knowledge, skill, and ability tests can be grouped into two subcategories of *achievement tests* and *aptitude tests*.[17] Achievement tests focus on measuring things people have learned in the past. Aptitude tests focus on measuring people's ability to solve problems that require interpreting information that is presented within the test itself. Ability tests are typically considered to be measures of aptitude, while knowledge and skills tests are considered to focus on achievement.

In reality, ability tests and knowledge and skills tests overlap quite a bit, since what we have previously learned influences the kinds of problems we can solve.

For example, math tests measure both mathematical principles we have learned in the past and our ability to apply these principles to solve new math problems. Nevertheless, the distinction between aptitude and achievement is a generally useful way to categorize these tests.

Ability Tests and Other Measures of Problem-Solving "Aptitude"

These measure an applicant's ability to process different types of information, solve problems, and learn new concepts. Most ability tests use questions that present candidates with different types of information and then ask them to solve problems based on this information. The following are examples of the kinds of questions one might find on an ability test:

- "If a person started facing north and then turned 90 degrees counterclockwise, and then turned 180 degrees clockwise, what direction is he facing?"
- "If there are twenty-six apples available at the store and each apple costs 25 cents, how much money would it cost to buy half of the available apples?"
- "Pick the best answer: 'Ocean' is to 'Sea' as (a) 'Car' is to 'Tire,' (b) 'Cat' is to 'Dog,' or 'House' is to 'Shack.'"
- "Five books are arranged on a shelf in five consecutive spaces ordered one to five from left to right. Two books are red, one is blue, one is green, and one is yellow. The red books must be placed next to each other. The green book cannot be next to a red book and must be to the left of the blue book. If the red books are in spaces 3 and 4, in what space is the yellow book?"

Ability tests are typically timed. Examples of attributes assessed by ability tests include verbal ability, math ability, spatial perception, inductive reasoning, deductive reasoning, dual or parallel information processing ability, and many other aspects of cognitive ability.

Ability tests are widely considered to be the single most effective type of assessment for predicting job success, particularly for jobs that require considerable on-the-job learning and problem solving.[18] However, many companies are reluctant to use ability tests due to the tendency for applicants from certain demographic groups to score lower on these tests. These differences in test scores can raise legal concerns about whether ability tests show "adverse impact" against certain legally protected groups of candidates. The concept of adverse impact is discussed in more detail in Chapter Six. There is considerable debate over why ability test scores differ across demographic groups (see sidebar "Demographic Group Differences in Assessment Scores" in Chapter Seven).[19] But despite these differences, the predictive accuracy and job relevance of ability tests has been extensively documented, and their value as staffing assessment tools should not be ignored.[20]

Knowledge and Skills Tests and Other Measures of Past Learning "Achievement"

These assess a person's knowledge and mastery of specific types of information and tasks. Examples of the kinds of candidate attributes evaluated by knowledge tests include familiarity with information related to a certain discipline or subject-matter area (for example, accounting guidelines, human resource policies and terminology, biomedical theories and concepts, Spanish language vocabulary). The following are examples of the kinds of questions and content one might find on knowledge tests:

- "What is the French translation of the word 'airplane'?"
- "Which of the following words is spelled incorrectly? (a) Conceive, (b) Exponential, or (c) Feasible?"
- "What does the computer term 'GUI' mean?"
- "What is the circumference of circle whose radius is 3 inches?"
- "What tools and parts do you need to overhaul the transmission of a 1996 Honda Accord?"

Skills tests measure people's ability to apply their knowledge in order to perform certain tasks. For example, asking a person to type a 1,000-word passage of text into a computer using a word processor, asking him to create a graph using MS Excel, or asking her to replace the hard drive in a computer. Each of these exercises involves performing specialized functions that require having certain types of knowledge and manual abilities necessary to use specific kinds of tools or machines. Skill tests that ask candidates to perform actual tasks that are performed in the job itself are called "work samples." Depending on their level of realism in recreating actual job tasks, some work samples may be considered more of a job simulation than an actual skill test.

The content of knowledge and skills tests ideally mimics the kinds of information and tasks that are actually used on the job. If you make these tests more job-relevant, candidates are less likely to react negatively to them. It is also important that questions contained in knowledge and skill tests be written at an appropriate level of difficulty. These assessments provide little value if they are passed or failed by virtually every person who takes them. Last, it is important to ensure that the tests accurately measure the attributes of interest and not some other aspect of knowledge or skill that may not be job-relevant. For example, candidates' scores on a written test designed to measure knowledge of cooking techniques will depend both on the ability to read as well as on actual knowledge of cooking. This could be a major issue if some candidates possessed the necessary cooking expertise required for the job but did not have high levels of literacy.

Another issue to consider when using knowledge and skills tests is whether they assess things that could be taught to candidates after they are hired (for example, teaching someone how to use a specific type of software program). If the costs of training employees on key skills and knowledge are not prohibitively high, it may make more sense to train employees after they are hired rather than screening out candidates based on knowledge and skills that they could learn on the job. Finally, although knowledge and skill tests tend to show lower levels of adverse impact than ability tests, they often do show adverse impact. Companies worried about disproportionately screening out candidates from certain ethnic groups may want to limit their use of knowledge tests to some degree.

Knowledge, skills, and ability tests are often the single most effective type of assessment for predicting job performance. But they also tend to receive much harsher criticism than other assessments. These tests are sometimes criticized as being illegal because they may show adverse impact against candidates with certain ethnic backgrounds. This criticism is usually false, given extensive evidence that shows that candidate scores on these assessments are often very predictive of job performance. These assessments also tend to be disliked by candidates.[21] This may be because these assessments are somewhat similar to tests commonly used for evaluating students in educational settings. For example, the Scholastic Aptitude Test (SAT) used for college placement is a type of knowledge, skills, and ability test. The similarity between these assessments and tests people encountered in school may raise anxieties that candidates encountered during childhood and formative years. Despite the adverse impact associated with these assessments and the fact that many candidates do not like them, companies should not ignore the wealth of research evidence demonstrating that knowledge, skills, and ability tests tend to be among the most valuable assessments for predicting job success.

SITUATIONAL MEASURES

This category includes assessments that ask candidates to respond to hypothetical or simulated situations for which there is not a single right answer based on objective logic or facts. Situational measures range from simple paper-and-pencil questionnaires asking how candidates would respond to various work-relevant situations to highly involved video-game-like simulations in which candidates must respond to situations that change second to second in real time. Candidate responses to situational measures are evaluated and scored using pre-defined criteria and scoring algorithms.

Situational measures can be broadly grouped into three categories: *low-fidelity simulations, high-fidelity simulations,* and *cognitive tasks.*

Low-Fidelity Job Simulations and Situational Judgment Tests

These ask candidates to read written descriptions of various job-relevant situations and answer different questions about the situations. The following is an example of the kind of question one might find on a low-fidelity job simulation:

- "Two of your employees formed a romantic relationship that recently took a turn for the worse. Now one of these employees regularly complains about the other's lack of honesty and insensitivity, saying that the person is not to be trusted and that he only care for himself. What actions should you take as a manager of these employees?

    a. Meet with both of them and tell them they need to put the past behind them. During this meeting, encourage the employees to learn and reflect on the problems inherent in having workplace romances.

    b. Hold a meeting with the employee who is complaining about the other employee and tell her that making critical comments about another staff member is not acceptable.

    c. Say nothing to either employee. Talk with the other employees to explain the situation and indicate that the person is just frustrated and is 'venting' and that she should not be taken seriously.

    d. Fire the employee who is regularly complaining about the other person."

Low-fidelity simulations are often used to measure candidate attributes similar to those measured by personality measures and biodata inventories. An advantage of simulations is they tend to be perceived as more job-relevant by candidates. As a result, candidates react more favorably toward them than they do toward personality or biodata measures. One of their disadvantages is that they require candidates to read much more material, compared to other assessments that simply ask candidates direct questions about their preferences, beliefs, and experiences. Situational judgment tests may take more time for candidates to read and complete compared to other types of assessments and may negatively impact candidates with lower levels of reading ability.

High-Fidelity Job Simulations, Including Assessment Centers and Work Samples

These simulations use audio, video, computer simulations, or human actors to re-create actual job situations. In the case of work samples, they may also include the use of job-specific machinery and equipment. Candidates are assessed based on how they react to these situations, for example, having candidates meet with an actor pretending to be a disgruntled customer and evaluating how they respond. High-fidelity job simulations usually engender very positive candidate reactions. However, they tend to be expensive to create and can be quite time-consuming to administer. It can also be difficult to figure out the most appropriate way to score candidate responses to high-fidelity situations.

Cognitive Task Simulations

Cognitive task simulations require candidates to perform simple tasks or "video games" that require the use of skills that influence job performance. These simulations can be designed to provide a highly realistic and job-relevant experience and have been found to be very accurate at predicting specialized job skills such as the ability to monitor and work on several specific tasks simultaneously or solve problems under time pressure,[22] for example, having candidates for air traffic controller positions complete a video game that requires them to direct and monitor different objects moving across a computer screen. Cognitive task simulations measure candidate attributes that are similar to those measured by knowledge, skills, and ability tests. These simulations are a relatively recent development in the field of assessments, and it remains to be seen whether they will show the same level of adverse impact as has been found with other forms of ability tests.

In addition to providing useful information for evaluating candidates, situational measures tend to be favorably perceived by candidates. They can also be used to provide candidates with a realistic preview of what it will be like to perform the actual job. Such previews can positively impact the job satisfaction and retention of those candidates who are eventually hired into the job.[23] The main limitations of situational measures is that they can be expensive to create, time-consuming to administer, and difficult to score. High-fidelity simulations that use human actors to portray different situations are particularly expensive. Simulations can also quickly become outdated if they focus on tasks that significantly change over time due to changes in technology or the basic nature of the job.

Table 3.1 provides a summary of strengths and weaknesses for the assessments in each of these seven categories. Every assessment has its good points and bad points, and no single type of assessment is inherently better or worse than any other assessment type. The effectiveness of an assessment depends as much on the types of job behaviors being predicted as it does on the actual assessment itself. For example, drug screens are an excellent way to identify candidates who are likely to use illegal drugs on the job, but may have no value for predicting sales performance. Conversely, a situational measure that explores how candidates respond to different sales situations might do an excellent job of predicting sales performance but may not predict on-the-job drug use. Assessments that may be useful in some hiring situations may also be impractical in others. For example, high-fidelity job simulations are often very predictive of performance and tend to be perceived quite favorably by applicants. But few organizations have the resources required to make extensive use of these sorts of simulations.

Assessment vendors tend to specialize in certain assessment categories. It is unlikely for any one vendor to excel in creating assessments across all seven categories listed in Table 3.1. Vendors specializing in different categories often form partnerships with each other in order to offer clients access to a more complete set of assessments. Unfortunately, it is not uncommon to encounter vendors who may oversell the value of tools in the categories they support while downplaying the value of assessments found in the other categories. For this reason, it is always a good idea to decide on the general kinds of assessments that you want to use before you begin engaging vendors in discussions around specific assessment solutions.

Vendors may also differ in terms of whether their assessments are designed for a single industry or job type, or are assumed to work across a wide variety of jobs. Assessments that measure candidate attributes that are assumed to predict performance across a wide range of jobs are referred to as "broad" assessments. These can be contrasted with "context-specific" assessments that are designed to focus on candidate attributes narrowly matched to a specific job or type of organization. The value of broad versus context-specific assessments is another thing that needs to be taken into account when evaluating the value of different types of assessments. This topic and other issues related to implementing assessments are discussed in more detail in Chapters Four, Five, and Seven.

BEHAVIORAL VERSUS DIRECT ASSESSMENTS

The previous discussion presented staffing assessments in seven categories based on how they collect information from candidates. Assessments can also be organized based on how the information collected from candidates is interpreted to make hiring decisions. Specifically, are you interpreting the assessment results directly by themselves or indirectly based on insight they provide into the likely job behaviors of candidates. For example, the results of a Social Security verification are virtually always interpreted directly. Companies may refuse to hire someone with an invalid Social Security number simply because it is invalid. In contrast, the results of ability tests are usually interpreted behaviorally. If companies choose not to hire someone with a low ability test score, it is usually not just because the test score is low. It is because low test scores are associated with poor job performance.

Figure 3.1 organizes assessments based on how they are usually interpreted. Assessments that are typically interpreted directly are on one end and those that are typically interpreted behaviorally are on the other. Assessments that are frequently interpreted in a direct manner include all types of investigations and physical exams. Assessments that tend to be interpreted behaviorally include most self-report measures, situational measures, and many types of knowledge, skills, and ability tests. Interviews, pre-screening questionnaires, resume screens, and reference checks tend to be interpreted both behaviorally and directly, depending on how they are designed and scored.

If you interpret assessment results directly, then you are assuming that the results are meaningful, regardless of whether they actually predict job performance. For example, candidates who complete a drug screen may be denied job opportunities if the drug screen results suggest that they have used illegal drugs in the recent past. Evidence of past drug use is considered adequate grounds for not hiring someone, regardless of whether past drug use actually predicts future job performance. If you interpret assessment results behaviorally, then you are only giving meaning to the assessment results insofar as they have been shown to predict job performance. For

Figure 3.1
Direct Versus Behavioral Assessments

Usually Interpreted Directly → / Usually Interpreted Behaviorally →

Social Security Verification
Drug Screens
Criminal Record Checks
Physical Ability Tests
Credit Reports
Reference Checks
Resume Capture and Reviews
Electronic Recruiting Agents
Pre-Screening Questionnaires
Unstructured Interviews
Structured Interviews
Knowledge and Skills Tests
Job Simulations
Integrity and Reliability Tests
Culture and Work Fit Inventories
Ability Tests
Personality Questionnaires
Biodata Inventories
Cognitive Task Simulations

example, a candidate who receives a high score on a personality measure might be given preferential treatment over another candidate who received lower scores. The reason the candidate is being given special treatment is not because he or she has a high personality score, but because previous research has shown that there is a relationship between these scores and job performance.

The order in Figure 3.1 is just a general guideline based on how different kinds of assessments are typically used. Any assessments can potentially be interpreted either behaviorally or directly. For example, a drug screen could be interpreted behaviorally, although I have never seen it done. In such an approach, candidates might be given scores based on the association between the use of different drugs and different levels of counterproductive job behavior (for example, candidates might receive a lower score for using methamphetamine than for using marijuana). Assessments like personality measures and ability tests that are usually interpreted behaviorally can also be interpreted in a highly direct manner, for example, deciding to hire only candidates who score above the 80th percentile on an ability test without having any clear basis showing that these candidates actually perform better than candidates with lower scores. It is risky to use behavioral assessments such as personality and ability tests in a direct manner without first testing the assumption that the assessments are actually relevant to job performance. Remember, just because an assessment is assumed to be relevant to job performance does not necessarily make it so.

Direct assessments such as physical exams and background investigations can be very effective for screening out candidates who do not meet minimum job requirements or who pose a significant hiring risk based on their past actions (for example, previous felony convictions). But these assessments are not as useful for predicting superior performance. For example, knowing that someone does not use drugs or has a valid Social Security number may tell us that he or she is an eligible candidate, but it tells us very little about whether the person will be a high-performing employee. In contrast, behavioral assessments can be constructed to predict both productive and counterproductive job behaviors. This makes them valuable tools both for screening out unqualified candidates and for identifying candidates with the greatest potential for success.

The biggest advantage of direct assessments over behavioral assessments lies in people's ability to understand them. Most hiring managers can readily grasp what it means if candidates have an invalid Social Security number, possess a criminal background, fail a drug test, or possess a college degree. They do not need a lot of explanation to comprehend how to use direct assessments to guide hiring decisions. In contrast, hiring managers often find it much harder to determine the value of using behavioral assessments such as personality measures or ability tests to screen and select candidates. They may wonder how the results of behavioral assessments should be used to guide hiring decisions. How do we know whether a high score on a personality measure is meaningful? What does it really mean to score in the 90th percentile on an ability test? These are not questions that lend themselves to simple, highly intuitive answers.

Behavioral assessments are arguably the most valuable assessments for selecting candidates because they can be linked to both counterproductive and productive job behaviors. But their complexity makes them less likely to be used in general, and more likely to be misused when they are deployed. For these reasons, this book emphasizes a lot of issues that are primarily related to the use of behavioral assessments. At the same time, the topics discussed in the remaining chapters apply to all staffing assessments to some degree, regardless of whether they are interpreted in a behavioral or direct manner.

CONCLUDING REMARKS: DIFFERENT TYPES OF ASSESSMENTS

All staffing assessments are designed to collect information from candidates to predict future job-related behaviors. But there are tremendous differences in how they accomplish this goal. The development of different methods for assessing candidates is a reflection of the complexity of both people and job performance. It is not possible to obtain a complete picture of a candidate's job potential by using a single type of assessment instrument. Direct assessments such as physical ability tests, drug screens, and criminal record and reference checks provide us with one view into candidate quality, while more behavioral assessments such as ability tests and personality measures provide quite another set of insights. Candidates often do well on one type of assessment, yet perform poorly on another.

I know of no staffing process that includes every conceivable type of assessment. Many highly effective hiring processes only utilize two or three different types of assessments. But anyone charged with developing a hiring process should provide some brief consideration to each of the different types of assessments. No assessment type is necessarily better or worse than any other, and it is unwise to limit one's view of assessments to just a few specific kinds of instruments.

Notes

1. Taylor, P.J., Pajo, K., Cheung, G.W., & Stringfield, P. (2004). Dimensionality and validity of a structured telephone reference check procedure. *Personnel Psychology, 57,* 745–772.
2. McDaniel, M.A., Lees, C.A., & Wynn, H.A. (1995). *Personal credit information in screening for personnel reliability.* Paper presented at the tenth annual conference of the Society for Industrial and Organizational Psychology, Orlando, Florida.
3. Glanz, J., & Rubin, E. (2006, February 2). Wide plot seen in guilty plea in Iraq project. *The New York Times.*
4. Taylor, P.J., Pajo, K., Cheung, G.W., & Stringfield, P. (2004). Dimensionality and validity of a structured telephone reference check procedure. *Personnel Psychology, 57,* 745–772.
5. Hausknecht, J.P., Day, D., & Thomas, S.C. (2004). Applicant reactions to selection procedures: An updated model and meta-analysis. *Personnel Psychology, 57,* 639–683.
6. Campion, M.A., Pursell, E.D., & Brown, B.K. (1988). Structured interviewing: Raising the psychometric properties of the employment interview. *Personnel Psychology, 41,* 25–41.

7. Huffcut, A.I., & Woehr, D.J. (1999). Further analysis of employment interview validity: A quantitative evaluation of interviewer-related structuring methods. *Journal of Organizational Behavior, 20,* 549–560.

8. Beach, L.R. (1996). *Decision making in the workplace: A unified perspective.* Mahwah, NJ: Lawrence Erlbaum Associates.

9. Janz, T., Hellervik, L., & Gilmore, D.C. (1986). *Behavioral description interviewing.* Boston, MA: Allyn & Bacon.

10. Huffcut, A.I., & Woehr, D.J. (1999). Further analysis of employment interview validity: A quantitative evaluation of interviewer-related structuring methods. *Journal of Organizational Behavior, 20,* 549–560.

11. George, J., & Marett, K. (2004, May). The truth about lies: Reminding interviewers that applicants lie may help screen out fabrications and exaggerations. *HRMagazine,* pp. 87–91.

12. Hunt, S.T., Gibby, R., Hemingway, M., Irwin, J., Scarborough, D., & Truxillo, D. (2004). *Internet pre-screening: Does it lead to better hiring decisions?* Paper presented at the 19th conference of the Society for Industrial and Organizational Psychology, Chicago, Illinois.

13. Kruger, J., & Dunning, D. (1999). Unskilled and unaware of it: How difficulties in recognizing one's own incompetence lead to inflated self-assessments. *Journal of Personality and Social Psychology, 77,* 1121–1134.

14. Hunt, S.T., Gibby, R., Hemingway, M., Irwin, J., Scarborough, D., & Truxillo, D. (2004). *Internet pre-screening: Does it lead to better hiring decisions?* Paper presented at the 19th conference of the Society for Industrial and Organizational Psychology, Chicago, Illinois.

15. Sackett, P.R., & Wanek, J.E. (1996). New developments in the use of measures of honesty, integrity, conscientiousness, dependability, trustworthiness, and reliability for personnel selection. *Personnel Psychology, 49,* 787–829.

16. Kristoff, A.L. (1996). Person-organization fit: An integrative review of its conceptualizations, measurement, and implications. *Personnel Psychology, 49,* 1–49.

17. Anastasi, A. (1974–1975, August). Harassing a dead horse. *The Review of Education,* pp. 356–362.

18. Lubinski, D., & Dawis, R.V. (1992). Aptitudes, skills, and proficiencies. In M.D. Dunnette & L.M. Hough (Eds.), *Handbook of industrial and organizational psychology* (2nd ed., pp. 1–59). Palo Alto, CA: Consulting Psychologists Press.

19. Angoff, W. (1988). The nature-nurture debate: Aptitudes and group differences. *American Psychologist, 43,* 713–720.

20. Gottfredson, L.S. (1994). The science and politics of race-norming. *American Psychologist, 11,* 955–963.
    Murphy, K.R., Cronin, B.E., & Tam, A.P. (2003). Controversy and consensus regarding the use of cognitive ability testing in organizations. *Journal of Applied Psychology, 88,* 660–671.

21. Hausknecht, J.P., Day, D., & Thomas, S.C. (2004). Applicant reactions to selection procedures: An updated model and meta-analysis. *Personnel Psychology,* pp. 639–683.
22. Joslyn, S. & Hunt, E. (1998). Evaluating individual differences in response to time-pressure situations. *Journal of Experimental Psychology: Applied, 4,* 16–43.
23. Buckley, M.R., Fedor, D.B, Verse, J.G., Wiese, D.S., & Carraher, S.M. (1998). Investigating newcomer expectations and job-related outcomes. *Journal of Applied Psychology, 83,* 452–461.

Evaluating the Effectiveness of Staffing Assessments

Whether you succeed in a job depends on a lot of different things. Your talents and capabilities, how you are treated by your boss, your relationships with co-workers, changes in the broader economy, your personal health and the health of your family, and many other variables can interact to influence your job performance. Given all these factors, nothing can perfectly predict whether you or any other candidate is going to be successful in a job. So if we cannot perfectly predict performance, why bother to use assessments? The reason is that hiring decisions made with assessments, assuming they are appropriately designed and deployed, are far more accurate than decisions made without their use.

Properly designed staffing assessments provide hiring decision makers with the most accurate information available for predicting a candidate's job performance. The predictive accuracy of assessments can be quite impressive. For example, it is possible to reliably predict employee theft based on how candidates answer fewer than one hundred short, multiple-choice personality questions written at a sixth-grade reading level.[1] A thirty-minute ability test containing general logic and pattern-recognition problems can predict substantial differences in how well employees learn new job skills and solve work-related problems.[2] Years of research have shown that appropriately designed and deployed assessments not only predict performance, but they predict performance surprisingly well.

You might wonder "What makes assessments so effective?" The truthful answer is that not all assessments are effective. No assessment is effective for staffing all jobs, poorly designed assessments may not be good for staffing any jobs, and even the best assessments will not work if they are not appropriately administered and interpreted. This brings up one of the major risks of using assessments. Effective assessments provide companies with powerful tools for systematically improving the quality of their workforces. However, use of ineffective assessments will systematically decrease workforce quality. For this reason, it is important to critically examine the design and effectiveness of all staffing assessments before using them to assist with hiring decisions.

Determining whether an assessment is effective is done by evaluating whether the design and deployment of the assessment meets two basic requirements:

1. *Does the assessment collect the right information from candidates?* This means making sure the information the assessment collects from candidates is relevant to performance of the job. You have to first analyze the job to determine what information you want to know about job candidates. You then have to make sure the questions or other data collection methods used by the assessment are gathering that information.

2. *Does the assessment accurately evaluate the information collected from candidates?* This means making sure the information collected by the assessment is being effectively interpreted. It is not enough to ask candidates the right questions, you also have to know how to evaluate their answers. This often involves developing mathematical scoring methods that evaluate candidate responses to an assessment based on their statistical relationships to measures of job performance.

   This chapter reviews fundamental issues related to these two requirements. We will discuss both how assessments work and how to examine an assessment's validity to determine whether it is working well. By the end of the chapter you should have a fairly good understanding of what it takes to determine whether an assessment is likely to be useful for selecting candidates for a particular job.

HOW ASSESSMENTS WORK

In order to distinguish between effective and ineffective assessments, it is important to first have a clear understanding of how staffing assessments work. The entire notion of staffing selection is based on the belief that candidates with certain attributes are more likely to be effective for some jobs. In other words, all candidates are not equally qualified for all jobs. The role of assessments is to determine which candidates are better for a given job. Assessments do not classify candidates into categories of "good" and "bad" in a general sense. They classify candidates as "good" or "bad" with regard to a certain job or group of jobs. They do this by indicating which candidates are most likely to display behaviors that are associated with successful job performance.

Figure 4.1 illustrates how assessments actually predict job performance. The bottom half of the figure illustrates why assessments work. What assessments measure are candidate *attributes*. These attributes influence employee *behavior*. These behaviors in turn influence performance *outcomes*. Recognizing this multi-step process of attributes influencing behaviors and behaviors influencing performance outcomes is critical to understanding how to evaluate whether an assessment is likely to be useful for selecting candidates for a specific job.

The top half of Figure 4.1 illustrates why assessments do not perfectly predict job performance. The main challenge to developing assessments is that many of the

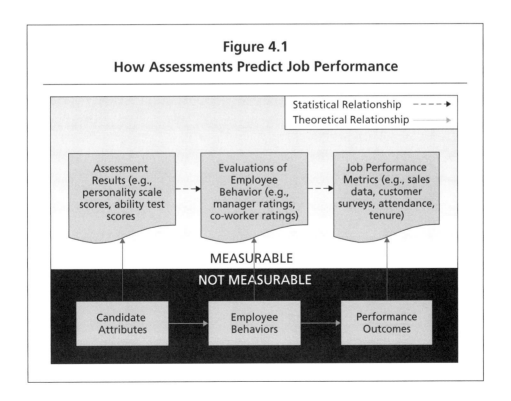

**Figure 4.1
How Assessments Predict Job Performance**

candidates attributes, employee behaviors, and job performance outcomes we wish to evaluate or predict cannot be measured directly. Because we cannot see many of the things we want to measure, we have to estimate them based on data from assessments, employee evaluations and ratings, and various job performance metrics. To illustrate this, imagine that you wanted to determine whether candidates for a bartender position had the math skills needed to quickly make change for customers without using a calculator. We cannot directly measure candidate math skills because mathematical ability is in abstract concept. We can give candidates an ability test that asks them to solve several math problems and then estimate their math skill based on how many questions they answered correctly (see sidebar, "A Crash Course in Psychometrics"). Similarly, it is probably not possible to directly measure how quickly and accurately employees make change for customers. Doing this would require directly observing or videotaping employees while they did their jobs. Instead, we might ask the employees' supervisors to rate the employees' ability to make change based in what they have seen them do at work. Such ratings will not be perfectly accurate measures of how well the employees make change, but they can give us some sense of which employees are the most effective. Even most performance outcomes such as "sales productivity" or "customer satisfaction" cannot usually be measured directly, but must be measured indirectly using performance indicators such as customer satisfaction surveys or point of sales data.

Developing assessments can be thought of as a two-step process reflecting the lower and upper halves of Figure 4.1. The first step is to define the underlying theoretical model upon which the assessment is based. This model defines hypothetical relationships between different candidate attributes, employee behaviors, and performance outcomes. It describes the things we are interested in but cannot measure directly. The second step is to validate the model using assessment and job performance data. This second step is where the real work comes in. It is one thing to say that certain candidate attributes are important for job performance. It is another to develop an assessment that accurately measures these attributes and conclusively demonstrate that there are reliable, statistical relationships between people's scores on the assessment and measures of their behavior and performance on the job.

Another thing to notice in Figure 4.1 is that what assessments measure and what companies care about are not necessarily the same things. Assessments measure candidate attributes. What companies care about are performance outcomes. Business leaders may not care what an assessment actually measures, as long as the data it provides predicts important performance outcomes and does not violate any employment laws.* Consider the example of the candidate attribute "extroversion." Extroversion is a broad personality trait that is partially a reflection of a person's sensitivity toward external stimulation.[3] It is associated with things such as being socially outgoing and talkative. The fact that psychologists have identified a personality trait called "extroversion" may be of relatively little interest to a business leader running a chain of retail stores. But this leader might be interested in knowing that extroverted candidates are more likely to display behaviors such as approaching customers and engaging them in conversation.[4] The leader's interest might further increase if he or she knew that socially outgoing behaviors associated with extroversion increased the likelihood of closing sales with customers. While there is little direct financial value tied to simply knowing that a candidate is extroverted, there is considerable financial value in knowing that candidates who score high on an assessment measuring extroversion are likely to close more sales.

In sum, the value of most assessments is gained solely through their indirect relationships to job performance outcomes (the exception is assessments that are interpreted directly and measure necessary requirements for employment, such as Social Security verifications). These assessments work by measuring candidate attributes that are associated with employee behaviors that drive job performance. Ensuring that all of these things come together can be a fairly challenging process. It is not an insurmountable challenge, provided one takes the appropriate steps during assessment design and deployment. But it does increase the danger of inadvertently building or deploying assessments that look like they should work, but that do not actually predict performance.

A CRASH COURSE IN PSYCHOMETRICS

One of the challenges to effective staffing is that many of the things we want to know about job candidates are psychological characteristics that are not visible to the naked eye. It is fairly easy to look at someone for a

*It is possible to build assessments that predict performance by measuring candidate attributes that may be illegal for use in job selection decisions. For example, it is conceivable that certain religious beliefs are associated with different types of potentially job-relevant behaviors (for example, willingness to work certain days of the week). Although it could be possible to construct an assessment to measure religious beliefs that predict aspects of job performance, use of such an assessment would be considered illegal in many employment settings.

few moments and estimate his or her height. It is quite another to meet with someone for thirty to sixty minutes and accurately estimate his or her ability to cope with stress, solve complex problems, or work long hours without stopping. But this is just the sort of thing that hiring managers are asked to do when making selection decisions. This task is also the core focus of a specialized branch of psychology called "psychometrics."

Psychometrics is a scientific discipline that studies how to measure intangible psychological characteristics such as ability, personality, and motivation. This field creates and evaluates the accuracy of techniques designed to assess various psychological traits. Most psychometric techniques involve measuring how people react to different situations or examining how people respond to different types of questions. Complex statistical methods are used to combine data collected by these measures to estimate a person's underlying "level" with regard to various psychological traits. Perhaps the most famous example of psychometrics is the use of reasoning and knowledge questions to estimate a person's overall intelligence quota (IQ).

Two particularly important concepts that come out of psychometrics are assessment *reliability* and assessment *validity.* Reliability reflects the degree to which people's assessment scores are stable over time. We expect that each time a person takes an assessment he or she should get approximately the same score, assuming there have not been any major changes since the last time he or she took the assessment. For example, imagine you complete a personality measure and receive a score saying you have a high level of emotional stability. If you completed this measure again six months later and the measure was reliable, then it should give you a similar score unless something happened during those six months that radically changed your underlying level of emotional stability (for example, experiencing some sort of traumatic event).

In most cases one does not expect assessment scores to change much from month to month or year to year. There are exceptions to this for certain types of assessments such as knowledge and skills tests, drug screens, and qualifications questionnaires that measure things people can more easily change. People's scores on these types of assessments might change considerably if they learn new information, accomplish certain things, or begin or cease using drugs since the initial time they took the assessment.

The most common methods for estimating reliability are the *internal consistency* method and the *test-retest* method. The test-retest method involves administering an assessment to the same people multiple times and then comparing their scores to see how much they change from one administration to the next. The test-retest method is the most accurate way to estimate reliability, but is not used that often because of the difficulty of getting people to complete the same assessment multiple times. The internal consistency method is the most common method used to estimate reliability. Reliability estimates based on the internal consistency method are often reported using a statistic called "Cronbach's alpha" or "alpha" for short. The statistical concepts associated with the internal consistency method go beyond the scope of this book. Interested readers are encouraged to read Cortina (1993) for more information on these concepts.[5] Reliability is usually reported using a class of statistical variables called *reliability coefficients.* Reliability coefficients typically range from 0 to 1. The larger the reliability coefficient, the more reliable the test. Most well-designed assessments have reliability coefficients between .60 and .90.[6]

Validity is an even more important psychometric concept than reliability. Validity refers to whether an assessment accurately measures what it is theoretically purported to measure. For example, it is one thing to say an assessment measures candidates' ability to perform effectively under stress, but it is quite another to demonstrate that candidates who score high on the assessment actually handle stress more effectively than candidates with lower scores. The concept of validity is discussed in greater detail elsewhere in this chapter. You may recall from Chapter One that the validity of an assessment is often represented by a statistic called a validity coefficient that can range between –1 and 1.

A common mistake made by people unfamiliar with assessment design is to confuse reliability coefficients and validity coefficients. Both are important, but they measure substantially different things. An assessment can be reliable without being valid, but cannot be consistently valid if it is not reliable. An analogy for understanding the concepts of reliability and validity is to think of them in terms of people throwing darts at the bulls eye on a dart board. An unreliable, invalid dart player will hit the board randomly each time he throws. He will rarely hit the bulls eye, and when he does it will be almost entirely by chance. A reliable dart player will hit the board in roughly the same place every time, but may not necessarily be hitting the bulls eye. A reliable and valid dart player will hit the bulls eye almost every time he throws.

Most well-designed assessments have reliability coefficients ranging between .60 and .90, and have validity coefficients ranging between .10 and .50.** Having a general, non-technical understanding of the psychometric concepts of reliability and validity is very useful for evaluating and analyzing the value and likely effectiveness of different types of assessments. But providing a full understanding of psychometric techniques and how they are used to evaluate assessments would require delving into statistical topics and methods that are beyond the scope of this book. For a more detailed discussion of psychometrics, the reader is encouraged to read either of the "classic" texts on the topic written by Nunnally and Cronbach.[7]

ASSESSMENT VALIDITY: HOW TO DETERMINE HOW WELL AN ASSESSMENT IS WORKING

Staffing assessments are only effective if the information they provide about candidates accurately predicts job-relevant behaviors and performance outcomes. Such assessments are said to be "valid" tools for making employee selection decisions. But assessments are never valid in a general sense. They are only valid for predicting certain types of job performance. For example, an assessment that is valid for predicting tenure in call center jobs might not be valid for predicting tenure in construction jobs. Similarly, an assessment that is valid for predicting attendance in retail jobs might not be valid for predicting customer service in the same jobs.

An assessment that is considered to be valid for evaluating candidates for a certain job is said to be "validated" or to "have validity" for that job. Assessments are validated for a job by performing a "validity study." Validity studies use various techniques to systematically compare the information collected by an assessment

***

**This is based on my personal experience analyzing the validity and effectiveness of hundreds of assessment instruments, coupled with direct and meta-analytically derived estimates of assessment validity and utility reported in the scientific literature.

with employee behaviors and performance outcomes associated with job success. The studies investigate whether the things the assessment measures about candidates are relevant to predicting their performance on the job.

There are four general types of validity studies, reflecting four different kinds of assessment validity: *face validity, content validity, criteria validity,* and *construct validity.*

Face Validity

Face validity is established by having people familiar with the job look at the content of an assessment and evaluate whether it seems relevant to the job based on its appearance. In other words, does the information collected by the assessment appear to be related to the kinds of things people actually do on the job? Face validity is usually established by simply asking employees or hiring managers whether they think the assessment is likely to be useful for evaluating candidates. For example, a knowledge test used to assess candidates for an accounting job might be considered face valid if current employees in this job felt that the questions it contained asked about the kinds of accounting information they used at work.

The problem with face validity is that it can be an overly simplistic way of evaluating the effectiveness of assessments. Just because hiring managers or employees feel that an assessment looks relevant for a job does not mean that it will actually predict performance. Conversely, many assessments that accurately predict job performance contain content that on the surface may appear to have little in common with the actual tasks performed in the job (see sidebar "Face Validity Versus Criteria Validity: The Case of the Raven").

Face validity is important for determining how hiring managers, employees, and applicants will respond to an assessment. If employees, hiring managers, and candidates perceive an assessment to be relevant to the job, they are more likely to accept it as a fair and accurate way to evaluate job candidates.[8] This can lead to greater use of the assessment by hiring managers, better reactions from candidates who are asked to take the assessment, and less risk of candidates seeking legal action against the company for using an assessment that they feel is unfair. But because face validity is based on relatively informal, subjective evaluations by subject-matter experts, it may not be considered to provide adequate evidence for establishing the job relevance of an assessment if its use were to be challenged in a court of law.

FACE VALIDITY VERSUS CRITERIA VALIDITY: THE CASE OF THE RAVEN

A common source of conflict that arises when evaluating assessments is the relative importance of face validity versus criteria validity. Face validity is determined based on whether the questions and content of an assessment look like they would be relevant to the job. Criteria validity is determined based on statistical relationships between the scores candidates receive on an assessment and measures of their performance or tenure in the job. Criteria validity depends on quantitative analysis of relationships between assessment data and performance data, while face validity depends on subjective evaluations of an assessment's apparent job relevance.

It is common to encounter assessments that have a high level of face validity but little to no criteria validity. For example, a pre-screening questionnaire for an accountant job might contain a question like "What is your skill level doing accounting: none, novice, intermediate, or expert?" This question appears relevant to working as an accountant and would probably be evaluated as having a high level of face validity. However, there is no guarantee that candidate responses to this question actually predict performance in accounting jobs. One might even argue that the question could be negatively associated with performance. As people become more skilled, they often become more critical in rating their skill levels. In other words, the more you know the more you realize what you do not know. From this perspective, the most skilled candidates might be hesitant to actually rate their skill levels as "expert." In contrast, there is nothing that prevents candidates with little experience in accounting from rating themselves as "experts."

Assessments that have little face validity can also have very high levels of criteria validity. An example of this are tests of general reasoning ability. General reasoning ability, also sometimes referred to as "general intelligence" or just "g," is a psychological trait that reflects people's ability to quickly solve problems using deductive and inductive reasoning. Candidates with high levels of general reasoning ability tend to perform well in jobs that require learning complex information and solving mentally challenging problems. One of the most famous measures of general

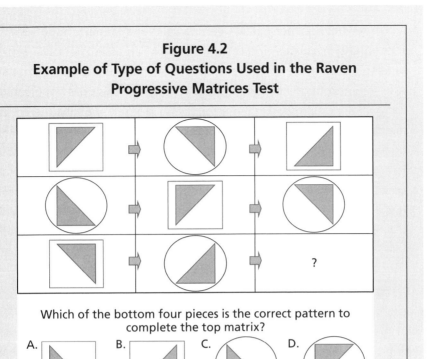

Figure 4.2
Example of Type of Questions Used in the Raven Progressive Matrices Test

Which of the bottom four pieces is the correct pattern to complete the top matrix?

A. B. C. D.

reasoning ability is the "Raven's Progressive Matrices" test.[9] The questions used in the Raven involve looking at a series of geometric shapes and then inferring the patterns that underlie their design. Figure 4.2 provides an example of the kind of questions contained in the Raven test. These questions can be quite complex, and it is very difficult to determine the correct answers to many of the questions on the Raven.

The Raven is an excellent tool for measuring general reasoning ability. Candidates' scores on this test tend to show strong criteria validity when used to predict performance in jobs that require working with complex information and solving difficult problems. But the questions on the Raven bear little in common with the actual types of information or problems found in most jobs. Even though the Raven test has strong criteria validity for a wide variety of jobs, people may be reluctant to use it because it has very little face validity.

From a financial perspective, criteria validity is far more important than face validity because it indicates that use of an assessment will actually lead to hiring more effective employees. There is little value in using assessments that do not show criteria validity. But this does not mean that face validity is unimportant. If assessments lack face validity, then people are likely to perceive them as not being relevant to the job. If hiring managers feel an assessment is not reflective of the job, they may resist using it. If candidates feel an assessment is not job-relevant, they may take negative actions such as litigation toward the hiring organization. As a result, it is desirable to use assessments that have strong criteria validity and at least moderate levels of face validity.

Content Validity

Content validity is established by showing clear theoretical links between the information collected by an assessment and different job-relevant behaviors. For example, imagine a math test was being used to screen candidates for cashier jobs in a movie theater. If movie cashiers performed simple addition and subtraction to make change for customers, and the math test included similar problems involving addition and subtraction, then it would be said to be content valid. But if the math test contained problems involving algebra, and employees never used algebra in the job, then the test might be said to lack content validity.

Content validity is similar to face validity in the sense that it is based on people's opinions about whether the content of the assessment is relevant to tasks employees perform on the job. But there are two noticeable differences. First, establishing content validity requires having a clear understanding of the candidate attributes measured by the assessment. In contrast, face validity simply focuses on examining the physical appearance of the assessment without specifically questioning what the assessment is actually measuring. For example, imagine a personality measure used to assess candidates for retail sales jobs contained the following questions: "Do you like going to parties?" and "Are you comfortable making formal presentations to large groups?" These questions lack face validity because going to parties and making presentations are not part of a retail sales job. However, suppose these questions were used to measure an underlying personality trait called "social confidence" that predicts job behaviors related to proactively approaching and talking to customers. These job behaviors are relevant to performing retail sales jobs, and so this measure would have content validity. In other words, an assessment can be content valid even if it is not face valid.

The other major difference between content validity and face validity lies in the processes used to evaluate validity. Content validity is established through conducting "job analysis" to define the behaviors and employee attributes that influence job performance. Job analysis is a broad term referring to various systematic measurement and observational techniques used to determine the specific types of employee knowledge, skills, behaviors, and attributes that influence performance in a job.[10] Job analysis is discussed in more detail in Chapter Five.

In sum, content validity is determined using clearly defined, rational arguments that utilize job analysis information to show the degree to which the candidate attributes measured by the assessment are theoretically related to employee behaviors that influence job performance. Because it is based on systematic, rigorous methods, content validity is often accepted as adequate grounds for establishing the job relevance of assessments in a legal setting. In contrast, face validity may not be accepted as appropriate evidence in a legal setting because it is usually established using relatively unstructured processes whereby people are simply asked for their opinions about the job relevance of the assessment.

Different job analysis methods can be used to evaluate an assessment's content validity. But they all require following well-defined processes to create detailed descriptions of the tasks, behaviors, and activities that influence job performance. Some job analysis methods take less than an hour, while others may take several weeks. Typical job analysis activities include reviewing existing job descriptive materials such as training manuals and performance management forms, observing employees performing the job, and interviewing or surveying employees and their managers about the types of tasks and activities they do on the job. Job analyses are usually conducted by people with some level of training in industrial-organizational psychology or related disciplines, although this is not a requirement. More information about job analysis is provided in Chapter Five in the section on defining and describing critical employee behaviors.

Criteria Validity

Criteria validity is established by using numerical data to demonstrate statistical links between people's assessment scores and measures of their performance on the job. For example, the criteria validity of a personality assessment used to select car salespeople could be demonstrated by showing that employees with higher scores on the assessment tended to sell significantly more cars. The name "criteria validity" refers to the job performance measures used to evaluate assessment accuracy. Such measures are called "performance criteria." Criteria validity may also be called "empirical" validity or "predictive" validity because it involves using empirical data to demonstrate how well an assessment predicts job performance.

Criteria validity is the only form of validity that provides a mathematical estimate of how accurately an assessment predicts job performance. By definition, criteria validity studies must involve collecting assessment data from either employees or candidates and then statistically comparing this data to measures of their job performance. Examples of job performance measures frequently used to calculate the criteria validity of assessments include tenure, supervisor ratings of employee behaviors, time and attendance data, accident data, and sales data. Collecting accurate measures of job performance is critical for effectively evaluating criteria validity. It is also often one of the most difficult challenges to performing criteria validation studies (see the sidebar at the end of this chapter, "Measuring Performance Is Harder Than You Might Think").

There are two basic types of criteria validity studies: *predictive* and *concurrent*. Predictive studies collect assessment data from candidates during the staffing process and then statistically compare it to job performance data collected from those candidates who end up being hired. Because predictive validation uses data collected from actual candidates during the hiring process, it provides the most accurate validation results. The downside is that it may require months or years before enough people have been hired to provide the data needed to compute meaningful predictive validation statistics.*** This makes predictive validation studies impractical for companies that want to examine the validity of an assessment in a relatively short amount of time.

Concurrent validation follows the same general approach as predictive validation, but collects assessment and performance data from existing employees all at

***A lot has been written on the sample sizes required to conduct accurate and meaningful criteria validation studies. If the data set is too small, then the statistical results are not likely to be reliable. But collecting large sets of data can be difficult, expensive, and time-consuming. It is hard to set a precise limit on how much data is needed to perform a criteria validation study. It depends on both the quality and nature of the performance measures being used in the study. But in general, most validation studies require assessment and performance data from a minimum of around one hundred employees.

one time. The advantage of concurrent validation is that it can be done relatively quickly. It does not require waiting for candidates to be hired and get up to speed in the job. The disadvantage is that how people respond to assessments may change, depending on whether they take the assessment as part of the hiring process or after they have already been hired.[11] In other words, employees do not respond to assessments in exactly the same way as candidates. However, the results of concurrent validation studies do tend to correspond pretty strongly with the results of predictive validation studies.[12]

The primary result of a criteria validity study is a statistical variable called a "validity coefficient" that can range from −1.0 to 1.0. Technically speaking, a validity coefficient is the correlation coefficient between employees' or candidates' scores on an assessment and a measure of their performance on the job. A validity coefficient of 0 means there is no relationship between people's assessment scores and measures of their job performance. If an assessment has a validity of 0, then knowledge of a candidate's score on the assessment provides no information about how well he or she is likely to perform on the job. A coefficient of 1.0 would mean there is a perfect relationship between a person's score on the assessment and a measure of his or her job performance. This would imply that whenever one candidate scored higher then another candidate on the assessment, the candidate with the higher score would *always* perform better on the job. Validity coefficients below 0 mean that candidates with higher scores on the assessment tend to have lower levels of job performance.

Because it is impossible to perfectly predict job performance, no assessment has a validity coefficient of 1, or even close to 1. Validity coefficients for a single assessment almost never exceed .50, and in most cases coefficients above .70 would be considered to be both unrealistic and unbelievable. Validity coefficients above .25 suggest that the staffing assessment is quite useful for predicting performance. Validity coefficients between .15 and .25 suggest that an assessment is fairly useful for predicting job performance. Assessments with validity coefficients below .10 are usually considered to have little to no value for predicting performance. But recall from Chapter Two that the validity coefficient is not the only factor that influences the value of an assessment. Assessments with seemingly small validity coefficients can still provide substantial value, depending on the number of hires they support, the performance variance of the job, and the size and quality of the candidate pool.

The size of a validity coefficient depends on both the assessment and the performance criteria it is being validated against. For example, an ability test might have a validity of .40 with a measure of employee performance in job training courses. This same test might have a validity of 0.0 with a measure of employee attendance.

Validity coefficients can be used to mathematically estimate the percentage of performance variance predicted by an assessment. (Discussion of the mathematical equations used to do this is beyond the scope of this book.) But validity coefficients are not the same things as percentages and should not be thought of in the same way. Saying that an assessment has a validity of .30 does NOT mean it is accurate 30 percent of the time! (see sidebar, "Describing Assessment Accuracy"). What it does mean is that the assessment is an effective tool for predicting job performance.

DESCRIBING ASSESSMENT ACCURACY

It is common for people to ask "How accurate are assessments?" This reasonable and seemingly simple question is actually fairly difficult to answer. First, it requires defining what people mean by "accurate." Assessments are not accurate in a general sense. They are accurate for predicting certain specific things. An assessment that is accurate at predicting whether people are likely to have good attendance might have no accuracy for predicting customer service performance. An assessment that is accurate for predicting performance in computer programming jobs might have no accuracy for predicting performance in real estate sales positions.

A second problem is the challenge of describing assessment accuracy in a way that people can easily understand. Most people struggle to understand what validity coefficients mean. They want a less technical answer such as "This assessment is right 90 percent of the time." But this requires defining what "right" means and figuring out how to measure different degrees of being right. Imagine someone wanted to know how accurate an assessment was for making the right hires in a call center job. Answering this requires defining what constitutes a "right" hire. Is it lasting more than thirty days? Is it not being fired? Suppose we agreed that a right hire was defined as "a hire that stayed in the job more than thirty days." Now suppose 70 percent of employees who failed the assessment lasted thirty days, compared to 75 percent of employees who passed the assessment. Even though this data gives some sense of the assessment's value, it still does not allow us to make a simple, definitive statement like "This assessment is right four out of five times."

When discussing assessment accuracy with people who have neither the time nor inclination to understand validity coefficients, I have found it is best to try two tactics. First, assuming data is available, create some simple bar graphs that show the average performance of people with different assessment scores. For example, a graph contrasting average sales of people whose assessment scores were in the top 25 percent of all the people who took the assessment versus people whose assessment scores were in the bottom 25 percent. These graphs often oversimplify the nature of relationships between assessments and performance and can be somewhat misleading. But they are things people can understand without having a course in statistics.

Second, I try to frame the conversation in terms people can understand. Usually this involves making analogies to common things that involve probability such as gambling, flipping coins, or predicting the weather. For example, you might say that using an assessment is kind of like gambling with loaded dice. You may not win every bet using loaded dice, but you will win more often than not. It's the same with assessments. In the absence of other more reliable information about candidates, selection decisions based on validated assessments tend to be substantially more accurate than decisions made without assessments. You may still make some bad hires from time to time, but for the most part your hires will be better than if you had not used the assessment.

A unique advantage of criteria validity is that it provides a direct, empirical estimate of the impact an assessment is likely to have on job performance outcomes. If you know the validity coefficient of an assessment and have some information on the financial value associated with different levels of employee performance, then it is possible to mathematically estimate the dollar value the assessment is likely to provide to a company's hiring process. Statistical techniques that estimate the financial value of assessments are commonly called "utility analysis." Readers interested in this topic can find more information on these techniques in books such as *Costing Human Resources*.[13]

Conducting utility analysis to estimate the financial benefits of an assessment cannot be done without first conducting some form of criteria validity study. This is because criteria validity is the only type of validity that provides a quantitative, empirically based estimate of how well the assessment predicts job performance. Face validity and content validity provide rational, subjective estimates of an assessment's likely relationship to performance outcomes. But only criteria validity provides the detailed information needed to mathematically estimate the strength of the relationship between assessment scores and performance metrics.

Criteria validation studies are considered the strongest test of an assessment's relevance to job performance. Discussions of criteria validity often play an important role in legal cases evaluating the job relevance of assessment methods. But criteria validation studies are also the hardest types of validation studies to conduct. Determining an assessment's criteria validity is a fairly complex exercise requiring considerable resources as well as technical knowledge of various measurement methods and statistical techniques. It cannot be done effectively without having some level of specialized training. Furthermore, criteria validation studies require access to data that may not exist or that may be impractical to collect for many jobs. It would be difficult to conduct a highly meaningful criteria validation study with data from fewer than twenty or so employees, and most criteria validation studies use data from over one hundred employees. In sum, while it is a good idea to conduct criteria validation studies whenever possible, it is not always operationally feasible or cost-effective to do so. As a result, content validation is used far more often than criteria validation to test and establish the job relevance of assessments.

Construct Validity

Construct validity focuses on determining what candidate attributes are actually measured by an assessment. For example, imagine you had a situational judgment test that asked candidates to read short paragraphs describing different customer service scenarios and then indicate how they would respond to each scenario. Scores on this test might depend on a candidate's past experience working in customer service jobs, differences in personality traits like empathy and emotional stability, their ability to read and interpret text written in English, or some combination of all three. The purpose of looking at this assessment's construct validity would be to determine which of these three attributes have the greatest impact on candidates' assessment scores.

Construct validity is different from the other forms of validity because it focuses on what an assessment measures, rather than on its ability to predict job performance. Construct validity is an important concept for assessment scientists who want to understand the theoretical relationships between assessment scores and different candidate attributes (see the sidebar, "Figuring Out What Assessments Really Measure"). But it is less relevant to practitioners whose primary interest is to simply predict and improve job performance. Such practitioners are usually satisfied simply knowing that an assessment has strong face validity, content validity, and/or criteria validity. They don't necessarily want or need to know what the assessment measures, they just want to know what it predicts.

FIGURING OUT WHAT ASSESSMENTS REALLY MEASURE: THE ROLE OF CONSTRUCT VALIDITY IN ASSESSMENT DESIGN

Companies use staffing assessments primarily for one reason: to improve financial results by hiring more effective employees. What business leaders want to know when evaluating an assessment is whether it predicts job performance and complies with relevant employment and hiring laws, and that it does not offend the applicants and hiring managers who use it. These things can be addressed solely through looking at face validity, content validity, and criteria validity. Consequently, these three kinds of validity are emphasized the most when evaluating the effectiveness of staffing assessments.

A fourth kind of validity called construct validity focuses on figuring out what an assessment actually measures. The word "construct" is a psychological term referring to the traits, characteristics, and other attributes that are measured by assessments. Evaluating construct validity is important to scientists who wish to understand the theoretical reasons why an assessment predicts performance. But construct validity is less important for evaluating whether an assessment has value for selecting employees.

It is possible to build staffing assessments that predict important job outcomes, meet legal requirements, and are acceptable to candidates and hiring managers without ever knowing exactly what theoretical constructs they measure.[14] When evaluating whether an assessment will improve hiring decisions, all that we really need to know is whether it predicts job performance. We do not need to know how or why the assessment actually works. This might be likened to taking drugs because we know they will improve our health, even if we are not certain of what they contain or what they actually do that makes us feel better.

Understanding the construct validity of an assessment is very useful for scientists who are seeking to develop new and better types of assessments. But it is considerably more difficult then evaluating face, content, or criteria validity. Determining construct validity requires investigating both what an assessment is measuring and what it is not measuring. It involves collecting the data needed to contrast one type of assessment against other types of assessments to show that they are not measuring the same things.

Because business leaders tend to have fairly little interest in investing the time and resources required to examine the construct validity of assessments, most construct validity research is done in academic settings or through academic partnerships with businesses. Readers who wish to learn more about the concept of construct validity may want to explore books such as *The Role of Constructs in Psychological and Educational Measurement.*[15]

The purpose of examining validity is to determine if an assessment is useful for evaluating candidates for a specific job or class of jobs. Face validity, content validity, and criteria validity represent three different methods for achieving this goal. Different people tend to emphasize each kind of validity when evaluating assessments. For example, candidates place a lot of emphasis on face validity when making decisions about whether an assessment is a "fair" way to evaluate them for job opportunities. Hiring managers tend to emphasize both face and content validity when deciding whether assessments are likely to be useful tools for helping them to make selection decisions. Criteria validity is the only type of validity that can provide a mathematical estimate of the financial value of using assessments, and it tends to be emphasized the most by business leaders charged with making decisions whether or not to invest in the use of assessments.

Both criteria validity and content validity are heavily emphasized by courts when they are asked to rule on the job relevance of assessments used for screening employees. Criteria validity is probably the best kind of validity for defending the job relevance of an assessment in a legal setting. But while content validity may not be as optimal as criteria validity, it is also considered to be acceptable for establishing the job relevance of an assessment, provided it is based on sound job analysis techniques. This requires collecting the necessary data and information needed to clearly articulate the relationships between the candidate attributes measured by the assessment and specific behaviors identified as being critical to job success.

One of the best ways to get a complete understanding of the different kinds of validity and how they are used is to examine the relevance of different assessments for a job or class of jobs. The following case study provides further insight into how validity information can be collected and used to determine an overall staffing assessment strategy for a specific position.

ESTIMATING VALIDITY: AN ILLUSTRATIVE CASE STUDY

To illustrate how different validation methods are used, we are going to examine a fictional case study involving a retail company expanding its operations into the southwestern United States. This new market contains a high proportion of Hispanic customers, many of whom do not speak English as their first language. The CEO asked the company's staffing director to ensure that the employees they hire will be effective at providing service to these Hispanic customers. This is where our story begins.

The staffing director asked her team for ideas on assessment measures that might be appropriate for identifying candidates who will be effective at providing customer service to Spanish speaking Hispanics. After talking with several staffing assessment vendors, the team presented four assessments they thought might work****:

The Cross-Cultural Qualifications Screen

This is an online pre-screening questionnaire that asks candidates questions to assess their experience and comfort working with people from different cultural backgrounds. Candidates are given an overall score based on how they respond to the questions. Sample questions include:

- Are you comfortable working with people who do not speak English as their primary language?
  A = Yes   B = Maybe   C = No

****The assessments described here are fictional but are similar in content and design to assessments that can be found in the market.

- Indicate how much experience you have had working in jobs in which you provided extensive customer service to people with the following ethnic backgrounds:

  Caucasian/White:
    A = 0 to 1 year   B = 2 to 3 years   C = over 3 years
  African American/Black:
    A = 0 to 1 year   B = 2 to 3 years   C = over 3 years
  Asian:
    A = 0 to 1 year   B = 2 to 3 years   C = over 3 years
  Hispanic:
    A = 0 to 1 year   B = 2 to 3 years   C = over 3 years

- How many languages do you speak in addition to your native language?

  A = None   B = One   C = Two D = Three or more

- What is your level of skill speaking Spanish?

  A = None   B = Novice   C = Intermediate   D = Expert

The Cultural Agility Behavioral Interview Guide

This is a structured interview containing questions designed to determine a candidate's ability to work with people from different cultures. Candidates are given scores based on how they answer the interview questions. Sample interview questions include:

- Tell me about a time you had to work with someone who came from a different cultural background than you. How did the differences in your background affect your relationship or interaction? How did you act differently when talking with the person? What did you do differently?

- Tell me about a time when you were having trouble understanding someone else—a time when you had to struggle to make sense of what someone was saying. What made it difficult to understand the person? What did you do to improve your level of communication and understanding? What was the result?

The Cultural Empathy Personality Measure

This is an online personality measure that asks candidates a series of questions about their interests, preferences, and beliefs. The questions are scored using a complex mathematical algorithm designed to measure a candidate's ability to recognize cultural differences and to adapt their behavior to fit in with people from different cultural backgrounds. Sample questions include:

- Indicate whether you agree or disagree with the following statements as accurate descriptions of you:

  I act the same way toward everyone.

  In reality, some cultures in this world are better than others.

  It's dishonest to change your behavior just to please others.

  I can always tell when someone is mad or angry.

  It is better to be honest than polite.

The Spanish Language Skills Test

This is a knowledge test that asks candidates to read passages of text written in Spanish and then answer questions about the text. The text in the assessment is written in a variety of styles, ranging from fictional stories to legal documents. The following is an example of a question from the test that has been translated into English:

[This text is written in Spanish on the actual test.] Please answer the questions below based on the information contained in the following passage:

Jorge and Mateo have known each other for years. They first met in elementary school when they were assigned seats next to each other during math class. They formed a strong friendship and came to think of each other as brothers. Now they are getting ready to graduate from high school. They will soon no longer be seeing each other every day, as they have over the past ten years. Jorge will be going to college in another city and Mateo will be staying to work in his father's restaurant.

The realization that they will soon be apart was starting to slowly creep into their daily conversations and thoughts.

Which of the following is not true?

A. Jorge and Mateo are brothers
B. Jorge and Mateo are classmates
C. Jorge and Mateo live in the same city
D. Jorge and Mateo have known each other since childhood.

Which of the following seems most likely based on this story?

A. Mateo is going to go to college after high school
B. Jorge is going to live at home after high school
C. Mateo is going to live at home after high school
D. Jorge will open a store in another city after high school

The vendors selling these assessments provided information attesting to the value and validity of their products for selecting employees to work with Hispanic customers. The challenge facing the staffing director was to determine which, if any, of these assessments will be the most effective at predicting employee performance in her company's stores. To address this challenge, the director decided to evaluate the face validity, content validity, and criteria validity of each assessment. (See Table 4.1.)

Face Validity

The staffing director examined the face validity of the assessments to get a sense of how hiring managers and applicants might react to their use. Knowing the face validity of the assessments could help her avoid using selection tools that hiring managers or applicants might perceive as being irrelevant or unfair for evaluating job candidates. To estimate the face validity of the assessments, she asked ten store managers working in the southwest market to evaluate each assessment based on the following question: "Do you feel that candidates' responses to the questions in this assessment will provide useful information for determining whether they are likely to be effective retail service employees?" Table 4.1 lists the overall evaluation of face validity made by these managers, along with comments managers made regarding each assessment. Only the qualifications screen and behavioral interview were considered to be highly face valid.

Content Validity

The staffing director employed a job analysis consultant to evaluate the content validity of the assessments. A job analysis study was performed to explore what employee behaviors and attributes are the most relevant to providing effective service for Hispanic customers. The job analysis process took about a week. The job analyst interviewed several store managers and employees individually. He also conducted a day-long focus group with a cross section of employees, managers, and human resource staff familiar with the job. The results of the job analysis identified three types of behaviors that are particularly relevant to providing effective customer service in these jobs:

- *Adapting to customers.* Store customers are from a wide range of cultural and socioeconomic backgrounds. The best employees are skilled at picking up on the unique concerns and expectations of each customer and adapting their behavior based on different customer needs and interests.
- *Sensitivity to Hispanic culture.* Although it would be incorrect to classify all Hispanic customers as being the same, there are common themes across many of the stores' Hispanic customers in terms of how they make major purchasing decisions. The best employees understand these themes and keep them in mind when working with Hispanic customers.
- *Speaking Spanish.* The majority of customers speak English very well. But many customers are also fluent in Spanish, and the ability to converse in Spanish can enhance the service experience for these customers.

The consultant reviewed each of the four assessments and estimated their content validity with regard to the three key behaviors identified by the job analysis. This information is provided in Table 4.1. The results of the content validity study suggest that the behavioral interview and personality test may be the most effective assessments. The consultant did note that, while the behavioral interview and personality measure appear to measure content valid candidate attributes, their effectiveness will depend on the degree to which they are accurate measures of these attributes.

Table 4.1
Summary of Validation Evidence

	Face Validity (Based on Hiring Manager Estimates)	Content Validity (Based on a Job Analyst's Examination of Relationships Between Job Tasks and Assessment Content)	Criteria Validity (Based on an Industrial-Organizational Psychologist's Statistical Analysis Comparing Assessment Scores to Job Performance Criteria)	Operational Resources (Based on a Staffing Manager's Review of Staffing Processes and Assessment Costs)
Cross-Cultural Qualifications Screen	Face Validity Estimate: High These questions ask about experiences and interests that are relevant to what people in this job do every day. Candidates who aren't comfortable working with people who speak Spanish are not going to be effective in these jobs.	Content Validity Estimate: Medium This assessment measures a person's past experience and interest in working with culturally diverse customers. But successful performance depends on more than simply having experience working with Hispanic customers. What is more critical is an employee's ability to recognize and adapt to a	Criteria Validation Coefficient with Customer Service Ratings: .04; Retention Past 90 Days: .13; Point of Sales Data: .02 This assessment showed little empirical relationship to performance. This may be because most candidates answered the assessment questions in the same way. For example, less than 1 percent of the applicants said they were uncomfortable working with	Resources Required: Low This assessment is administered to candidates through a simple online screening system. Candidates take fifteen minutes to complete the assessment off-site prior to being interviewed. There are costs associated with building the technology platform, but few costs associated with ongoing use of the assessment. This assessment

Cultural Agility Interview Guide	Face Validity Estimate: High I like these questions. They ask about situations that are similar to what employees in these jobs encounter working in the stores.	customer's cultural expectations. This assessment may be useful for predicting employee tenure by measuring comfort working with culturally diverse customers, but does not seem as useful for predicting actual employee performance. Content Validity Estimate: High This assessment provides information on how candidates performed in past jobs working with culturally diverse individuals. This assessment seems valid based on the assumption that past performance is a good predictor of future performance. The assessment may select out people who would be good in this job but who have not had previous opportunities to work in culturally diverse environments. The assessment's effectiveness will also be limited by the skill of the interviewer.	customers who did not speak English as a first language. There was a small relationship between this assessment and retention past ninety days. Criteria Validation Coefficient with: Customer Service Ratings: .26; Retention Past 90 Days: .16; Point of Sales Data: .18 This assessment showed some empirical relationships with all three criteria. The strongest validity was with customer service ratings.	will save hiring managers time by reducing interviews with unqualified candidates. Resources Required: High Hiring managers must complete a six-hour course on behavioral interviewing to effectively use the assessment. The structured interviews require thirty minutes with each candidate, compared to about fifteen minutes for the unstructured interviews we currently use.

(Continued)

Table 4.1 *(continued)*

	Face Validity (Based on Hiring Manager Estimates)	Content Validity (Based on a Job Analyst's Examination of Relationships Between Job Tasks and Assessment Content)	Criteria Validity (Based on an Industrial-Organizational Psychologist's Statistical Analysis Comparing Assessment Scores to Job Performance Criteria)	Operational Resources (Based on a Staffing Manager's Review of Staffing Processes and Assessment Costs)
Cultural Empathy Personality Measure	Face Validity Estimate: Low I'm not sure what these questions get at. I can't see the relationship between these questions and what people do on the job. I don't know how to interpret questions like "It's better to be honest than polite."	Content Validity Estimate: High Assuming this assessment accurately measures cultural empathy, then it should be useful for identifying candidates who have the ability to recognize and adapt their behavior to fit the cultural norms and expectations of different customers.	Criteria Validation Coefficient with: Customer Service Ratings: .27; Retention Past 90 Days: .22; Point of Sales Data: .32 The personality assessment showed moderate or high relationships with all three performance measures. It was particularly effective for predicting sales.	Resources Required: Medium This assessment is administered to candidates through an online system. Candidates spend thirty minutes completing the assessment off-site prior to being interviewed. There are few up-front costs associated with using the technology. A company is charged a small fee each time a candidate completes the assessment. Use of this assessment will reduce time hiring managers spend interviewing unqualified candidates. Hiring managers must complete a two-hour course on how to interpret the assessment results.

Spanish Language Skills Test	Face Validity Estimate: Medium	Content Validity Estimate: Medium	Criteria Validation Coefficient with: Customer Service Ratings: .24; Retention Past 90 Days: .17; Point of Sales Data: .36	Resources Required: Medium
	Understanding Spanish is definitely a plus in these positions, but the problems on this test aren't that relevant to the job. We want our employees to be able to answer questions about our products, not learn about people's childhood friendships!	The best employees in these stores are able to carry on conversations in Spanish with their Spanish-speaking customers. However, all the written materials used in this job are in English and employees are never asked to actually read anything in Spanish. This assessment will only be valid to the degree that the ability to read Spanish is related to the ability to speak Spanish. It is also difficult to determine what level of reading skill is actually necessary for the job. There may be little difference in performance between candidates who have a rudimentary ability to read Spanish and those who are highly fluent.	The reading skills test was particularly effective for predicting sales and moderately effective for predicting customer service.	This assessment is administered to candidates through an online system. Candidates spend thirty minutes completing the assessment off-site prior to being interviewed. There are few up-front costs associated with using the technology. A company is charged a small fee each time a candidate completes the assessment. Use of this assessment will reduce time hiring managers spend interviewing unqualified candidates. Hiring managers must complete a one-hour course on interpreting the assessment results.

Criteria Validity

The staffing director decided to investigate the assessments' criteria validity to determine which ones have the most value for predicting job performance. A consultant with expertise in the field of industrial-organizational psychology was employed to conduct criteria validation studies for each of the assessments. The staffing director decided to conduct a predictive validation study using three job performance measures as criteria: (1) supervisor ratings of employee performance on various customer service behaviors, (2) employee retention past ninety days after their hire date, and (3) point-of-sales data indicating how much sales revenue each employee generated per hour worked. Assessment data was collected from candidates during the hiring process. Supervisor performance ratings and point-of-sales data were collected for employees who remained on the job at least ninety days.

The industrial-organizational psychologist recommended that the company collect a sample of data from at least one hundred employees before conducting the validation analysis. This took approximately five months. Validation coefficients were then computed for each assessment against the three types of job performance criteria. A summary of the criteria validation study results is provided in Table 4.1.

The strongest validation results were for the personality measure and the reading skills test. To examine the potential value of using the personality measures and reading test together, the industrial-organizational psychologist computed the criteria validity for a combined score created by averaging the scores from both of the assessments. The validation coefficients for the combined assessment score were .41 with customer service ratings, .35 with retention, and .43 with sales. The fact that the validation coefficients for the combined assessment are higher than the coefficients for either measure by itself suggests that these two assessments have "incremental validity" over one another. In other words, the assessments are measuring different types of candidate attributes that predict job performance. As a result, using both assessments together provides a more accurate measure for predicting a candidate's performance than using either assessment by itself.

The director critically reviewed the validation study results across all of the assessments to determine whether any should be removed from the staffing process. She considered two things in this review: (1) the overall validity of the assessments, and (2) the operational resources required to use the assessments. Operational resources were calculated by reviewing the costs, time, and technological resources required to implement each assessment into the company's current hiring processes.

Table 4.1 summarizes the face validity, content validity, criteria validity, and operational resources associated with each of the four assessments. This table illustrates one of the realities of choosing assessments. Rarely is one single assessment solution clearly superior to all other alternatives. The most valid assessments often require the highest operational resources. The assessments hiring managers find to be the most face valid may not have the strongest criteria validity. Companies almost always have to make tradeoffs when deciding what assessments to use. The challenge is figuring out which tradeoffs make the most sense given a company's particular business needs and operating environment. What tradeoffs would you make if you were the staffing director in this example? Which assessments would you deploy? Which ones would you get rid of?

CONCLUDING REMARKS: CHOOSING WHAT ASSESSMENTS TO USE

The basic way that assessments work is not that complicated. Assessments measure candidate attributes that influence job-relevant behaviors that in turn influence performance outcomes. But because candidate attributes, employee behaviors, and performance outcomes are largely intangible concepts that must be measured indirectly, care must be taken to ensure that assessments are truly measuring things that are relevant to predicting job success. Do not assume an assessment works simply because someone says it is valid.

Given the impact hiring decisions have on company performance, no staffing assessment should ever be used without first taking a somewhat critical look at its validity. This does not necessarily mean doing a thorough review of all the different kinds of assessment validity. In fact, several of the actions described in the previous case study would not make financial sense or even be operationally feasible in many employment settings. But some attention should always be taken to address the following four key issues:

1. *Face validity:* Do the contents of the assessment appear job relevant to hiring managers and candidates?

2. *Content validity:* Is the assessment measuring candidate attributes that are relevant to job performance?

3. *Criteria validity:* Do assessment scores show a statistical relationship to measures of job performance?

4. *Operational costs:* Does the value of the assessment justify the costs and resources required to use it?.

Failing to consider any of these issues could lead to selecting employees based on inaccurate or incomplete assessment data, offending candidates, frustrating hiring managers, or encumbering the hiring process with unreasonably costly, difficult, or time-consuming assessment methods.

Assessment vendors should be able to provide data demonstrating the validity of their assessments. When talking with staffing assessment vendors, ask them for summaries of validation studies conducted to test the job relevance of their assessments. These summaries should include the types of job used in the study, the number of people included in the study, and the validity coefficients between people's scores on the assessment and performance criteria. Some of this information may not make a lot of sense to someone who is not fairly well versed in assessment science. If there is no one in your organization who is able to make sense of validity information, you may want to consider consulting a qualified industrial-organizational psychologist. The money you spend enlisting an outside expert is likely to be negligible compared to the financial gains associated with using appropriate staffing assessments, not to mention avoiding the risks and financial costs of implementing an invalid assessment.

The use of assessments poses both an opportunity and a risk. The risks are associated with deploying a poorly designed assessment that systematically selects the wrong people, offends candidates and hiring managers, or is overly difficult and expensive to use. This risk is controlled by carefully examining assessment validity and operation utility. Use of well-validated and efficiently designed assessments will ensure that you gain the opportunities provided by more effective hiring practices: a better-quality workforce, more efficient and fair staffing decisions, and happier and more productive employees and hiring managers.

MEASURING PERFORMANCE IS HARDER THAN YOU MIGHT THINK

Nothing impacts the success of an organization more than the performance of its employees.[16] However, few companies accurately measure employee performance. Most companies have relatively little data that tells them what their employees are actually doing each day they come to work. This is not because companies do not value performance, but because performance is actually a very difficult thing to measure.

Collecting accurate measures of performance is one of the biggest challenges to developing and validating staffing assessments.[17] The following are just a few of the issues that need to be considered when identifying and developing performance measures.

Are You Measuring Performance at the Right Level?

Staffing assessments are designed to predict the performance of individual employees. But many organizations are more interested in the performance of teams, departments, stores, or other groups of people, rather than the actions of individual employees. For example, all large retail companies track sales and customer service data at the store level, but many do not track the performance of specific employees working within the stores. These companies know a lot about overall store performance, but know very little about actual employee performance.

One might assume that one way to evaluate the impact of assessments in these companies would be to simply average the assessment scores of employees working in a store and compare that to overall store performance. Unfortunately, from a statistical standpoint there are a lot of problems with this approach.[18] For example, store performance is affected by a lot of things that are outside of the control of individual employees such as geographic location or store manager behavior. This is just one of many problems that limits the ability to analyze individual level assessment data at a more aggregated group level. Although these problems are not always insurmountable, they are far more challenging than one might initially suspect.

Are the Measures of Performance Statistically Predictable?

Just because we can measure something does not mean we can predict it, and if we cannot predict it, then we cannot expect to improve it through the use of staffing assessments. Many performance measures cannot be reliably predicted due to various statistical issues associated with the data they provide. Some reasons why performance measures may be unpredictable include:

- *Low performance variance.* Some types of job performance change very little from one employee to the next. If almost all employees perform at roughly the same level, then it is very difficult for assessments to have a noticeable effect on employee performance.[19] This is because performance does not vary much depending on who is selected into the job. For example, imagine the average attendance record for a group of employees was 99 percent, with 100 percent being perfect attendance. It might take a very long time before the use of an assessment would noticeably increase employee attendance because there is not actually much difference between the average employee and the perfect employee.

- *Low base rate.* Some performance measures track events that occur very infrequently. You may need very large samples in order to be able to detect a meaningful change in these types of performance measures.[20] This often occurs with measures of theft and safety where incidents are rare and many of the incidents that do occur are never reported or measured.

- *Low reliability.* Some performance measures change considerably over time, but not in any stable or predictable fashion. Such measures are very hard to predict with assessments. Low reliability tends to be a problem with performance measures that are heavily influenced by random or uncontrollable factors. This frequently occurs in sales environments in which performance in one quarter may not show strong relationships to sales performance the following quarter. It can also occur in measures of retention that are highly susceptible to external factors such as changes in the economy.

Many of the statistical problems caused by low variance, base rate, or reliability can be remedied simply by increasing the size of the sample being studied. However, some performance measures are so unpredictable that they simply cannot be used to accurately guide or evaluate the design of staffing assessments.

Are People Putting In the Time and Energy Needed to Provide Accurate Performance Data?

Just because data is labeled "performance data" does not mean it accurately measures performance. The problem of inaccurate criteria often occurs when using behavioral ratings of performance gathered from employees' supervisors or co-workers. A massive amount of research has been done looking at the accuracy of performance ratings.[21] This research has shown that to collect accurate ratings it is important to follow some careful practices around the design of the rating forms and use of rater training. The kinds of performance management data commonly collected by companies often shows relatively little relationship to actual employee behavior.[22] This is not that surprising when you consider that the primary purpose of most performance management ratings is not to measure what employees have done in the past, but to influence what employees do in the future or to justify future actions related to things such as compensation, promotions, and terminations.

Because assessments work by predicting employee behaviors, the best performance measures for validating assessments are often ratings from managers, co-workers, or customers that evaluate the behavior of individual employees. People sometimes argue that these behavioral ratings are overly subjective or too time-consuming to collect. It is true that performance ratings based on a manager's memory of past employee behaviors are subjective.[23] On the other hand, they are probably no more subjective than budget numbers scribbled on a white board based on vague predictions about future business performance. Few companies would dismiss the need for budget estimates because they are too time-consuming and subjective. But many companies put little emphasis on the importance of collecting accurate performance ratings. This is somewhat illogical, given that most financial numbers are a direct result of employee behaviors. If companies wish to systematically influence financial measures, they might do well to get more serious about collecting accurate behavioral measures of employee performance. This means putting resources into creating effective behavioral rating forms, and then providing managers with adequate training and time to accurately rate the performance of their employees.

Are You Evaluating Performance Solely Based on Existing Performance Levels?

Performance of employees is usually evaluated partially or wholly on comparisons to other employees in the same job or organization. While there are advantages to using comparisons to measure performance, there is also the danger that these comparisons may not capture the full range of performance that could occur if different employees had been hired into the company. The statistical term for this problem is "range restriction."[24]

Range restriction can mask the true value of a staffing assessment. For example, a drug screen assessment may be very good at screening out particularly bad employees, but may have no value for differentiating between average and good employees. Consequently, a study that compares the performance of current employees with their drug screen results might conclude that the assessment has no relationship to performance because it did not include performance data from those candidates who were never hired because they failed the drug screen during the application process.

Range restriction is a particularly important issue when conducting studies to establish performance "benchmarks" based on a company's existing high-performing employees. Companies that benchmark based solely on examining existing performance levels may settle for performance levels below what might be found if they were examining another group of employees outside of the organization. It is possible that a company's current high performers are not actually achieving the highest levels of performance possible. When considering performance, it is always important to differentiate between performance of current employees and levels of performance that might exist if a different method had been used to select those employees in the first place.

Are You Assuming That More Is Always Better When It Comes to Performance?

There are points at which increasing certain performance-relevant behaviors no longer helps improve job results. In some cases, an increase in behavior may even begin to negatively impact results. For example, while high levels of attendance are certainly preferable to low levels, companies do not necessary benefit from employees who maintain perfect attendance by coming to work, even when they are extremely sick. In job settings such as food service, this sort of attendance behavior could even have catastrophic job outcomes (handling food while suffering from an infectious illness). Virtually any candidate strength can at some point turn into a weakness. Staffing assessment strategies should take into account that more is not always better when it comes to performance.[25]

These are just some of the challenges to defining, measuring, and predicting performance. Many other issues and concerns may need to be addressed, depending on the unique nature of each organization and job. The key is to approach the issue of performance measurement with an open and critical mind. If possible, work with someone who has expertise in this area. Also be prepared for the reality that the best ways to deal with most performance measurement challenges usually involve developing new performance measures, collecting a larger data sample, collecting data over a longer time period, or some combination of all three. But if you truly want to systematically predict employee performance, you need to be willing to put the time and energy needed to define and measure exactly what it is you want to predict.

Notes

1. Ones, D.S., Viswesvaran, C., & Schmidt, F.L. (1993). Comprehensive meta-analysis of integrity test validities: Findings and implications for personnel selection and theories of job performance. *Journal of Applied Psychology, 78,* 679–703.

2. Schmidt, F.L., Ones, D.S., & Hunter, J.E. (1992). Personnel selection. *Annual Review of Psychology, 43,* 627–670.

3. Zuckerman, M. (1984). Sensation seeking: A comparative approach to a human trait. *Behavioral and Brain Science, 7,* 413–471.

4. Deb, M. (1983). Sales effectiveness and personality characteristics. *Psychological Research Journal, 7,* 59–67.

5. Cortina, J.M. (1993). What is coefficient alpha? An examination of theory and applications. *Journal of Applied Psychology, 78,* 98–104.

6. Nunnally, J.C. (1978). *Psychometric theory.* New York: McGraw-Hill.

7. Cronbach, L.J. (1990). *Essentials of psychological testing* (5th ed.). New York: Harper and Row.
   Nunnally, J.C. (1978). *Psychometric theory.* New York: McGraw-Hill.

8. Bauer, T.N., Truxillo, D.M., Sanchez, R.J., Craig, J.M., Ferrara, P., & Campion, M. (2001). Applicant reactions to selection: Development of the selection procedural justice scale (SPJS). *Personnel Psychology, 54,* 387–419.

9. Grubb, W.L., Whetzel, D.L., & McDaniel, M.A. (2004). General mental ability tests in industry. In J.C. Thomas & M. Herson (Eds.), *Comprehensive handbook of psychological assessment, Vol. 4, Industrial and organizational assessment.* Hoboken, NJ: John Wiley & Sons.

10. Harvey, R.J. (1991). Job analysis. In M.D. Dunnette & L.M. Hough (Eds.), *Handbook of industrial and organizational psychology* (2nd ed., pp. 873–919). Palo Alto, CA: Consulting Psychologists Press.

11. Becker, T.E., & Colquitt, A.L. (1992). Potential versus actual faking of a biodata form: An analysis along several dimensions of item type. *Personnel Psychology, 45,* 389–406.

12. Moorman, R.H., & Podsakoff, P.M. (1992). A meta-analytic review and empirical test of the potential confounding effects of social desirability response sets in organizational behavior research. *Journal of Occupational and Organizational Psychology, 65,* 131–149.

13. Cascio, W.F. (2000). *Costing human resources: The financial impact of behavior in organizations.* Cincinnati, OH: South-western.
    A somewhat briefer discussion of utility analysis can also be found in J.W. Boudreau (1991). Utility analysis for decisions in human resource management. In M.D. Dunnette & L.M. Hough (Eds.), *Handbook of industrial and organizational psychology* (2nd ed., pp. 621–745). Palo Alto, CA: Consulting Psychologists Press.

14. Klimoski, R.J., & Brickner, M. (1987). Why do assessment centers work? The puzzle of assessment center validity. *Personnel Psychology, 40,* 243–260.

15. Braun, H.I., Wiley, D.E., & Jackson, D.N. (2002). *The role of constructs in psychological and educational measurement.* Mahwah, NJ: Lawrence Erlbaum Associates.

16. Collins, J. (2001). *Good to great: Why some companies make the leap … and others don't.* New York: HarperCollins.

17. Austin, J.T., & Villanova, P. (1992). The criterion problem: 1917–1992. *Journal of Applied Psychology, 77,* 836–874.
    Robertson, I.T., & Kindner, A. (1993). Personality and job competencies: The criterion-related validity of some personality variables. *Journal of Occupational and Organizational Psychology, 66,* 225–244.
18. Dansereau, F., & Markham, S.E. (1987). Levels of analysis in personnel and human resources management. *Research in Personnel and Human Resources Management, 5,* 1–50.
19. Schmidt, F.L., & Hunter, J.E. (1998). The validity and utility of selection methods in personnel psychology: Practical and theoretical implications of 85 years of research findings. *Psychological Bulletin, 124,* 262–274.
20. Austin, J.T., & Villanova, P. (1992). The criterion problem: 1917–1992. *Journal of Applied Psychology, 77,* 836–874.
21. Murphy, K.R., & Balzer, W.K. (1989). Rating errors and rating accuracy. *Journal of Applied Psychology, 74,* 619–624.
22. Landy, F.J., & Farr, J.L. (1980). Performance rating. *Psychological Bulletin, 87,* 72–107.
23. Olson, J.B., & Hulin, C. (1992). Information processing antecedents of rating errors in performance appraisal. *Journal of Vocational Behavior, 40,* 49–61.
24. Campbell, J.P. (1990). Modeling the performance prediction problem in industrial and organizational psychology. In M.D. Dunnette & L.M. Hough (Eds.), *Handbook of industrial and organizational psychology* (2nd ed., Vol. 1, pp. 687–731). Palo Alto, CA: Consulting Psychologists Press.
25. Sinclair, R.R., Banas, C., & Radwinsky, R. (1999). *Non-linearity in personality-performance relations: Theory, assessment methods, and empirical evidence.* Paper presented at the 14th annual meeting of the Society for Industrial and Organizational Psychology, Atlanta, Georgia.

Defining Job Performance and Its Relationship to Assessments

Assessments are never valid in a general sense. They are only valid for predicting certain kinds of job performance. You cannot determine whether an assessment is good or bad for selecting employees into a job until you first determine the things you want the assessment to predict. This requires clearly defining what effective job performance looks like in that specific job.

This chapter discusses how to define and describe job performance and how to use this information to determine which assessments to use. The chapter also discusses how to monitor assessments over time to ensure they optimally predict key aspects of job performance. These topics are addressed as steps in an overall process for designing and implementing a staffing assessment system. Since many readers of this book may be more likely to purchase assessments from vendors, rather than developing them "in-house," the steps include guidelines for evaluating assessment vendors to determine whether their assessments are likely to be effective for predicting different types of job performance.

The process for developing an effective staffing assessment system consists of four general steps:

1. *Identify key performance outcomes.* This requires defining business outcomes you wish to improve through making better staffing decisions. Some of the outcomes assessments can influence include hiring people who tend

to stay on the job longer, avoid accidents, sell more products, calm down angry customers, solve difficult technical problems, or simply show up to work on time. Which performance outcomes are most important will vary from job to job.

2. *Use job analysis to define and describe critical employee behaviors.* This involves determining what employee behaviors actually drive the business outcomes defined in Step 1. In other words, what is it that high-performing employees do on the job that makes them more effective than average or poor-performing employees? The behaviors that drive performance often vary from job to job. For example, highly creative, "out-of-the-box" behaviors that might drive productivity in an entrepreneurial sales job with few standard work policies could negatively affect productivity in a manufacturing job that emphasizes highly structured, systematic work processes.

3. *Choose an assessment that is valid for predicting critical employee behaviors.* This involves either developing a new assessment or identifying existing assessments that predict the kinds of employee behaviors and performance outcomes identified in Steps 1 and 2. This step often involves reviewing assessment solutions offered by different assessment vendors to ensure they meet your organization's needs.

4. *Appropriately collect and interpret assessment data.* Determining what assessment to use is only part of developing an effective assessment solution. It is equally important to deploy the assessment in a manner that ensures appropriate collection and interpretation of assessment data. This includes tracking data to make sure the assessment continues to optimally predict critical employee behaviors and business outcomes over time.

The most common mistake in designing assessment systems is to skip the first two steps of defining performance outcomes and conducting job analysis and go directly to the step of choosing assessment instruments. Doing this is like buying shoes for someone without first finding out the person's size, gender, or how he or she intends to use the shoes. You may end up buying a very attractive, nicely made pair of men's size 13 hiking boots, only to find out that what was needed were women's size 4 high heels to go with a formal evening gown. You cannot possibly know what assessment to use if you do not first clearly determine what job-relevant behaviors and performance outcomes it should predict. With that in mind, we now turn to the first step: identify key performance outcomes.

STEP 1. IDENTIFY KEY PERFORMANCE OUTCOMES

If anyone ever asks you "What is the best assessment for evaluating job candidates?", your response should always be "It depends on what business outcomes you want to influence." The reason for using assessments is to improve performance outcomes. Assessments do this by evaluating candidates, but evaluating candidates is a secondary goal. Companies do not use assessments simply because they want to learn more about candidates. They use them to influence business results by making better hiring decisions. And the best way to do this is to use assessments that provide accurate insight into the match between candidates' attributes and the demands of the job they are applying for.

Determining what assessment to use starts with determining what specific outcomes you want to influence through better hiring decisions. Is your goal to improve employee retention, increase productivity, provide better customer service, achieve higher sales revenue, or to impact some other performance outcome? Answering this question may require making some difficult choices around business priorities. This is because assessments that positively impact some performance outcomes often negatively impact others (see sidebar, "No One Is Good at Everything").

The process of selecting assessments should be part of a broader strategic discussion looking at overall business goals and objectives. This discussion often involves making decisions to emphasize certain outcomes over others. Fairly in-depth analysis may be needed to determine the optimal balance of outcomes for your organization's strategy and business model. For example, one common tradeoff when developing assessments is whether to focus on productivity versus retention. The most highly productive employees in jobs can be among the first to leave.[1] These employees are often driven by a desire to move on to increasingly challenging positions, tend to have more job opportunities elsewhere, and may quickly tire of jobs after they master them. While there is value in having highly productive, short-time employees, there is also value in having a stable workforce. But the financial value of retention varies substantially, depending on a company's business model. Companies that spend a lot of resources to train employees gain greater value from increasing retention. In contrast, companies that invest in simplifying jobs so little training is needed to perform them may not gain as much from increased retention.[2] Discussions around the relative value of various business outcomes such as these are an important part of the process of determining what assessments will make the most sense for your company.

Effective staffing requires making choices between the relative importance of different candidate attributes. There are some candidate attributes that are probably universally counterproductive across virtually every type of job. For example, it is hard to imagine a legitimate job for which superior performance is associated with attributes related to outright theft and dishonesty. But it is also hard to envision a candidate attribute that is always desirable, regardless of the job. Attributes that are strengths for some job behaviors are usually also weaknesses for others. For example, being agreeable and respectful may be desirable traits when applied to things like fostering teamwork and getting along with others, but can be weaknesses for job roles that require taking a firm stance on an issue or holding others accountable for their behavior.

When designing staffing methods, it is good to remember that there is no such thing as a single type of "ideal" candidate. Candidates who excel at some aspects of a job will invariably be less effective in other areas. This was illustrated once when I was helping a group of hiring managers design a staffing system to identify people who shared the same attributes as their high-performing, "superstar" sales people. The hiring managers responded that, while having this type of information would be useful, in reality they did not want to hire a team entirely made up of these superstars. The attributes like competitiveness and independence that make these people great at winning sales deals also made them very difficult to manage. They don't "play nice" with others and tend to ignore any aspects of the job that do not directly help them achieve their goals. The managers said that they always want a few of these people on their teams, but if they had to deal with more than about three of these superstars it would probably cause them and the rest of the people in their groups to quit.

The underlying point made by these managers is that an effective organization requires people with diverse attributes and skills. Because no one is good at everything, you need to focus on hiring candidates whose mix of skills complement each other. Assessment can help avoid hiring people who have "fatal flaws" associated with catastrophically bad performance. They can also help identify each candidate's unique strengths. But they cannot replace the role hiring managers play in terms of hiring those specific employees whose particular blend of strengths and limitations best complement the existing skill set of their team.

When discussing business outcomes, be realistic about whether they are likely to be impacted by staffing strategies. Assessments only impact outcomes if they are influenced by differences in employee behavior. Many business outcomes are driven by variables that have little to do with what employees actually do on the job. For example, sales levels for some retail jobs are driven largely by an employee's work schedule. How much an employee sells depends more on the number of customers who come to the shop during the person's shift then the person's actual sales skills. Similarly, employee turnover is often driven more by broader economic trends, corporate policies, or actions of individual store managers than differences in employee attributes and behaviors. It is futile to try to use staffing assessments to influence things that are determined almost entirely by situational variables that lie outside the control of individual employees (see sidebar, "Staffing Jobs No One Wants").

STAFFING JOBS NO ONE WANTS

Organizational leaders occasionally approach staffing assessments as if they were a "magic bullet" that can fix broader human resource problems within their company. These leaders hope, wrongly, that if they just hire the right people then more systematic problems in their company will simply go away. One place this often occurs is in the area of turnover. While hiring the right people can significantly reduce turnover, it cannot overcome problems caused by jobs that provide people with a fundamentally unpleasant or unrewarding work experience. For example, an organization once asked me for an assessment that would decrease turnover in one of their entry-level jobs. This was a part-time minimum-wage job without health care benefits. Employees were required to wear an uncomfortable, heat-resistant suit and shovel heavy lumps of metal into a hot furnace over the course of an eight-hour shift. When the hiring manager was asked who would want this sort of job, his reply was, "I don't know; I can't imagine anyone who would enjoy this." This company was looking for an assessment that could identify people who would remain in a job that virtually no one who had any type of career choice would want. Although the company did not want to admit it, their problem was not an issue of staffing but an issue associated with how they were designing their jobs and compensating their workers. The company was hoping staffing assessments could fix their turnover problem so they could avoid having to invest the resources required to actually make the job desirable. This won't work.

STEP 2. USE JOB ANALYSIS TO DEFINE AND DESCRIBE CRITICAL EMPLOYEE BEHAVIORS

In this step you determine what employee behaviors influence the business outcomes you identified in Step 1. For example, if you want to identify candidates who achieve higher sales revenues, then you have to determine what specific employee behaviors are associated with increased sales. Some companies sell products by having employees engage in friendly and social behaviors to build strong customer relationships, while others rely on more aggressive, transactional and persuasive behaviors to close deals. An employee who is effective in one sales environment might be highly ineffective in the other. It is unwise to assume that behaviors that drive performance outcomes in one job or company are identical to the behaviors that drive these outcomes in another job or company. Deploying an assessment to evaluate candidates without first clearly defining the behaviors that drive performance is like shooting an arrow without first identifying the target; you may be successful, but your success will depend largely on luck.

Developing a clear understanding of the behaviors that drive job performance can be harder than you might expect. When you ask managers "What makes a great employee?" they tend to answer in vague generalities about passion, dedication, and "can do" attitude. These things sound good, but they tell us next to nothing about what it is that high-performing employees actually do that makes them different from average or poor employees. Fortunately, there are various job-analysis techniques you can use to quickly and accurately define the key employee behaviors and characteristics that drive job performance (see the sidebar "Job Analysis and Competency Modeling"). Job analysis is not an overly complex thing to master, and there are many books available that walk you through different job analysis methods.[3] But unless you plan to design a lot of assessment processes, it probably makes more sense to enlist help from someone who specializes in conducting job analyses rather than learning how to do it yourself.

Assessments do not predict job performance outcomes directly; they predict the employee behaviors that influence those outcomes. To build maximally effective staffing assessments, it is critical to clearly describe the specific employee behaviors that drive job performance outcomes. The methods used for developing these descriptions are commonly referred to as "job analysis" techniques.[4] Job analysis has historically been a somewhat laborious process involving extensive on-site job observation by trained job analysts coupled with use of lengthy job analysis questionnaires. Fortunately, the last decade has seen significant advances in the development of shorter, less labor-intensive job analysis methods based on a technique called competency modeling.

Competencies are groups of job-relevant behaviors that tend to occur in combination for the purpose of achieving different job objectives. "Negotiating," "adhering to policies and regulations," and "maintaining physical endurance" are examples of competencies. Research over the last several years has identified many of the competencies that influence performance in most jobs. This has made it possible to create competency libraries that provide basic building blocks for describing performance in different jobs.[5]

Table 5.1 lists examples of the kinds of competencies that are often contained in a competency library. An actual competency library would also include detailed descriptions of effective and ineffective behaviors associated with each of these competencies. Various processes and techniques have been created to help subject-matter experts review competency libraries and select those competencies that are most critical for driving business outcomes in a specific job.[6]

Competency modeling provides a relatively simple but effective means for identifying key employee behaviors that determine job success.[7] Thanks to competency modeling methods, companies no longer have to view job analyses as a highly time-intensive endeavor. As a result, job analysis and assessment development projects that used to take weeks or months to conduct can now be completed in a matter of days.

Table 5.1
Sample Competency Library

Action-Oriented Competencies	Interpersonal Competencies	Intellectual Competencies
Driving results	Setting direction	Thinking commercially
Following procedures	Building relationships	Interpreting complex information
Taking decisive action	Displaying ethical behavior	Applying technical knowledge
Dealing with change	Influencing others	Analyzing problems
Managing stress	Communicating information	Thinking creatively
Planning and	Working across cultures	Developing strategies

Any worthwhile job analysis method will require direct involvement from hiring managers, employees, or other subject-matter experts familiar with the job being staffed. Most methods require subject-matter experts to review different kinds of behaviors and indicate how relevant they are to job performance. Subject-matter experts might also be asked to provide examples of actual things employees have done on the job that illustrate effective or ineffective behavior. Such examples are sometimes referred to as "critical incidents" of productive or counterproductive performance.[8]

Gaining access to subject-matter experts in order to conduct a job analysis can be challenging. But failing to conduct appropriate job analysis can lead to the development of assessment systems that systematically ignore, overlook, or improperly weight important candidate attributes. A thorough job analysis also significantly decreases legal exposure should your assessment methods be challenged in court.[9] The following are a few additional things to consider when conducting job analysis.

Balance Different Types of Performance

Successful performance in almost all jobs depends on multiple types of behavior.[10] Employees who excel at one type of performance may struggle at another. For example, employees who are good at learning technical skills are not necessarily good at working with people. Employees who are highly reliable may struggle with change. A common mistake when developing staffing assessment strategies is to over-emphasize one type of job performance while overlooking others. This can lead to hiring candidates whose performance is very good in some areas but detrimental in others. To be maximally effective, staffing assessment processes must predict different types of performance to ensure that newly hired employees do not succeed at one aspect of the job but fail in another.

Attend to the Changing Nature of Performance

The nature of job performance can change across work situations or at different points in an employee's career. For example, the behaviors that drive performance during an employee's first two weeks learning the job may not be the same as the behaviors that influence performance four months later once the job has become more routine.[11] Companies that only focus on hiring people based on how they perform during the first month on the job may end up with employees who are excellent at mastering new tasks when they first start the job but who are not very good at maintaining tasks once they have been learned.[12] Conversely, companies that only look at the performance of longer-tenured employees may not adequately emphasize the importance of behaviors that may be critical to the performance of newly hired employees such as learning new tasks.

Distinguish Between Maximal and Typical Performance

It is often important to distinguish between the value of employees' typical day-to-day performance and the value of their maximal performance when they are under pressure. For example, a grocery cashier who can process forty transactions an hour during peak hours but only processes ten per hour during slow times may be more valuable than a cashier who processes fifteen transactions per hour throughout the day but cannot process more than thirty per hour during peak times. Making these subtle distinctions in performance is important to designing a maximally effective staffing assessment process.

Creating an assessment process that effectively identifies the best candidates requires taking time to clearly describe what effective job performance "looks like." This is the purpose of job analysis. Companies that fail to invest the time and resources required to conduct a thorough job analysis run a significant risk of implementing assessments that may fail to predict critical behaviors that drive job performance. For this reason, many assessment vendors insist that clients conduct some form of job analysis before they will allow them to use their assessment tools. This is not just because they wish to charge clients extra fees. It is because the vendors take pride in providing a quality product, and they know that the only way to ensure an assessment will work is to take the time to understand the job. In addition, these vendors may not want to expose their assessment instruments to potential legal risks that can arise from deploying assessments without first conducting job analysis to document their relevance to the positions being staffed.

Some staffing assessment vendors are willing to sell assessments with little concern about whether the assessments are actually appropriate for a given job. Certain vendors may even downplay the importance of job analysis because they view it as a barrier to sales. Providing assessments to a company without first conducting some form of job analysis is like a doctor prescribing medicine without first taking time to diagnose the patient. It may work, but it may hurt you too. Companies that use assessments without conducting job analyses may initially feel that the assessments are adding value, but could eventually discover that what the assessments are predicting has little bearing on actual job performance. These companies also place themselves at much greater risk should their assessment practices ever be legally challenged as being unfair or irrelevant to the job. Given all of these things, it is always worth the time and cost to do some form of job analysis before implementing a new assessment, even if the job analysis process is relatively simple and abbreviated.

STEP 3. CHOOSE AN EFFECTIVE ASSESSMENT

This step involves selecting or building assessments that measure candidate attributes that predict the employee behaviors and performance outcomes you identified in Steps 1 and 2. This step can be quite complicated due to the technical nature of assessments and the number of assessments available in the marketplace. At the time this book was written, there were hundreds of assessment vendors in the United States selling thousands of different kinds of assessments. Most of these assessments are effective for predicting certain types of employee behaviors. But all of these assessments only predict a subset of the possible behaviors and performance outcomes you might be interested in. No assessment predicts everything. In addition, not all assessment tools are built to the same quality standards. Some work far better than others, and a few may not work at all. Distinguishing between well-designed and poorly designed assessments and determining which of these assessments have the most value for a company's specific hiring needs can be difficult, even for highly trained assessment professionals.

The key to choosing an effective assessment is to use a systematic process clearly centered around the ultimate goal: finding an assessment that will help you efficiently hire people who will display the behaviors that the job analysis conducted in Step 2 identified as being critical for driving the business outcomes identified in Step 1. Determining whether an assessment will meet this goal requires answering two basic questions. First, does the assessment predict the employee behaviors and performance outcomes you care about? Second, does the assessment meet key operational requirements and constraints related to the broader staffing process? These questions will be discussed separately, although in practice they can often be addressed simultaneously.

Does the Assessment Predict Key Employee Behaviors and Performance Outcomes?

When choosing assessments, always maintain a steady focus on what matters the most: Does the assessment predict the employee behaviors and job outcomes that are critical to your organization? Be cautious of assessment vendors who discuss the virtues of their assessments, what they look like, and what they measure, but who spend very little time asking about what specific employee behaviors and job outcomes you actually want to predict. Choosing assessments based on vendor explanations of why their assessments are important can place a company at risk of systematically selecting candidates based on attributes that sound desirable, but that may not be that relevant for job performance (see sidebar "The Emotional Intelligence Fad").

THE EMOTIONAL INTELLIGENCE FAD

Discussions of what staffing assessments measure should be secondary to discussions of the employee behaviors and performance outcomes they actually predict. Unfortunately, it is not uncommon for staffing assessments to be deployed based primarily on hype around what they measure, with far too little focus on whether they actually predict employee behaviors that drive job performance. One example of this occurred in the late 1990s with assessments designed to measure "emotional intelligence."

Emotional intelligence reflects differences in people's ability to effectively monitor, manage, and utilize emotional behavior in themselves and others.[13] Emotional intelligence was a hot topic in human resources during the late 1990s. Emotional intelligence as originally defined in the scientific research literature is clearly relevant to performance on many jobs. On the other hand, like most attributes, its relevance to jobs varies widely, depending on what employee behaviors are most critical for job success.

The core concept of emotional intelligence is actually very difficult to measure. It requires evaluating people's ability to both recognize emotions in others and to appropriately regulate or change their own emotional responses in real time. In spite of the difficulty in measuring such a specialized skill, several self-report assessments marketed in the late 1990s were purported to measure emotional intelligence. Many of these measures were sold as staffing assessment tools, even though little data was provided showing that they actually predicted employee behaviors or job performance outcomes. Rather than focusing on emotional intelligence as a means to predict specific aspects of job performance, vendors marketed emotional intelligence as being important in and of itself, regardless of the job being staffed. In a sense, some emotional intelligence assessments were sold as a "wonder drug" that cures all staffing ills. These assessments did not deliver on the promises made by these vendors, and fewer than ten years later one rarely finds mention of emotional intelligence assessments.

The emotional intelligence fad illustrates the danger of deploying assessments based on the supposed virtues of an assessment itself, rather than the relationships between the assessment and specific aspects of job performance. This approach puts companies at risk of using assessments that have little to do with actual employee behaviors or performance outcomes.

The process of choosing an assessment should not begin with assessment instruments. It should begin with carefully defining what employee behaviors and job performance outcomes drive job success. Only then should companies begin discussing different assessments. These discussions should remain firmly focused on evaluating the relationships between assessments and job-relevant behaviors and outcomes. Beware of assessment vendors who focus more on selling the virtues of their assessments than on discussing the ability of their assessments to predict the things you have identified as important. As a general rule, if a vendor recommends an assessment to your company without first discussing what behaviors you want to predict, then you may want to consider finding another vendor.

The key to finding the most appropriate assessments is to approach assessment vendors with a very "job-performance-centric" mindset. Do not ask vendors for information about what their assessments are or what they measure. Instead, request information about how well their tools predict the things you want to influence through better staffing. For example, instead of asking vendors for a measure of customer service skills, you might ask whether they have assessments that predict whether candidates will be effective at engaging customers in pleasant conversations. Let the vendors determine which of their tools will be the most effective for predicting the employee behaviors and performance outcomes you describe. Then ask them to provide evidence showing why these tools are likely to work. What assessments are called, what they look like, and what they are purported to measure are all secondary to the kinds of employee behaviors and performance outcomes they actually predict.

Most assessment vendors will be fairly straightforward about the kinds of employee behaviors their assessments have been shown to predict. Sadly, this is not the case for all vendors. As long as there is money to be made selling staffing tools, there will be people willing to sell tools that do not work. The best way to tell whether an assessment actually does what it is supposed to do is to examine its criteria validity. Criteria validity was discussed in a fair bit of detail in the previous chapter. To quickly review, criteria validity shows the statistical association between the information collected from candidates by an assessment (that is, their assessment "scores") and data reflecting their subsequent performance on the job. The best assessment vendors will be able to provide criteria validity data that illustrates how well their assessments predict specific types of job performance. When looking at this data, keep in mind that the *only* way to establish criteria validity is to compare people's scores on an assessment with measures of their performance on the job.* If the vendor has never statistically compared people's assessment scores with independent data collected on their performance, then the vendor is showing you an assessment with no demonstrated criteria validity.

*Some assessment vendors present data from a statistical technique called employee profiling as though it were the same as criteria validity data. This technique summarizes assessment scores of different types of employees or candidates, but does not actually show direct links between employees' assessment scores and measures of their actual performance. See the sidebar "Profiling and the Dangers of Cloning High-Performing Employees" in Chapter Seven for a more detailed discussion of the difference between validation and profiling.

When it comes to staffing, criteria validity is what matters most. That's not to say that the other forms of validity such as face and content validity are unimportant, just that they are usually of less importance compared to criteria validity. Later in this chapter I will discuss some situations in which content validity may provide sufficient justification for using an assessment without any criteria validation evidence. But these exceptions are rare for more general behavioral assessments such as ability tests and personality measures. Vendors selling these kinds of assessments should have done the work required to gather some evidence demonstrating the criteria validity of their assessment.

The methods for evaluating the criteria validity of assessments are fairly well understood, although not always used.[14] High-quality staffing assessment vendors can usually provide standard summaries of criteria validity studies that have been conducted to test the effectiveness of their tools. These validation summaries should include the following kinds of technical information:

- The types of jobs used in the validation studies, including descriptions of the kinds of companies participating.

- The number of employees and/or candidates used in the studies.

- The performance criteria used to validate the assessment (for example, supervisor ratings of performance, tenure, sales performance, and so on).

- Statistics indicating relationships between peoples' scores on the assessment and relevant job performance criteria. These statistics will ideally appear in the form of "validity coefficients" that were discussed earlier in Chapter Four. Statistics may also be reported in the form of percentage differences in performance across groups of people who scored high or low on the assessments.

- Equal Employment Opportunity Commission (EEOC) statistics indicating potential differences in assessment scores across various demographic groups. These provide insight into whether an assessment may adversely impact applicants with certain demographic backgrounds. See Chapter Six for additional information on employment laws pertaining to the EEOC and adverse impact.

Any quality assessment vendor should be able to provide this sort of validation information. At the very least, vendors should be familiar with the concept of validity and should be able to explain what steps they take to ensure the validity of their assessments. If you ask an assessment vendor for validity evidence and the reply contains a lot of scientific or business jargon and very few actual validation numbers, it may be time to start looking for some other vendors.

There are some situations in which content validity alone is considered sufficient to warrant use of an assessment without any criteria validity evidence. For example, when using direct assessments to evaluate whether candidates meet certain, well-defined qualifications or requirements for the job, or when operational constraints make it impractical or impossible to conduct a criteria validation study (e.g., building an assessment for a job when there are not enough existing employees to collect adequate validation data). You may recall from Chapter Four that content validity is based on using qualitative data to demonstrate that what an assessment measures is related to key job behaviors. Content validity is not as desirable as criteria validity, but does constitute legally acceptable and scientifically defensible evidence for an assessment's effectiveness and job relevance.

Content validity is frequently used to demonstrate the job relevance of assessments that measure relatively well-defined aspects of a candidate's knowledge, skills, experiences, or qualifications. Knowledge and skill tests and pre-screening questionnaires are two types of assessments for which content validity may be acceptable in lieu of criteria validity. These types of assessments are often used to assess "hard skills" or requirements that a person must possess in order to perform a job. For example, in order to be hired on as a truck driver, a candidate may need to possess a valid driving license and be able to pass a test demonstrating knowledge of rules and regulations related to truck driving. It is often possible to determine whether assessments effectively measure these specific sorts of qualifications and knowledge merely by studying the properties of the assessments themselves, without actually comparing assessment scores to performance data. In contrast, it is much more difficult to use content validity as a means to evaluate the job relevance of behavioral assessments such as personality and ability tests that measure less-well-defined characteristics such as "reliability" or "safety mindedness."

When evaluating the content validity of an assessment, focus on examining the degree to which the content of the assessments is based on systematic job analysis information collected from qualified subject-matter experts. Ask: "What processes were used to ensure that kinds of questions on the assessment are relevant to the types of qualifications, knowledge, and experiences needed to perform the job?" "What actions are taken to keep the content of the assessment up-to-date and reflective of current knowledge, skills, or requirements for the job?" Last, "What data has been collected to make sure the assessment questions are at an appropriate level of difficulty for the position?" The key to creating content valid assessments is to use systematic, detailed methods to build and continually test assessments based on the specific needs of different jobs. Vendors that do not follow such methods are much more likely to build assessments that may look job-relevant, but that actually assess things that are tangential or unimportant to job performance.

Does the Assessment Meet Key Operational Requirements?

When selecting assessments, it is critical to consider how the assessment will be used and who will be using it. Even the most accurate and valid assessment will be useless if hiring decision makers do not use it or use it incorrectly. Assessments can also hurt an organization if candidates find them to be overly offensive or inappropriate.

The following five questions should be considered when examining whether an assessment meets an organization's operational requirements:

1. *Will hiring managers accept the assessment as appropriate and useful?* Hiring managers often resist the introduction of new staffing assessments into the hiring process. These managers are the ones who have to live with any hiring mistakes that may occur if the assessment does not work as promised. Hiring managers who have never used assessments before are frequently skeptical about their value. Some hiring managers feel they are better at evaluating candidates than assessments are (although this is unlikely; see the sidebar in Chapter Six, "Why Assessments Are More Accurate Than People"). Other hiring managers may have had bad experiences with other assessment tools they used in the past.

   There are several ways to increase the chances of hiring managers accepting an assessment. First, try to use assessments that have higher levels of face validity so that managers perceive them to be clearly job-relevant. Second, consider using assessments that are similar to ones hiring managers may have used and accepted in the past. This is one of the advantages of structured interviews, since all managers have some experience conducting interviews. Last, communicate how the assessment was chosen and provide evidence regarding its value for predicting job performance. These things will not guarantee that all hiring managers will embrace the use of assessments, but they lessen the chance of assessments being rejected outright.

2. *Is the assessment easy to administer?* When choosing an assessment, it is important to think about how it will be given to candidates. Can you administer the assessment to candidates in a way that will not place an excess burden on people in the organization responsible for supporting the staffing process? Similarly, the administration process should not be overly burdensome on the candidate. For example, some vendors insist that their assessments only be administered in a proctored setting where candidates are supervised in order to make sure they do not cheat, steal, or otherwise display unethical behaviors when completing the assessment. While there are often good reasons to proctor assessments, requiring candidates to report to specific, supervised locations to complete assessments at a specific time may cause a lot of candidates to drop out of the hiring process.

   The advent of online, web-based staffing has made it much easier to administer assessments to candidates. But there are significant differences in the ease of use associated with different assessment technology platforms. In addition, some assessments such as physical exams still need to be administered in person. These issues need to be considered when choosing assessments. There is no sense in deploying an assessment if people are unable to effectively use it.

3. *Is the assessment easy to interpret?* Some assessments provide information that can be interpreted with little or no training. For example, some pre-screening questionnaires classify candidates as "green" or "red" based on whether they meet minimum job requirements. Most people can quickly grasp how to use this information in the hiring process. In contrast, the information provided by other assessments can be highly complex. People may need to complete several hours of training before they are able to effectively interpret the results of many kinds of ability tests, personality assessments, and structured interviews.

   When choosing an assessment, it is important to think about who will receive the assessment results and what sort of training they will need to interpret these results appropriately. Also consider turnover among the people who will be interpreting the assessment results. Remember, each time someone new uses the assessment he or she will need to first receive training on how to use it.

4. *Is the assessment affordable?* The cost of assessment solutions varies widely, depending on both the type of assessment and the vendor. Some assessments

carry no charge beyond initial set-up costs. Others require ongoing licensing or usage fees of $100 or more per candidate. Before deciding on an assessment, it is important to review assessment costs that take into account the number of times the assessment is likely to be administered to candidates.

5. *How will candidates react to the assessment?* There are no fixed rules when it comes to evaluating how candidates will react to assessments. Some candidates will happily complete lengthy assessments, while others bristle at the request to complete any type of structured assessment (the issue of candidate reactions to assessments is discussed in much more detail in Chapter Six). At a general level, efforts should be made to avoid using assessments that candidates may perceive as inconvenient, inappropriate, or unfair. A failure to consider candidate reactions may result in the loss of good candidates, creation of negative attitudes among candidates toward your company, and a greater risk of litigation based on perceptions of unfair hiring practices.

These five questions cover most of the major issues that affect the operational use of assessments. Other issues that may warrant consideration include the desire to integrate technology used to administer assessments with other staffing and HR technology systems, the need to deploy assessments in multi-lingual or international settings, and potential legal concerns that may affect use of certain kinds of assessments in certain states or countries. Remember that staffing assessments are not "stand-alone" tools. They must effectively fit into the larger staffing process and organizational environment to be useful and supported over the long run.

STEP 4. APPROPRIATELY COLLECTING AND INTERPRETING ASSESSMENT DATA

Steps 1 through 3 focused on how to determine what assessments to use for staffing certain jobs. This last step focuses on how to make sure that assessments are used effectively after they have been deployed. This step includes a discussion of how to track assessment data over time and use it to strengthen the relationship between assessments and job performance.

Systematically Collecting and Interpreting Assessment Information

The accuracy of assessments depends on gathering and interpreting candidate information in a highly structured manner. This requires collecting and interpreting information from all candidates using consistent methods. Systematic collection and interpretation of candidate data is one of the primary reasons why assessments are often more accurate than people at predicting job performance.[15] Failure to systematically collect and interpret staffing assessment data greatly reduces the accuracy of staffing decisions.

The best way to ensure systematic data collection is to use computer-based systems that automatically administer and score assessments. A technology-based approach works particularly well for self-report measures and knowledge, skills, and ability tests. Use of other assessments such as interviews that cannot be easily automated can be made more consistent by providing hiring decision makers with training and guidelines on how to administer and interpret assessments.

The important thing is to make sure that all candidates go through the same basic assessment process when applying for a job. This is not only important for ensuring the accuracy of staffing decisions, but it also reduces the risk of candidates filing legal action against a company based on the perception of preferential or unfair hiring practices that inappropriately favor some candidates over others.

Tracking and Improving Assessment Performance Over Time

Assessments that worked well in the past may not always continue to work well in the future. Businesses change over time. These changes may alter the employee behaviors that are needed for successful job performance. This in turn can change the kinds of candidate attributes associated with success in these jobs. All these changes may serve to reduce or even eliminate the effectiveness of certain assessments.

The key to maintaining an effective staffing process is to periodically revisit and test underlying assumptions about the accuracy of the assessments used in the process. In most cases, this means re-evaluating the content validity of assessments from time to time. But in cases in which large numbers of employees are being hired based in part on assessment results, it is possible to establish ongoing criteria validation processes to test how well existing assessments are working and to find ways to make them even more effective. This results in turning the staffing process into a data-driven continuous improvement process.[16] The application of mathematically driven staffing processes can also lead to discoveries of unrecognized candidate attributes associated with success, which in turn can lead to greater access to high-potential candidates (see sidebar, "Baseball and Staffing Assessment"). The concept of applying empirical, continuous improvement techniques to staffing processes is discussed in more detail in Chapter Seven in the section on assessment optimization.

CONCLUDING REMARKS: LINKING ASSESSMENT PROCESSES TO JOB PERFORMANCE

Designing and implementing an effective assessment process is rarely a simple undertaking. It requires paying careful attention to what performance outcomes are critical to job success, what employee behaviors influence those outcomes, which assessments best predict those behaviors, and what methods will ensure appropriate deployment of those assessments. On the other hand, designing an assessment process need not be a daunting, overly complex undertaking either. The key is to undertake the process with a firm appreciation of the various steps and issues that influence the accuracy and value of assessments, coupled with a clear focus on what matters most: the employee behaviors and performance outcomes that you want to impact through better hiring.

BASEBALL AND STAFFING ASSESSMENT

The book *Moneyball*[17] describes how the Oakland A's major league baseball team was able to consistently finish among the top-performing teams over several years, despite having a relatively smaller budget to recruit and retain players. A key theme in the book is the A's use of statistics to identify players who possessed unique attributes associated with key performance outcomes. For example, the management of the A's realized that the key to winning games was not how many hits players had, but how often players got on base. Players can get on base either by getting a hit or by being walked. Most teams focused on finding players who excel at getting hits. In contrast, the A's also looked for players who had a high percentage of walks. These players did not have the batting style of traditional baseball "superstars" who get a lot of hits. However, the A's determined statistically that players who showed certain often somewhat peculiar batting styles were more likely to be walked, even if they did not fit the stereotypical mold of a great baseball player. As a result, the A's were able to recruit several highly effective players at much lower wages then they would have had to pay if they had gone after the kinds of players most teams viewed as having the highest potential.

Examples like those found in *Moneyball* illustrate the sort of benefits that come from taking a highly empirical approach toward the development of staffing assessment systems. By identifying specific performance outcomes and then using mathematical techniques to identify employee behaviors and candidate attributes associated with those outcomes, companies are able to identify and hire high-performing employees that may be overlooked by other companies who rely on more traditional "gut feel" methods to select candidates. This can lead to hiring better employees at substantially lower costs.

Notes

1. Hom, P.W., & Salamin, A. (2005). In search of the elusive U-shaped performance-tenure relationship: Are high-performing Swiss bankers more liable to quit? *Journal of Applied Psychology, 90*, 1204–1216.
2. Glebeek, A.C., & Bax, E.H. (2004). Is high employee turnover really harmful? An empirical test using company records. *Academy of Management Journal, 47*, 277–286.
   Shaw, J.D., Gupta, N., & Delery, J.E. (2005). Alternative conceptualizations of the relationship between voluntary turnover and organizational performance. *Academy of Management Journal, 48*, 50–68.
3. Brannick, M.T., & Levine, E.L. (2002) Job analysis: Methods, research, and applications for human resource management in the new millennium. Thousand Oaks, CA: Sage.
   Gael, S. (1988). *Handbook of job analysis for business, industry, and government.* Hoboken, NJ: John Wiley & Sons.
4. Harvey, R.J. (1991). Job analysis. In M.D. Dunnette & L.M. Hough (Eds.), *Handbook of industrial and organizational psychology* (2nd ed., pp. 873–919). Palo Alto, CA: Consulting Psychologists Press.
5. Examples of competency libraries can be found in the following books, among others: Davis, B.L., Skube, C.J., Hellervik, L.W., Gebelein, S.H., & Sheard, J.L. (1996). *Successful manager's handbook.* Minneapolis, MN: Personnel Decisions International.
   Lombardo, M.M., & Eichinger, R.W. (1996). *For your improvement: A development and coaching guide.* Minneapolis, MN: Lominger Limited, Inc.
   Spencer, L.M. (1993). *Competence at work: Models for superior performance.* Hoboken, NJ: John Wiley & Sons.
6. Lucia, A.D., & Lepsinger, R. (1999). *The art and science of competency modeling: Pinpointing critical success factors in organizations.* San Francisco, CA: Jossey-Bass.
7. Lievens, F., Sanchez, J.I., & De Corte, W. (2004). Easing the inferential leap in competency modeling: The effect of task-related information and subject-matter expertise. *Personnel Psychology, 57*, 881–904.

8. Anderson, L., & Wilson, S. (1997). Critical incident technique. In D.L. Whetzel & R. George (Ed.), *Applied measurement methods in industrial psychology* (pp. 89–112). Palo Alto, CA: Davies-Black.

9. Sparks, C.P. (1988). Legal basis for job analysis. In S. Gael (Ed.), *Handbook of job analysis for business, industry, and government* (Vol. 1, pp. 14–29). Hoboken, NJ: John Wiley & Sons.

   Thompson, D.E., & Thompson, T.A. (1982). Court standards for job analysis in test validation. *Personnel Psychology, 35,* 865–874.

10. Campbell, J.P., McCloy, R.A., Oppler, S.H., & Sager, C.E. (1993). A theory of performance. In N. Schmitt, W. Borman, and Associates, *Personnel selection in organizations* (pp. 35–70). San Francisco, CA: Jossey-Bass.

11. Helmreich, R.L., Sawin, L.L., & Carsrud, A.L. (1986). The honeymoon effect in job performance: Temporal increases in the predictive power of achievement motivation. *Journal of Applied Psychology, 71,* 185–188.

12. Ackerman, P.L. (1993). Intelligence, attention, and learning: Maximal and typical performance. In D.K. Detterman (Ed.), *Current topics in human intelligence: Volume 4: Theories of intelligence.* Norwood, NJ: Ablex.

   Kanfer, R., & Ackerman, P.L. (1989). Motivation and cognitive abilities: An integrative/aptitude-treatment interaction approach to skill acquisition. *Journal of Applied Psychology, 74,* 657–690.

13. Goleman, D. (1994). *Emotional intelligence: Why it can matter more than IQ.* New York: Bantam.

14. Handler, C., & Hunt, S.T. (2004). Distinguishing between assessment science and snake oil. Electronic Recruiting Exchange. www.erexchange.com.

15. Westen, D., & Weinberger, J. (2004). When clinical description becomes statistical prediction. *American Psychologist,* pp. 595–613.

16. Hunt, S.T. (2006). Using metrics to guide staffing strategies across dispersed workforces. *Journal of Corporate Recruiting Leadership, 2,* 3–17.

17. Lewis, M. (2003). *Moneyball: The art of winning an unfair game.* New York: W.W. Norton.

Common Criticisms of Staffing Assessments

Companies use staffing assessments because they accurately predict job performance. But just because something predicts job performance does not mean it should influence hiring decisions. For example, height shows a remarkably strong relationship with general career success. Yet there are legal, social, and scientific reasons why companies might not want to make job selection decisions based specifically on candidate height.[1] Similar criticisms can and often are made against the use of certain types of staffing assessments. This chapter discusses several of these criticisms, specifically claims that staffing assessments:

1. Are not very accurate;

2. Can be faked by applicants;

3. Are not worth the cost required to use them;

4. Pose a legal risk;

5. Are an unfair way to evaluate people;

6. Are offensive to candidates; and/or

7. Add too much time to the hiring process.

All these criticisms have some truth to them, but they also have some noticeable flaws. The goal of this chapter is not to prove that these criticisms are either right or wrong. It is simply to examine the viewpoints upon which they are based. While I might argue that the value of using assessments far outweighs their risks, it would be disingenuous to imply that there is no potential downside to their use. Before making the decision to use assessments, you should carefully consider both the benefits and risks they pose.

CRITICISM 1: STAFFING ASSESSMENTS ARE NOT VERY ACCURATE

People often point out examples in which assessments classified highly successful employees as being poor candidates or vice versa. These examples emphasize the fact that assessment data, just like any other information that might be used to guide hiring decisions, is not perfectly accurate. Just because assessments are not perfect does not necessarily discount their value for guiding hiring decisions. The question is: Are they accurate enough to warrant being used to select employees?

A massive amount of research has investigated how well staffing assessments predict employee performance.[2] Much of this research has been conducted by companies that seek to sell these tools, and as such might fall under some suspicion. At the same time, an equal amount of work has been done by independent academic researchers, many of whom have been highly critical of assessments. Literally thousands of articles addressing the effectiveness of staffing assessments have been published in peer-reviewed academic journals. Some of the more common staffing assessment methods such as interviews, personality measures, and ability tests are subject to hundreds of research studies every year. A sample of these research studies can be seen in the *Journal of Applied Psychology, Personnel Psychology, International Journal of Selection and Assessment, Journal of Organizational Behavior, The Academy of Management Journal, Organizational Behavior and Human Decision Processes, Journal of Personality and Social Psychology,* and many other academic peer-review publications.

The clear answer that has emerged from this research is that, when appropriately designed and deployed, staffing assessments do predict job performance.[3] What is more, the accuracy of assessment data is often far higher than the accuracy of other information commonly used to select candidates. In particular, standardized assessments tend to be much more accurate at predicting candidate performance than subjective evaluations made by hiring managers or recruiters (see sidebar, "Why Assessments Are More Accurate Than People").

The accuracy of assessments does vary considerably depending on the type of assessment, how it is used, and the nature of the job. Some staffing assessment methods do not appear to work at all regardless of the job (for example, graphology/handwriting analysis).[4] Others predict performance across virtually all jobs and job settings (general ability tests).[5] The accuracy of assessments can range from predicting no measurable differences in performance to predicting as much as 50 percent of the differences in performance across employees.[6]

An additional factor that often plays a role in people's evaluations of assessment accuracy is what they are comparing the assessment against. Assessment results are often criticized as "wrong" because they do not align with how people evaluate individuals based on their own personal knowledge and experience. I have had many conversations where hiring managers made statements such as, "An employee I worked with for the past 5 years took the assessment and his results were way off. The assessment suggested he might not be the best employee for this job, but I know from personal experience that he's a great performer." There are two basic problems with these sorts of criticisms of assessment accuracy. First, it is unrealistic to expect an assessment to provide as much detailed information about a person as you could gain from working closely with him or her for several months or years. Assessments can be remarkably accurate at describing people, given the information they utilize. Usually this information is limited to things such as how the person answered a hundred multiple choice questions administered as part of the job application. But you should not necessarily expect an assessment to be as accurate as the evaluations one might make based on months or years of first-hand observation of a person's behavior.

In most hiring situations, the only information available on candidates is data that can be collected during the application process. This is because the first time most candidates meet hiring managers is during the job application process itself. Consequently, hiring managers are rarely able to evaluate candidates based on memories of previous experiences working with them. Research suggests that assessments tend to provide the most accurate information for predicting job performance in hiring situations where hiring managers do not have previous experience with a candidate, and often, even in cases where they do.

Second, assessment results for an individual may be more accurate than they initially appear when compared to a surface-level evaluation of that person. Many assessments measure underlying attributes that a person may intentionally manage or "hide." For example, I once provided assessment feedback to a high level sales executive whose responses to a personality measures suggested that he was fairly shy and reserved. This struck me as odd, because my interactions with him suggested that he was a relatively outgoing individual. I asked him about this particular result and his response was that it was actually quite accurate. He explained that his natural tendency was to be a fairly shy person, but he realized early in his career that success in his sales roles required him to proactively approach people and engage them in conversation. Over the years, he had actively worked to modify his behavior to overcome his natural tendency to be reserved in social settings. Although examples of people consistently acting in ways that are counter to their underlying psychological characteristics are rare, they do exist. As discussed in Chapter Two, assessments provide an indication of what people are likely to do, given their natural tendencies. However, this does not necessarily imply that everyone will always follow these tendencies.

In sum, the answer to the question "Are staffing assessments accurate?" is "Yes, as long as you are using the right assessments in the right way and have realistic expectations regarding their level of accuracy." Even though no assessment is perfectly accurate, most well-designed assessments are considerably more accurate than other methods frequently used to evaluate candidates.

WHY ASSESSMENTS ARE MORE ACCURATE THAN PEOPLE

Few things are more important to us than the actions of other people. Our happiness and success depend largely on what other people say and do. For this reason, many people think they are fairly good at evaluating and predicting what other people are likely to do in different situations. But psychological research indicates that people actually make a lot of mistakes when trying to judge others.[7] Many of us may think we are good at "sizing up others," but few of us truly are.

There are many reasons why people are lousy at evaluating other people. First, predicting people's behavior is complex. There are a lot of reasons why we do what we do. It's hard to figure out what information we should look at when evaluating people and how this information should be interpreted. For example, imagine we learned that a job candidate quit his last job. What does that actually tell us about his future job commitment and tenure? Is it a sign that he will give up easily when faced with challenges, or is it a sign that he is willing to take action to change his situation when he is dissatisfied? Maybe his previous boss did something highly offensive, but the candidate is not sharing this information because he doesn't want to complain about a previous employer. Knowing that a person had previously been fired almost certainly has some value for predicting the person's future behavior. But it is not easy to figure out how the information should be interpreted.

One of the major advantages of many assessments is their ability to optimally weigh different types of candidate information in order to predict job performance. When people make hiring decisions, they tend to combine candidate information in a highly ineffective and idiosyncratic manner. Hiring managers and recruiters frequently over-emphasize the importance of more specific characteristics such as the college a person went to or past job titles, while undervaluing other more subtle behavioral cues that may provide more information about a person's likely job performance.[8] In contrast, assessments can be configured to always combine information in the way that past history has shown to be the most predictive of actual job performance. Assessments that use appropriately developed statistically derived scoring algorithms are more effective at predicting people's behavior than even highly trained professional psychologists.[9]

Another reason people make mistakes when evaluating other people is because our decisions are invariably influenced by non-job-relevant aspects of the candidate and environment. Many times these influences are at an unconscious level and affect our decisions without us even realizing it. For example, how we perceive people is influenced in part by their race, gender, and physical appearance. This happens whether we are aware of it or not.[10] Our decisions are also influenced by whether we are tired, hungry, happy, or sad.[11] These are things that candidates have no control over, that are probably not related to job performance, and that should not be used as a basis for hiring decisions. But as people, we are unable to control these unconscious and physiological factors that affect how we make decisions. At best we can make ourselves aware of them, but we can never completely eliminate them.

When people evaluate job candidates, many of these evaluations depend more on biases, perceptions, and other characteristics of the people doing the evaluating than on the attributes of the actual candidates. In contrast, the only things that influence the scores of automated assessment instruments are differences in the characteristics of the candidates themselves. The quality of assessment data collected through an automated assessment system remains constant over time, regardless of what the candidate looks like, the mood of the hiring manager, or whether the assessment was administered in the morning or afternoon.

Evaluating other people is a complex task. It requires appropriately collecting and interpreting a diverse range of information about the person while simultaneously ignoring or controlling for non-relevant biases and situational factors that might influence our decisions. Assessments tend to be more accurate than people because (1) they take a highly systematic, thorough, objective, and often very complicated approach toward collecting and interpreting candidate information and (2) they only focus on information gathered from the candidate and are not influenced by other non-job-relevant information or situational factors. This is not to say that people's evaluations of candidates are unimportant. People's opinions and decisions about candidates are at the heart of the hiring process. After all, assessments do not hire people, people hire people. But people's hiring decisions tend to be much more accurate if they utilize assessment information as part of the decision-making process.

CRITICISM 2: STAFFING ASSESSMENTS CAN BE FAKED BY APPLICANTS

Many staffing assessments ask applicants to respond to questions about their interests, skills, attitude, and past behaviors. Self-report measures designed to assess personality, motives, interests, and experiences frequently ask questions such as "Do you tend to take the lead during conversations with others?" "Have you managed large teams?" and "Do you like constant change?" A common criticism of these types of assessments is that candidates will fake their responses to make themselves look good to the hiring organization. In psychological research, this sort of faking behavior is referred to as socially desirable responding, impression management, or response distortion.

A lot of research has been done looking at the effects that faking has on the accuracy of assessments.[12] Some of the more interesting findings of this research include the following.

Applicant Faking Is Not the Same As Lying

Most applicant faking does not involve making statements that are objectively untrue (for example, saying you have a college degree when you did not complete college). Instead, it is associated with applicants expressing subjective opinions about themselves in a way they feel will make them look better to the hiring organization (for example, a candidate saying, "I work harder than most people" even though she knows that others might describe her as being somewhat lazy). These sorts of efforts to make oneself look good are not the same as lying or outright dishonesty.[13] To some degree they reflect socially intelligent behavior in terms of trying to present oneself in the best possible light—sort of like rolling down one's sleeves to hide tattoos before a job interview.

Many Applicants Do Not Fake

Although it is difficult to estimate a precise number, the majority of applicants do not appear to radically distort their response to assessments just to make themselves look good.[14] There are at least three reasons why applicants do not fake more often:

1. Applicants may feel that intentionally faking is ethically wrong. These applicants feel morally obliged to respond in an open and candid manner.

2. Applicants may believe that they will be caught if they try to fake. Research indicates that applicants are less likely to intentionally change their answers if they are warned that an assessment is designed to detect faking.[15]

3. Applicants may prefer to describe themselves in a candid manner. They do not feel a need to purposefully fake their responses in order to be hired. These candidates would prefer not to be hired if it means working in a job that does not fit their personal styles, motives, or skills.

Most Applicants Who Fake Are Not Very Good at It

To effectively fake an assessment, candidates have to know how to respond to make themselves look good. Yet the questions on many assessments do not have a clearly correct response. Applicants may not know what behaviors are associated with effective performance in the jobs they are applying for or how these behaviors relate to assessment questions. As a result, applicants do not know how to fake their responses. For example, the correct answer to the question "Do you like to take risks" depends on the degree to which the job requires risk-taking behavior. Figuring out the right amount of risk taking for a job is probably not something most candidates are able to accurately estimate.

Efforts to fake also fail due to the fact that many people think their personal views and beliefs are similar to those of most other people. Even someone who holds very extreme beliefs may not think of himself as extreme.[16] As a result, when people fake they may not do so to the point of it actually being effective. For example, applicants who use illegal drugs can provide surprisingly revealing responses to questions like "How many times have you used illegal drugs in the past year?"[17] One reason why some applicants openly admit to drug use may be because they believe that almost everyone uses drugs to some degree. They assume that saying that they never used drugs would be perceived as unrealistic. The same is true when you ask candidates about whether it is okay to steal from their employer. Some candidates appear to assume that almost everyone steals, so they do not see anything wrong with admitting that they steal as well.

Some Faking Is Not Faking But a Lack of Self-Awareness

There are several reasons why applicants may provide inaccurate responses to assessment questions. On one hand, they may truly be faking in an attempt to pass the assessment. On the other hand, they may simply be unaware of their true skills, interests, and capabilities. For example, a candidate once answered "yes" to the pre-screening question "Are you an expert at Excel?" even though all she had ever done was enter data into Excel for several years. She did not know Excel had other functions or features beyond simple data entry, so from her perspective she truly believed she was an expert.[18] Lack of self-awareness can also influence the results of personality measures for candidates who do not have realistic perceptions of themselves (for example, applicants describing themselves as being highly creative, even though others might describe them as lacking creativity).

Faking Can Significantly Affect the Scores of Some Assessments

Some assessment questions are easier to fake answers for than others. For example, most applicants could guess the correct answer to questions like "Do you have strong people skills?" or "Are you an expert typist?" Assessments that contain questions for which the correct answer is fairly obvious are called "transparent." Transparent assessment questions can be very susceptible to problems of faking, particularly when they are used to rank order candidates based on their assessment scores.[19] In such cases, applicants who fake may receive much higher scores than better-qualified applicants. The result is an assessment that rewards candidates who fake over candidates who provide candid and accurate self-appraisals of their skills, interests, and capabilities.

Applicant faking may significantly influence the results of any assessment that asks candidates to provide information about their skills, interests, experiences, and capabilities. Virtually all self-report assessments fall into this category, regardless of whether they are designed to measure personality, past experiences, qualifications, or interests. Through careful design and analysis, it is possible to build and score these sorts of assessments in a way that helps control the effects of faking, but the influence of faking can never be completely removed.[20]

It is worth noting that the effects of faking are not limited to self-report assessments. Faking can and does affect other aspects of the hiring process. For example, it has been estimated that more than 10 percent of resumes contain outright fabrications.[21] Interviews are also susceptible to applicant faking, particularly when the interviews are not well structured. The results of highly objective assessments such as background investigations can and are faked by applicants using false or stolen legal documents. A small industry even exists to provide applicants with prosthetic devices and drug-free urine samples to fake the results of drug screens that utilize urinalysis. In sum, applicant faking is an important issue that must be taken into account when designing any staffing processes, not just processes that use self-report measures such as personality tests and pre-screening questionnaires.

In sum, the question is not whether applicants will fake. Research clearly indicates that some, but not all of them, will. Better questions to ask include how prevalent applicant faking is, how much it affects the assessment results, and whether it affects the results enough to render the assessment useless. These questions should be considered when designing and evaluating any proposed process for evaluating candidates. This includes processes that use highly structured assessments such as personality measures and pre-screening questionnaires. But it also includes processes that use less systematic techniques for evaluating candidates such as reading resumes and conducting interviews.

CRITICISM 3: STAFFING ASSESSMENTS ARE NOT WORTH THE COST REQUIRED TO USE THEM

Depending on the size and complexity of the selection process, it can cost from less than $500 to well over $100,000 to develop staffing assessment systems.[22] Many staffing assessment systems also have ongoing costs related to things such as licensing fees, training, and time spent by the recruiters or hiring managers using the assessments. All of these costs and resources add up. Some large companies spend over $1 million per year on the use of assessment tools and related staffing systems. It is reasonable to ask whether the value provided by using assessments is worth these costs.

Like most questions focusing on the financial value of people, determining precise answers to questions about assessment costs and value is difficult. The main financial benefit of staffing assessments comes from hiring employees who effectively support business processes and strategies. But it is hard to calculate the precise value of a "good hire" or the cost of a bad one. Most companies simply do not track performance data at the level of detail needed to compute the financial value generated by using staffing assessment tools.[23]

Even if the financial value of making better hiring decisions could be accurately calculated, it is unlikely that company financial reports will ever attribute these gains specifically to the use of better assessment tools. The behavior of employees is the main reason for the financial success of organizations. But rarely is the revenue generated by employees attributed to the processes that led to hiring them in the first place. It would be surprising to see company financial reports include statements such as "Profits increased 10 percent in the fourth quarter due to the improved quality of the interview guides we used to hire employees in the first quarter."

Despite these challenges, it is necessary to estimate the financial value associated with assessments if one is to make a strong business case for their use. Such estimates often focus on looking at one or more of the following benefits associated with the staffing assessments:

- *Hiring employees who are more successful at their jobs.* The main value of assessment tools comes from increasing the average performance of newly hired employees. Imagine the impact of increasing the average performance of a company's employees by 5 percent. Years of private and public research have shown that the use of well-designed staffing assessment tools can provide these sorts of results.[24]

- *Avoiding "catastrophic" hires.* While good employees can be a company's greatest asset, the wrong employees can be a company's largest liabilities. Assessments such as drug screens, background checks, and certain personality measures can substantially reduce the risk of hiring employees who engage in highly counter-productive activities such as theft, violence, sabotage, or fraudulent insurance claims.[25]

- *Increased retention.* Many assessment tools are specifically designed to help organizations reduce turnover and increase retention. When designed properly, assessment tools can increase retention of employees by as much as 5 percent or more.[26] These sorts of increases significantly reduce turnover costs associated with workflow disruptions caused by staff vacancies, recruiting candidates, and selecting and training new employees.

- *Increased staffing efficiency.* The most visible short-term benefit associated with assessment tools is the reduced time spent filling job positions. There are three main reasons for this. First, because many assessments are scored automatically, they reduce the amount of time hiring decision makers have to spend time reading through applications or resumes to find good candidates. Second, many assessments can be delivered to candidates over the Internet and used to automatically screen out poorly qualified candidates. This allows hiring managers to spend time meeting only with those applicants who have the highest potential for success. Third, using automated assessments often makes it easier for candidates to apply for a job. Companies implementing web-enabled assessments frequently see increases in applicant volumes and a subsequent decrease in the time needed to fill vacant positions.

The financial value assessments provide through increased performance, decreased catastrophic hires, improved employee retention, and greater staffing efficiency vary across different jobs and companies. The calculations required to estimate this value can be fairly complex. It may require measuring how differences in employee performance affect profitability, the cost of turnover caused by things such as workflow disruptions or increased recruiting and training costs, and time spent interviewing and selecting job candidates. Fortunately, there are a variety of sources available to assist with calculating these sorts of ROI estimates.[27] These range from easy-to-use, but somewhat overly simplistic ROI formulas, to highly sophisticated mathematical algorithms.[28]

Regardless of the method used to calculate the costs and financial benefits of using assessments, it is rare to find cases in which the financial value associated with the use of a well-designed and validated assessment process does not justify the costs. This is particularly true when the alternative is to continue with a staffing process that does not utilize assessments at all. If an assessment allows your company to avoid one catastrophically bad hire or leads to one or two great hires that you might otherwise have missed, then there is a fair chance that it has more than paid for itself.

CRITICISM 4: STAFFING ASSESSMENTS POSE A LEGAL RISK

If you spend much time working with assessments, at some point you will probably hear questions such as "Aren't tests illegal?" or "Didn't a company get sued for using a test like this?" The following is a discussion of some of the ways assessments come under legal scrutiny. This is for general information purposes only, and is not intended to provide actual legal advice. Readers who are concerned with legal issues related to assessments should consult their own legal counsel on their use.

Several major legal cases have centered around the use of staffing assessments. Many of these cases have found the use of staffing assessments to be appropriate and legal. On the other hand, some cases have led to rulings against companies using assessments.[29] When assessments have been found to be in violation of employment laws, it is usually for one or both of the following reasons:

- The assessment disproportionately screens out applicants from demographic groups protected by governmental regulations *and* measures candidate characteristics that are not considered to be essential attributes relevant to performance of the job, for example, evaluating candidates using an assessment whereby white applicants tend to score higher than Hispanic applicants without demonstrating that the assessment actually predicts job performance.

- The assessment collects information from candidates that is considered to be legally inappropriate for evaluating candidates and making hiring decisions, for example, asking candidates about their marital status or religious affiliation without showing that this information is relevant to a "bona fide occupational requirement" for the job.

The majority of legal actions in the United States concerning assessments are directly or indirectly related to two major acts of legislation: Title VII of the 1964 Civil Rights Act and the Americans with Disabilities Act of 1990 (ADA). These acts and related state and county laws emphasize that it is illegal to make hiring decisions in a way that systematically reduces the likelihood for people from certain protected groups to gain employment, unless the reason for the hiring decisions are based on criteria that are clearly job-relevant and consistent with business necessity. Candidate groups protected by these acts and the various government regulations and policies that have stemmed from these acts include people with certain ethnic backgrounds, genders, religious beliefs, physical or mental disabilities, age, military status, and family characteristics. Hiring practices that significantly screen out candidates from these protected groups are said to show "adverse impact."

Entire books have been written to discuss the impact that the Civil Rights Act, Americans with Disabilities Act, and related laws and Equal Employment Opportunity (EEO) regulations have on hiring practices.[30] Some of the major points found in these books relate to things discussed below.

Using the Four-Fifths Guideline to Evaluate Adverse Impact

The threshold used to establish potential evidence of adverse impact is typically based on something called the "80 percent" or "4/5ths" guideline. This states that a hiring process is under suspicion of displaying adverse impact if, on average, fewer than four applicants from a protected group are hired for every five non-protected applicants hired into the same position. For example, imagine a company hired 50 percent of all white applicants who applied for a position. If this company did not hire at least 40 percent of the applicants from a protected group who applied for this position (for example, Hispanics, Asian, or black applicants), then it would be considered to be in violation of the 4/5ths guideline. This is because 40 percent divided by 50 percent is equal to 4/5ths. If the company only hired 10 percent of all white applicants, it would need to hire at least 8 percent of protected applicants to comply with the 4/5ths guideline (10 percent divided by 8 percent = 4/5ths).

Companies can be held liable for adverse impact regardless of whether it was done on purpose or happened as an inadvertent consequence of using a certain staffing method. Adverse impact does not have to be intentional to be illegal. This issue becomes even further complicated by the fact that violations of the 4/5ths guideline can often occur simply by chance alone.[31] Companies may also be held legally responsible for tracking staffing data to ensure their hiring systems do not display adverse impact. Whether companies are held responsible for tracking this data depends on their size, whether they do work with federal or state governments, and other local and federal laws. For more information about adverse impact and other EEO-related topics, readers can visit www.EEOC.gov.

Job Relevance

Companies do not necessarily have to stop using an assessment that displays adverse impact, but they must demonstrate its job relevance. This is usually done through demonstrating that the assessment is valid for predicting critical job behaviors and performance outcomes. Companies must also make good-faith efforts to consider using alternative assessment methods that are equally valid but that do not show adverse impact, although in reality such alternative methods rarely exist.[32] For example, suppose candidates for a job that required lifting one-hundred-pounds boxes were assessed using a physical ability test that asked them to lift one-hundred-pound weights. This assessment might display adverse impact against female candidates. But it could still be considered legal because it is directly related to key job requirements. Furthermore, it is hard to imagine an alternative assessment method for predicting the ability to lift one-hundred-pound boxes that would have the same level of validity as this type of physical ability test, but that would not show similar levels of adverse impact against women.

Prohibited Information

The Civil Rights Act, Americans with Disabilities Act, and related laws and regulations explicitly prohibit collecting certain kinds of information from candidates for the purposes of making hiring decisions, regardless of relationships this information might have with job performance. Information that cannot be used as the basis for making hiring decisions includes things pertaining to applicant gender, age, ethnicity, religion, family status, and disability status. For example, because people tend to become physically weaker as they grow older, the age of candidates might show statistical relationships to performance in a job that requires lifting one-hundred-pound boxes. But being young is not actually a requirement for this job. The requirement is the ability to lift one-hundred-pound boxes. For this reason, a company would not be allowed to use age as a variable in selecting candidates, despite its relationship to job performance. The courts will make exceptions to this legislation for certain jobs for which prohibited information is directly relevant to bona fide occupational requirements. For example, asking about a candidate's religious beliefs is probably acceptable when hiring pastors for a church. However, these exceptions are rare and very narrowly defined.

The legislation and resulting government policies and guidelines created by the Civil Rights Act and Americans with Disabilities Act apply to all hiring practices, regardless of whether they use staffing assessments. Nothing about staffing assessments makes them intrinsically more or less legally defensible than other employee selection methods. The use of staffing assessments does introduce some potential benefits and risks from a legal standpoint. One benefit of assessments is the standardization and centralization they create in a company's hiring practices. This can decrease the potential for hiring managers and recruiters to do or say something that could get a company into legal "hot water." Technology-enabled staffing assessment systems also facilitate collection of data needed to calculate adverse impact and validation statistics that are used to examine the legal defensibility of a company's hiring practices. On the other hand, because staffing assessment systems can collect massive amounts of data, it may be easier for plaintiffs to challenge the legality of these systems in comparison to other less-structured staffing methods for which such data does not exist.[33] In addition, because many staffing assessments are deployed over the Internet, if they contain any legally risky content it may receive fairly widespread exposure in the public.

While there are no specific legal reasons not to use assessments, companies must be careful to use them in a legally appropriate manner. Fortunately, the requirements for creating legally defensible assessments are largely the same as the requirements for designing valid and effective assessments. These requirements include:

- *Understand and clearly document hiring needs.* This is accomplished by using job analysis to identify, verify, and document job performance requirements. Assessment tools that are not based on well-defined job analysis data are more likely to measure things that are not job-relevant. Such assessments place companies at considerably higher risk in terms of legal defensibility.

- *Demonstrate the job relevance, accuracy, and appropriate nature of assessments.* It is important to be able to explain links between assessments used to evaluate candidates and key job-performance requirements and outcomes. At the very least, this involves establishing and documenting the content validity of an assessment. The strongest evidence for job relevance is usually considered to come from conducting a criteria validation study that statistically demonstrates associations between assessment scores and measure of performance or retention on the job. Assessments should also be reviewed to ensure that they do not ask questions or collect information that might be considered to be legally inappropriate (for example, asking about someone's mental health or marital status).

- *Effectively translate online assessment results into hiring decisions.* Staffing assessment tools only provide information about job candidates. Assessments do not actually select employees. It is ultimately up to people to translate assessment data to make hiring decisions. These decisions should be made following a clearly documented process to ensure that assessment data is evaluated in the same manner across all applicants. This is typically done by creating easy-to-interpret assessment reports and providing clear guidelines and training on the use of assessments.

- *Monitor assessment data over time.* It is important to periodically examine staffing assessment data to ensure they are not displaying unjustifiable adverse impact. This point regarding "unjustifiable" adverse impact is important. Assessments that display adverse impact are not considered to be illegal if they are (1) job-relevant, (2) predict employee performance, (3) do not measure any applicant characteristics expressly prohibited by law, and (4) there are no reasonable and readily available alternative methods for evaluating candidates that shows similar levels of job-relevance and predictive validity. This is illustrated by the ongoing use of ability tests for police and fire selection. Ability tests have been shown to among the best predictors of police and fire job performance, and they are used widely for employee selection, even though certain protected groups consistently receive lower average scores on these types of assessments.[34]

- *Design or deploy assessments so that candidates perceive them as job-relevant.* Candidates are more likely to interpret assessments as offensive or inappropriate if they feel they are not relevant to the job they are applying for.[35] If candidates dislike an assessment or think it is unfair, then they are more likely to seek legal action challenging its use. The key to avoiding this is to use assessments that have a high level of face validity. Another method is to communicate to candidates the reasons why the assessment is being used as part of the hiring process.

Following these practices will help ensure the legal defensibility of assessments and reduce the risk of legal challenges. But they cannot guarantee that a company's assessment tools will never be challenged. This is virtually impossible. Any selection method can potentially be challenged for any number of reasons. The question is whether its use can be effectively defended in court.

Staffing assessments are neither more nor less legally defensible than other selection methods. They are held to the same set of legal standards as any other process used to make employment decisions. The burden of ensuring that these processes meet legal standards is carried by the organization. Although the systematic nature of assessments can reduce legal risks that arise from using less-structured staffing practices, if a company cannot demonstrate the job-relevance of its assessment tools, or uses these tools in an inconsistent or biased manner, the legal defensibility of their selection process will be jeopardized.

CRITICISM 5: STAFFING ASSESSMENTS ARE AN UNFAIR WAY TO EVALUATE PEOPLE

People frequently state that assessment tools are unfair because they do not perfectly predict performance. While such criticisms may be rooted in noble sentiments about treatment of candidates, they ignore the realities of job selection (see sidebar, "The Cult of Personality and the Realities of Staffing"). These realities include the facts that companies often have far more applicants than job openings, some applicants are clearly better-suited than others to perform certain jobs, and neither the company nor the applicants have the time and resources required to conduct a full and complete evaluation of each person applying for the job. When people criticize the use of assessments, what they are often actually criticizing is the use of any job-selection processes that evaluate people on less-than-perfect information. But there is no way to perfectly predict people's job performance. Perhaps from a fairness perspective it would be better if companies did not select candidates at all but instead just hired every person who applied for a job and kept those who liked the job and performed successfully. But such an approach is clearly unrealistic.

THE CULT OF PERSONALITY AND THE REALITIES OF STAFFING

A good example of the disconnect that often occurs between criticisms of staffing assessments and the realities of staffing can be found in the book *The Cult of Personality* by Annie Murphy Paul.[36] While this book raises valid points about the risks and limitations of using personality tests, it demonstrates limited understanding of the actual reasons why companies use personality assessments to support staffing decisions. First, the author fails to acknowledge the extensive research literature exploring the accuracy of personality-based staffing assessments. Second, she concludes with a suggestion that personality testing be abandoned for

> a "life story" method of assessment that, in the author's own words, is "just about useless for the purposes of sorting and screening" (p. 219). An assessment method that is useless for sorting and screening is also useless to companies faced with the challenge of efficiently selecting the best job candidates from hundreds or thousands of applicants.

Selection choices must be made, and they must often be made based on limited and sometimes woefully incomplete data. There are significant limits to the time and resources companies can spend with candidates to collect information to assist with selection decisions. There are also limits to the time candidates will spend providing this information. Even if these limits did not exist, it still would not be possible to collect enough information during the hiring process to perfectly predict candidate performance. It is important to avoid confusing the issue of whether companies should use staffing assessments with the issue of whether companies should evaluate candidates using imperfect information. The latter issue was resolved thousands of years ago when the first hiring manager found that he had more job applicants than job openings (see sidebar, "A Brief History of Staffing Assessment"). This hiring manager, just like current hiring managers, had to make a decision based on the information available, perfect or not.

A BRIEF HISTORY OF STAFFING ASSESSMENTS

> Although staffing assessments tend to be thought of as an invention of the "information age," their use goes back almost to the dawn of written history. The government of China used standardized achievement tests to select bureaucrats as early as 1115 BC.[37] The Old Testament describes how Gideon selected three hundred soldiers from an applicant pool of ten thousand by systematically assessing their alertness based on how they drank water from a stream.[38] There is also evidence of the use of standardized methods for job placement in ancient Islamic societies.[39]
>
> Modern scientifically based assessments can largely be traced back to work done by Sir Francis Galton and Alfred Binet in Europe during the late 19th and early 20th centuries.[40] The work done by Binet focused on educational assessment with the goal of better understanding differences

in student capabilities. Galton's assessment work was influenced by an interest in Darwinian evolution and how it relates to differences among people.

Some of the first assessments designed specifically to support staffing where created by the U.S. government during World War I to place people into different military jobs. One of the first assessments developed specifically for commercial staffing was created in the 1920s to predict performance of insurance sales people.[41] The insurance industry's pioneering use of data-driven employee selection methods is perhaps not that surprising given the actuarial nature of insurance.

World War II represented something of a "golden era" for assessment science as the United States sought to place thousands of people into a wide variety of specialized military roles. The broader commercial use of staffing assessments first really took off after World War II when private companies began leveraging assessment knowledge gained from military research. Many staffing assessment instruments widely in use today are based directly or indirectly off of work done during the 1940s and 1950s.

As staffing assessments became more common in the 1950s, a growing trend developed around using personality measures to guide selection decisions. This trend resulted in improper use of many personality tests, as well as a proliferation of personality tests with questionable scientific value. These problems led to a virtual abandonment of personality testing for commercial staffing in the late 1960s and early 1970s. The abandonment of personality tests was reversed starting in the late 1980s when several well-designed studies showed that personality assessments are quite effective for selecting candidates when they are appropriately constructed to predict specific job-relevant behaviors.[42]

Since the mid-1980s there has been a steady increase in the use of staffing assessments. This is probably due in part to the shift in the United States from a manufacturing to a knowledge and service-based economy. This shift has increased the importance of human capital and created more attention around the value that assessments provide for helping to make accurate hiring decisions. Growth of Internet staffing practices starting in the late 1990s also fueled the use of staffing assessments.[43] Internet staffing increased the volume of applicants companies must manage, thereby increasing the need for efficient tools for screening and sorting candidates. The Internet also greatly facilitated the ability to quickly administer assessments to candidates.

Staffing assessments are seeing more use now than ever before. Assessment companies currently administer tens of millions of assessments to candidates each year. Given the somewhat cyclical nature in the use of the assessments over the past, one might question whether the current trend toward greater use of assessment will continue. But even if use of assessments temporarily slows down, it is unlikely they will ever disappear completely. More than three thousand years of use demonstrate that assessments have clearly "stood the test of time."

The purpose of staffing assessment tools is not to provide perfect information about candidates, but to ensure that staffing decisions are based on the best information available, given the constraints of the hiring situation. When deciding whether to use staffing assessments, companies should not ask: "Do staffing assessments provide a *perfectly* fair, *completely* accurate, and legally *unchallengeable* way to evaluate candidates?" No selection process will ever meet this standard. Instead, the question should be: "Will the use of staffing assessments provide a selection process that is more accurate, efficient, fair, and legally defensible than other alternatives we use or might consider?"

Hiring managers have to make selection decisions whether they have staffing assessment data or not. In the absence of assessment data, these decisions will probably be based on highly subjective, unsystematic, personal opinions about whether someone is "good." Is it fairer to evaluate someone using a standardized assessment that provides an imperfect, but objective appraisal of a candidate's likely success on the job or to rely on a hiring manager's highly subjective, personal estimations about someone's quality? While answering questions of fairness ultimately depends on personal values and not just scientific data, it seems clear which of these two selection methods is likely to be more systematic, objective, and consistent across candidates.

CRITICISM 6: STAFFING ASSESSMENTS ARE OFFENSIVE TO CANDIDATES

Another common objection to using assessments is that candidates may react negatively to being asked to "take a test" as part of the hiring process. This criticism does not focus on whether assessments are effective for predicting performance, but rather on whether candidates will perceive them as fair and appropriate. It is one thing to justify the use of assessments to companies based on their accuracy for predicting performance. It is another to design and deploy assessments so they will be perceived positively by candidates.

The hiring process is not simply a matter of companies evaluating candidates; it is equally about candidates evaluating companies.[44] Candidates may seek employment elsewhere if they are asked to complete assessments that they feel are irrelevant, invasive, unfair, or otherwise inappropriate. Many companies' candidates are also their customers and should be treated with the same level of care and respect as would be provided to any customer. Last, as mentioned previously, asking candidates to complete an assessment they may find unpleasant or invasive increases the likelihood of employment litigation.[45] For these reasons, it is important to consider applicants' perceptions of assessments. However, this must be balanced against the company's need to collect the necessary information required to make accurate hiring decisions.

The strongest criticisms of assessments regarding applicant reactions often come from recruiters. Some recruiters advocate what cynically might be called the "prima donna" approach toward recruiting. Candidates are deemed so valuable that they should not be subjected to any form of rigorous, systematic evaluation during the selection process lest it offend them in some way. A recruiter arguing against the use of a well-designed assessment solely because it might damage relationships with a candidate is like a real estate agent arguing against doing a housing inspection because it might offend the seller. The goal of recruiting should not just be to fill positions, it should be to fill positions with people who have the greatest potential for success.

The question should not be whether to use staffing assessments. It should be how assessments can be used so that candidates view them as a positive, effective, and fair method to ensure the job is right for them. Remember, assessments are not just good for companies because they lead to hiring better employees. They are also good for candidates because they help them avoid the trauma that comes from being hired into the wrong jobs. The challenge lies in getting candidates to see assessments as a tool for ensuring career success and not merely a barrier to employment.

Over the course of my career, I have talked with hundreds of candidates who have taken staffing assessment tools for positions ranging from entry-level hourly to senior executive jobs. The content of these conversations suggests that candidate attitudes toward staffing assessments are surprisingly similar, regardless of the job type or job level. These attitudes tend to fall into four different groups:

- *The indifferent (the largest group).* Most candidates simply accept assessments as part of what one has to do to get a job. They view them as neither good nor bad. It's just another step in the selection process.

- *The enthusiastic.* Some candidates express positive attitudes toward the use of assessments. They approach assessments as an opportunity to demonstrate their skills and capabilities. They may also appreciate the company's rigorous approach toward hiring the best people possible.

- *The anxious.* A few candidates express high levels of anxiety toward completing assessments. This is most likely to happen when using assessments that remind people of tests they took in school.

- *The annoyed (the smallest group).* A small number of candidates will openly express frustration or annoyance with assessments. Their complaints tend to focus on the time needed to complete the assessment or on the perceived lack of job relevance of the assessment questions.

It would be nice if all candidates taking assessments could end up in the enthusiastic category. It is more realistic to focus on avoiding having candidates in the annoyed category. The best approach to achieve this is to use assessments that are job-relevant, interesting, and engaging.

Candidates are most likely to react favorably toward assessments if they believe they are effective measures of their potential to perform the job.[46] Unfortunately, sometimes the most effective and efficient assessments for predicting job performance are not ones that applicants find to be particularly entertaining or clearly job-relevant. For example, one of the most effective ways to predict the ability to perform jobs that require rapidly learning new tasks and processing information is to give candidates assessments that measure something called "abstract reasoning ability." Many of these assessments, while very effective for predicting performance, are about as fun and job-relevant as you might expect from something called an "abstract reasoning test" (see the sidebar in Chapter Four, "Face Validity Versus Criteria Validity: The Case of the Raven").

Candidates will usually accept assessments if they believe the assessments are valid tools for predicting job performance. One way to achieve this goal is to use assessments that have high levels of face validity. But this is not the only way to get candidates to accept the use of assessments. Another method is to clearly answer any questions candidates may have about the assessments being used to evaluate them. This is particularly important when using ability tests, because these tend to receive some of the most adverse candidate reactions.[47] Listed below are four questions candidates commonly ask about assessments. Answering these in advance will go a long way toward improving candidate perceptions of assessments:

- *Why is the organization using assessments?* Explain the value of assessments in terms of how they improve staffing decisions and support more objective, consistent treatment of candidates. Let candidates know that the organization is concerned about treating candidates in a fair, accurate, and consistent manner. Also tell them that the company uses assessments to make sure people are placed in jobs that fit their particular interests and skills.

- *Why are these particular assessments being used?* Explain the process used to develop the assessments. Indicate that assessments were chosen based on an analysis of the job and work environment and focus on job-relevant knowledge, skills, interests, and abilities.

- *How do the assessments work?* It is good to briefly touch on this topic if you are using assessments with low face validity that may not have clearly visible relationships to the job. You never want candidates wondering, "Why are they asking me this?" You may even go so far as admitting that the assessment may ask some seemingly odd questions, but indicate that these questions tap into underlying characteristics and interests that are critical to the job.

- *How will the results be used?* Explain the role the assessment plays in the hiring decision. To reduce candidate anxiety, try not to imply that the assessment is scored as "pass-fail," unless it actually is used this way. Describe the assessment as "one piece in the puzzle" that goes into the overall hiring decision. It is an important piece, but just one piece of many.

Following these guidelines will help reduce the number of candidates who react negatively toward assessments. The sidebar, "How to Take a Staffing Assessment," provides additional information that can be given to candidates to help reduce potential concerns and anxiety they may have.

While much can be done to improve candidate perceptions of assessments, no matter what efforts are made to demystify, justify, and explain their use, companies will still encounter some candidates who respond negatively to requests to complete assessments. In these cases, companies need to make a choice of whether they want to hire someone who is reluctant or unwilling to go through a formal, standardized evaluation process. When someone says he does not want to take an assessment, a natural question that should arise in the mind of hiring decision makers is "Why? Does he have something to hide?"

An additional thing is worth noting regarding applicant reactions. One of the most common complaints applicants make regarding hiring processes is the lack of feedback from companies regarding their application status.[48] Applicants want to know whether they got the job, or at least when they are likely to find out. This does not mean providing them with their results on a specific assessment. In fact, there are a variety of reasons why it is not a good idea to share assessment results with applicants, including potential misinterpretation of results and increased risk of legal action against the assessment. It does mean letting applicants know where they stand in the selection process as quickly as possible. Assessments can help with this because they allow companies to more rapidly sort through candidates and make hiring decisions. This gain in staffing speed can positively influence applicant reactions if it is used to more rapidly share information with candidates regarding where they are in the hiring process.

HOW TO TAKE A STAFFING ASSESSMENT: A MESSAGE TO CANDIDATES

More and more companies are using staffing assessment tools to screen and select candidates. These questionnaires and tests allow companies to efficiently identify candidates who have the greatest potential for job success. Over fifty years of personnel-selection research indicate that, when properly used, these assessments greatly increase our chances of ending up in the right jobs. This is largely because, unlike evaluations made by people, evaluations made by assessments aren't influenced by idiosyncratic and largely irrelevant facts such as whether you look like the hiring manager, went to the "right school," or come from the same hometown as the chief executive officer.

The fact is that assessments improve the accuracy of hiring decisions. This isn't surprising when you consider the alternatives—for example, having a recruiter evaluate your resume with a five-second glance. They also speed up the staffing process. Instead of having to wait weeks to hear from an employer, your application may be evaluated within minutes.

Despite their value, few people probably look forward to completing staffing assessments. So what's the best way to respond if you are asked to take an assessment as part of the hiring process? The following are a few general guidelines and strategies for helping you effectively complete assessments.

1. *Respond positively to the request.* The use of staffing assessments shows that a company takes hiring seriously. Don't respond with the attitude that you're too important to complete the assessment, or that you think it's a waste of time. At best, you'll come across as a prima donna who thinks he or she is too important to follow the company's policies. At worst, you'll be perceived as someone who's trying to hide something. Either way, these aren't characteristics companies typically associate with good candidates.

2. *Don't be afraid to ask about the assessment.* You should view assessments as an additional source of information about the company and the job. Feel free to ask why the company decided to use an assessment, what it measures, and how the results will be used. But guard against asking questions that might make you appear accusatory, skeptical, or defensive toward the company's decision to use assessments.

3. *Approach the assessment in the same way you'd approach a job interview.* The results of the assessment will be used to evaluate your match with the job. Take it seriously. Schedule adequate time to complete the assessment in a quiet, distraction-free environment. Be thoughtful in your answers. If asked questions that have a clear right-or-wrong answer, put in the mental effort to make sure you answer them correctly. Follow any instructions regarding suggested use of scratch paper, calculators, or other reference materials.

4. *Be honest.* Your goal in taking an assessment should be to provide a realistic picture of your strengths and limitations. Don't purposefully fake your responses in an effort to look good. A lot of assessments can detect faking, and purposefully distorting your answers may seriously damage your efforts to get the job. There is also little

value in selling yourself into a job to which you're ill-suited. For example, if an assessment asks, "Do you find it easy to stay calm in tense situations," and you know you have difficulty managing stress and anxiety, don't answer "yes." You'll only be setting yourself up for failure. There's little value in being hired merely to be fired.

5. *Don't be humble.* Be honest, but don't be overly self-critical. Play up your capabilities and accomplishments. For example, if you have excellent math skills and are asked, "Are you an expert at working with numbers?" don't hesitate to say "yes," even if you don't have a degree in math. Use the following approach when providing self-evaluations:

- Think of specific examples of things you've done that relate to the question. For example, if you are asked, "How much experience do you have leading teams?" take a few seconds to think of what you've done that involved leading teams. Focus on what you actually did, without worrying about job titles and whether you were formally designated "team leader."

- When responding to questions that ask you to rate your performance, compare yourself against your peers. Use this as the basis of your self-evaluation. For example, if asked, "Are you an expert in Excel?" think about whether the ways you've used Excel are more advanced than the ways your previous co-workers used it. Be careful to compare your skills against those of other likely candidates for the job. What constitutes expertise in Excel is likely to be different for receptionists than for database administrators.

- When making your final evaluation, think about how you'd respond if you were asked to justify your self-rating in an interview. Could you effectively explain why you consider yourself to be an "expert" at something?

Following these strategies may not increase the likelihood that you'll pass every online assessment, but they'll increase the chances that you'll sail through assessments used for jobs that you're well-suited to perform. Remember, the goal of a job hunt isn't simply to find a job, but to find a job in which you'll be successful. Assessments may never be something you enjoy, but if approached correctly they can help you achieve a more successful career.

CRITICISM 7: STAFFING ASSESSMENTS ADD TOO MUCH TIME TO THE HIRING PROCESS

One of the more pervasive operational criticisms of assessments is that they take too long for candidates to complete. If assessments are too long, they may cause candidates to drop out of the hiring process or needlessly increase the time needed to fill positions. But if assessments are too short, they are unlikely to accurately predict performance. The challenge lies in determining at what point an assessment becomes too long or too short.

Research suggests that candidates do not hold strong opinions about how long assessments should or should not be. Many applicants will spend two hours or more completing assessments, provided they are interested in the job and perceive the assessments to be job relevant.[49] Research also suggests that it is not the length of an assessment that causes applicants to drop out, but the content. For example, a study found that few hourly job candidates dropped out of the application process when asked to answer dozens of general personality type questions (for example, "Do you like to take risks?").[50] In contrast, these same candidates were much more likely to quit the process when asked a single question about their willingness to provide reference information, take a drug test, or submit to a background check.

This does not mean that assessment length is unimportant. Certainly there is a point at which applicants will simply say "Enough is enough" and quit answering assessment questions. But the length of assessments does not appear to be a major issue, provided that candidates are truly interested in the position and understand why they are being asked to complete the assessment. While it might be unwise to use a ninety-minute assessment in the first step of the hiring process, assessments taking ninety minutes or longer can be effectively used later in the process after candidates have been initially screened and recruited and are more fully engaged toward being considered for the job.

There can be strong reasons to include longer assessments in the hiring process based on the importance of making accurate hiring decisions. Many highly predictive types of staffing assessments require sixty minutes or more to complete.

These assessments cannot be shortened without severely damaging their accuracy (see the sidebar, "Assessment Length and Assessment Accuracy"). If the main goal of staffing decisions is to hire candidates who will succeed in the job, then staffing assessments should be designed to take as long as is needed to get the information required to accurately predict job performance. Asking how long an assessment needs to be to provide accurate information about a candidate is like asking how long a housing inspection should take before purchasing a home. The appropriate length depends on the financial value, scope, and complexity of the decision. Larger, more expensive houses typically require longer inspections. The same is true for staffing assessments. Assessments designed to predict performance for simpler jobs tend to be shorter, while those designed for more complex jobs tend to take longer.

ASSESSMENT LENGTH AND ASSESSMENT ACCURACY

The accuracy of a staffing assessment always depends in part on its length. This dependency is a result of the statistical properties of assessments. In general, the longer the assessment, the better its value for predicting job performance. Simply put, you can only learn so much about a candidate from asking him or her one single question. This is because no question is perfect. To really learn about candidates you need to ask them lots of different questions and then look for patterns in their responses.

Assessment length is particularly important for developing behavioral assessments that measure things that cannot be seen directly (for example, personality measures or ability tests). These assessments evaluate candidates by making inferences about underlying characteristics based on how candidates respond to different questions. For example, it is not possible to directly measure a person's level of "social confidence." Intangible attributes such as social confidence must be statistically estimated by asking candidates a variety of questions that each reflect some aspect of the underlying attribute (for example, "Do you like being the center of attention?" "Are you comfortable talking to large groups?" "Are you usually the first to speak in team meetings?"). By measuring trends in people's responses to these questions, it is possible to get a fairly accurate estimate of the underlying attribute.

In general, the more questions an assessment asks, the more accurate it tends to be. On the other hand, there is a point at which asking additional questions ceases to provide much additional information beyond what has already been collected. One of the more complex aspects to building staffing assessments is determining how many questions are needed to get an acceptable level of accuracy with minimum assessment length.

An analogy might be made to trying to determine whether the average temperature of New York is higher than the average temperature of Philadelphia. One might start by taking the average temperature for both cities on a single day and comparing the two. But because temperatures in cities go up and down considerably from one day to the next, this might lead to the wrong conclusion. A more accurate method would be to collect temperature readings on additional days and average them to determine which city is warmer. But eventually a point will be reached at which gathering additional daily temperature readings provides diminishing new information. There is some optimal number of daily readings that balances the likelihood of getting an accurate estimate of temperature while limiting the total number of readings required. The same is true for assessments. If they are too short, they have little value for predicting performance. If they are too long, they needlessly increase the length of the hiring process and become overly tedious for candidates. The challenge is figuring out the point at which an assessment becomes too long or too short.

In sum, there do not appear to be any hard-and-fast rules about assessment length. An assessment that may be considered too long for some jobs may be considered too short in others. For example, many companies put candidates for senior-level executive positions through lengthy assessment center exercises that may take a day or more to complete. Such exercises would certainly be inappropriate for evaluating candidates for entry-level hourly jobs. However, few companies would be willing to base hiring decisions for their senior managers on using the limited types of information that can be collected from the short, thirty-minute assessments they may use to screen hourly job applicants. Determining appropriate assessment length, like so many other things related to assessments, must ultimately be decided on a situation by situation basis.

CONCLUDING REMARKS: SHOULD COMPANIES USE STAFFING ASSESSMENTS?

There are both benefits and risks associated with the use of assessments. These should be openly discussed within a company when addressing the question of whether to use assessments. When all is said and done, the ultimate answer to the question of whether to use assessments is likely to largely hinge on whether a company accepts the following assertions:

- *Assessments accurately predict performance.* The use of appropriately designed staffing assessments leads to more accurate hiring decisions than hiring decisions made using less systematic selection methods.

- *Assessments are resistant to applicant faking.* Although some applicants can influence their assessment results by faking, applicant faking does not eliminate the value assessments provide for predicting job performance.

- *Assessments are worth the cost.* There is enough financial value associated with hiring better-quality employees to warrant investment in the use of staffing assessments, even if this value cannot always be directly measured or recorded on a company's financial reports.

- *Assessments are legal.* The benefits staffing assessments provide through improving the quality of hiring decisions outweigh the legal risks that use of these measures might create.

- *Assessments are fair.* It is fairer to evaluate candidates using standardized assessment methods than to rely solely on unsystematic, subjective opinions formulated by hiring decision makers.

- *Assessments are not overly offensive to applicants.* Assessments can be designed and used in a manner that is acceptable to the majority of applicants.

- *Assessments are efficient.* The accuracy gained by using assessments justifies the time they add to the staffing process and the time applicants must spend to complete them.

A person who flatly rejects any of these assertions is unlikely to ever endorse the use of assessments, regardless of arguments that can be made in their favor. For people who do generally accept these assertions, the question changes from "Should companies use assessment tools?" to "What kind of assessment tools should companies use and how should they use them?"

Notes

1. Judge, T.A., & Cable, D.M. (2004). The effect of physical height on workplace success and income: Preliminary test of a theoretical model. *Journal of Applied Psychology, 89,* 428–441.
2. Schmidt, F.L., & Hunter, J.E. (1998). The validity and utility of selection methods in personnel psychology: Practical and theoretical implications of 85 years of research findings. *Psychological Bulletin, 124,* 262–274.
3. Schmidt, F.L., & Hunter, J.E. (1998). The validity and utility of selection methods in personnel psychology: Practical and theoretical implications of 85 years of research findings. *Psychological Bulletin, 124,* 262–274.
4. Rafaeli, A., & Klimoski, R.J. (1983). Predicting sales success through handwriting analysis: An evaluation of the effects of training and handwriting sample content. *Journal of Applied Psychology, 68,* 212–217.
5. Murphy, K.R., Cronin, B.E., & Tam, A.P. (2003). Controversy and consensus regarding the use of cognitive ability testing in organizations. *Journal of Applied Psychology, 88,* 660–671.
6. Schmidt, F.L., & Hunter, J.E. (1998). The validity and utility of selection methods in personnel psychology: Practical and theoretical implications of 85 years of research findings. *Psychological Bulletin, 124,* 262–274.
7. Landy, F.J., & Farr, J.L. (1980). Performance rating. *Psychological Bulletin, 87,* 72–107.
8. Ackerman, P.L., & Humphreys, L.G. (1990). Individual differences theory in industrial and organizational psychology. In M.D. Dunnette & L.M. Hough (Eds.), *Handbook of industrial and organizational psychology* (2nd ed., Vol. 1, pp. 223–282). Palo Alto, CA: Consulting Psychologists Press.
9. Westen, D., & Weinberger, J. (2004). When clinical description becomes statistical prediction. *American Psychologist,* pp. 595–613.
10. Banaji, M.R., & Greenwald, A.G. (1993). Implicit stereotyping and prejudice. In M.P. Zanna & J.M. Olson (Eds.), *Psychology of prejudice: The Ontario symposium on personality and social psychology.* Mahwah, NJ: Lawrence Erlbaum Associates.
11. Peters, E., Vastfjall, D., Garling, T., & Slovic, P. (2006). Affect and decision making: A "hot" topic. *Journal of Behavioral Decision Making, 19,* 79–85.
12. Ones, D.S., Viswesvaran, C., & Korbin, W.P. (1995). *Meta-analyses of fakability estimates: Between-subjects versus within-subjects designs.* Paper presented in F.L. Schmidt (chair), Response distortion and social desirability in personality testing and personnel selection. Symposium conducted at the 10th annual meeting of the Society of Industrial and Organizational Psychology, Orlando, Florida.
13. McCrae, R.R., & Costa, P.T., Jr. (1983). Social desirability scales: More substance than style. *Journal of Consulting and Clinical Psychology, 51,* 882–888.
14. Hough, L.M., Eaton, N.K., Dunnette, M.D., Kamp, J.D., & McCloy, R.A. (1990). Criterion-related validities of personality constructs and the effect of response distortion on those validities. *Journal of Applied Psychology, 75,* 581–595.

15. Griffith, R.L., Frei, R.L., Snell, A.F., Hamill, L.S., & Wheeler, J.K. (1997). *Warning versus no-warnings: Differential effect of method bias.* Paper presented at the 12th annual meeting of the Society of Industrial and Organizational Psychology, St. Louis, Missouri.

16. Mattern, J.L., & Neighbors, C. (2004). Social norms campaigns: Examining the relationship between changes in perceived norms and changes in drinking levels. *Journal of Studies of Alcohol, 65,* 489–493.

17. Sackett, P.R., Burris, L.R., & Callahan, C. (1989). Integrity testing for personnel selection: An update. *Personnel Psychology, 42,* 491–529.

18. Hunt, S.T., Gibby, R., Hemingway, M., Irwin, J., Scarborough, D., & Truxillo, D. (2004). *Internet pre-screening: Does it lead to better hiring decisions?* Paper presented at the 19th conference of the Society for Industrial and Organizational Psychology, Chicago, Illinois.

19. Graham, K.E., McDaniel, M.A., Douglas, E.F., & Snell, A.F. (1997). *Biodata validity decay and score inflation with faking: Do item attributes explain variance across items?* Paper presented at the 12th annual conference of the Society for Industrial and Organizational Psychology, St. Louis, Missouri.

20. Paulhus, D.L. (1991). Measurement and control of response bias. In J.P. Robinson, P.R. Shaver, & L.S. Wrightsman (Eds.), *Measures of personality and social psychological attitudes* (Vol. 1; pp. 17–59). San Diego, CA: Academic Press.

21. Cullen, L.T. (2006, May 1). Getting wise to lies: Alarmed about the prevalence of resume padding employers are turning fib detection into an industry. *Time.*

22. Handler, C., & Hunt, S.T. (2003). *Rocket-hire buyer's guide to online screening and staffing assessment systems.* Saint John, WA: PubSync.

23. Fitz-Enz, J. (2000). *The ROI of human capital: Measuring the economic value of employee performance.* New York: AMACOM.

24. Handler, C., & Hunt, S.T. (2003). *Rocket-hire buyer's guide to online screening and staffing assessment systems.* Saint John, WA: PubSync.

25. Woolley, R.M., & Hakstian, A.R. (1993). A comparative study of integrity tests: The criterion-related validity of personality-based and overt measures of integrity. *International Journal of Selection and Assessment, 1,* 27–40.

26. Martin, S.L., & Boye, M.W. (1998). Using a conceptually based predictor of tenure to select employees. *Journal of Business and Psychology, 13,* 233–243.
    Weiner, J. (2005). *Targeting turnover: Development and validation of a pre-employment attitude assessments.* Paper presented at the 20th annual conference of the Society for Industrial and Organizational Psychology, Los Angeles, California.

27. Boudreau, J.W. (1991). Utility analysis for decisions in human resource management. In M.D. Dunnette & L.M. Hough (Eds.), *Handbook of industrial and organizational psychology* (2nd ed., pp. 621–745). Palo Alto, CA: Consulting Psychologists Press.

28. For an example of some fairly simple ROI formulas, see C. Handler & S.T. Hunt. (2002), *Estimating the financial value of staffing assessment tools.* www.workforce.com/archive/article/23/40/88.php?ht=handler%20handler.

For an example of a more sophisticated set of ROI formulas, see K.D. Carlson, M.L. Connerly, & R.L. Mecham, III. (2002). Recruitment evaluation: The case for assessing the quality of applicants attracted. *Personnel Psychology, 55,* 461–490.

29. Terpstra, D.E., Mohamed, A., Amin, K., & Bryan, R. (1999). An analysis of federal court cases involving nine selection devices. *International Journal of Selection and Assessment, 7,* 26–34.

30. Allison, L.K. (1996). *Employee selection: A legal perspective.* Alexandria, VA: Society for Human Resource Management.
   Ledvinka, J., & Scarpello, V.G. (1991). *Federal regulation of personnel and human resource management.* Boston, MA: PWS-Kent.

31. Roth, P.L., Bobko, P., & Switzer, F.S., III (2006). Modeling the behavior of the 4/5ths rule for determining adverse impact: Reasons for caution. *Journal of Applied Psychology, 91,* 507–522.

32. Gottfredson, L.S. (1994). The science and politics of race-norming. *American Psychologist, 11,* 955–963.

33. Gutman, A. (2002). *Review of legal case law and implications for assessing work experience and developing, validating, and using work experience screens.* Presented at the 17th annual conference of the Society for Industrial and Organizational Psychology, Toronto, Ontario.

34. Hausdorf, P.A., LeBlanc, M.M., & Anuradha, C. (2002). Cognitive ability testing and employment selection: Does test content relate to adverse impact? *Applied Human Resource Management Research, 7,* 41–48.

35. Bauer, T.N., Truxillo, D.M., Sanchez, R.J., Craig, J.M., Ferrara, P., & Campion, M. (2001). Applicant reactions to selection: development of the selection procedural justice scale (SPJS). *Personnel Psychology, 54,* 387–419.

36. Paul, A.M. (2004). *The cult of personality.* New York: The Free Press.

37. DuBois, P. (1976). A test-dominated society: China 1115 B.C. 1905 A.D. In N.L. Barnette, Jr. (Ed.), *Readings in psychological tests and measurements.* Baltimore, MD: The Williams & Wilkins Company.

38. Faw, H.W. (1990). Does scripture support standardized testing? *Perspectives on Science and Christian Faith, 42,* 86–93.

39. Carson, A.D., & Altai, N.M. (1994). 1000 years before Parsons: Vocational psychology in classical Islam. *Career Development Quarterly, 43,* 197–206.

40. Hothersall, D. (1995). *History of psychology* (3rd ed.). New York: McGraw-Hill.

41. Katzell, R.A., & Austin, J.T. (1992). From then to now: The development of industrial-organizational psychology in the United States. *Journal of Applied Psychology, 77,* 803–835.

42. Barrick, M.R., & Ryan, A.M. (2003). *Personality and work: Reconsidering the role of personality in organizations.* San Francisco, CA: Jossey-Bass.

43. Handler, C., & Hunt, S.T. (2003). *Rocket-hire buyer's guide to online screening and staffing assessment systems.* Saint John, WA: PubSync.

44. Crispin, G., & Mehler, M. (2003). *The job seeker's experience: Who really cares?* CareerXroads white paper.

45. Hausknecht, J.P., Day, D., & Thomas, S.C. (2004). Applicant reactions to selection procedures: An updated model and meta-analysis. *Personnel Psychology,* pp. 639–683.

46. Bauer, T.N., Truxillo, D.M., Sanchez, R.J., Craig, J.M., Ferrara, P., & Campion, M. (2001). Applicant reactions to selection: Development of the selection procedural justice scale (SPJS). *Personnel Psychology, 54,* 387–419.

47. Hausknecht, J.P., Day, D., & Thomas, S.C. (2004). Applicant reactions to selection procedures: An updated model and meta-analysis. *Personnel Psychology,* pp. 639–683.

48. Crispin, G., & Mehler, M. (2006). *The candidate experience: Black hole or north star?* www.careerxroads.com/news/2006FortuneStudyWhitepaper.pdf.

49. iLogos Research. (2001). *Perception vs. reality: Job seeker behavior online.* San Francisco, CA: Recruitsoft, Inc.

    Mael, F.A., Connerley, M., & Morath, R.A. (1996). None of your business: Parameters of biodata invasiveness. *Personnel Psychology, 49,* 613–650.

50. Unicru (2003). *Applicant dropout rates in different phases of the hiring process.* Internal research paper. Beaverton, OR: Unicru Inc.

Choosing Among Different Assessment Methods

Companies interested in using staffing assessments can draw on a variety of assessment methods for evaluating candidates. Assessment methods vary considerably in terms of the quality and type of information they provide, the costs and resources required to use them, and the degree of legal risk they may pose. They range from things as simple as giving candidates a short online knowledge test downloaded from the Internet to putting them through a multi-day assessment center incorporating several types of assessments and requiring extensive consulting support. Determining which assessment method is best depends on the nature of the job, the staffing resources available to the company, and a variety of other factors.

This chapter discusses how to determine which assessment methods are likely to be the most effective for different hiring situations. Designing effective assessment methods largely comes down to balancing two competing objectives:

1. *Maximizing hiring accuracy through increasing assessment validity.* This requires investing time and energy to implement assessment methods tailored to your specific hiring situation.

2. *Maximizing efficiency and cost savings.* This is achieved by using simpler, somewhat "generic" assessment tools that can be deployed with minimal custom development or configuration.

Determining how to strike this balance must be done on a case-by-case basis through studying both the job and the hiring process. No method works equally well for all jobs in all situations. This is for two reasons. First, many assessments only work well for a limited range of jobs.[1] For example, assessments that evaluate people's ability to rotate visual representations of objects in their heads can be very useful for predicting success in jobs that require reading maps or performing mechanical tasks, but have questionable value for predicting performance in jobs that do not require these sorts of activities. Second, the effectiveness of an assessment method depends in part on a company's operational issues and constraints. Highly interactive, video-based job simulations are a good case in point. These simulations can be very good predictors of job performance and tend to generate fairly positive applicant reactions. They are also expensive to construct and relatively difficult to administer. As a result, it is not feasible to use them in many hiring situations. In sum, there are no "best practices" for which assessments to use because what is best for one job or company may not be the best for another.

The only correct answer to the question of "Will a particular assessment method work well for our needs?" is "It depends on your needs." Whether an assessment is appropriate will vary based on the financial impact associated with making a good versus a bad hire, the number of hires, the types of candidates, the skills of the recruiters and hiring managers who will be using the assessments, and many other financial, technological, and operational resources and constraints. Fortunately, there is a basic order companies can follow when choosing assessment methods.

Table 7.1 lists several assessment methods in rough order of easiest to most complex. The methods in Table 7.1 start with simple actions such as structuring the hiring process and deploying broad, somewhat generic assessments that are readily available on the market. These take advantage of some general truths about staffing that hold across virtually all jobs and organizations. They can also be implemented without investing the resources required to develop more tailored assessment tools used in subsequent methods. The methods in Table 7.1 become increasingly involved as they move toward more integrated, highly tailored assessment processes and scoring algorithms. Each additional method adds value through better assessment validity and subsequent hiring accuracy, but also increases the cost and complexity of the assessment process. Methods that make sense for one job or hiring environment may not be cost-effective or operationally feasible for other situations.

The methods listed in Table 7.1 build on one another in a logical fashion. But it is not always necessary to implement earlier methods before implementing later methods. For example, a company could go directly from no assessment (Method 1) to integrated, context-specific self-report measures and knowledge, skills, and ability tests with advanced, non-linear scoring (Methods 12 and 13). However, such a leap would require considerable investments in assessment design.

The right-hand column of Table 7.1 lists the estimated percentage of performance variance predicted by different assessment methods. This indicates the ability of a particular assessment method to accurately distinguish among candidates who will be highly successful in a job versus those whose job performance will be of lesser quality. Assessment methods that predict higher percentages of performance variance have a greater impact on a company's business performance through increasing the accuracy of staffing decisions. The estimates of performance variance predicted are based on research data examining statistical relationships between assessment scores and measures of job performance. These estimates reflect scientific research, but vastly oversimplify the actual relationships between assessments and workforce quality (see sidebar, "The Operational Impact of Assessments"). The estimates reflect what are considered to be average levels of validity that one might expect for different assessment types. In reality, the percentage of performance variance predicted by the same kinds of assessments can vary considerably. For example, I have seen broad self-report assessments (Method 5) predict from as little as 1 percent to as much as 15 percent of the performance variance in jobs, depending on the design of the assessment and the nature of the job.

The estimates of performance variance predicted listed in the right-hand column of Table 7.1 can serve as a high-level guide to the relative value of different assessment methods. The estimates range from a low of 0 percent for unstructured interviews to 40 percent for integrated knowledge, skills, and ability tests and self-report measures using advanced, non-linear scoring. This 40 percent level is slightly below the 50 percent improvement in employee performance that is felt to be around the maximum impact an assessment strategy is likely to ever have on workforce quality (see Chapter Two for more discussion on this concept). The estimates in Table 7.1 do not reach this upper limit, as it would require an extensive use of assessments that is probably unrealistic in most staffing environments.

Implementing multiple assessment methods usually results in predicting higher levels of performance variance than using a single method by itself. However, the estimates of performance variance predicted are unlikely to simply add together. For

Table 7.1

Assessment Methods for Incrementally Improving the Accuracy and Efficiency of Hiring Decisions[1]

Assessment Method	Estimated % of Performance Variance Predicted*
1. No standardized assessment (e.g., unstructured interviews)	0 to 1 Percent
2. Self-report qualifications screening (e.g., pre-screening questionnaires)	1 to 3 Percent
3. Applicant investigations (e.g., background checks, drug screens)	2 to 4 Percent**
4. Structured interviews (e.g., behavioral-based interviewing)	5 to 10 Percent
5. Broad self-report and situational judgment measures (e.g., off-the-shelf personality tests)	5 to 10 Percent
6. Broad knowledge and skills tests (e.g., software skills tests, general job knowledge tests)	5 to 10 Percent**
7. Broad ability tests (e.g. reasoning, math, and literacy tests)	10 to 15 Percent
8. Integrated broad self-report measures and knowledge, skills, and ability tests	15 to 25 Percent
9. Localized scoring***	Add 5 Percent
10. Context-specific self-report and situational judgment measures (e.g., configured personality tests)	10 to 15 Percent
11. Context-specific knowledge, skills, and ability tests (e.g., work sample tests, job-specific skill tests)	20 to 30 Percent
12. Integrated context-specific self-report measures and knowledge, skills, and ability tests	25 to 35 Percent
13. Advanced, non-linear scoring***	Add 5 Percent

*Reflects the percentage of performance variance accounted for based on directly estimated and meta-analytically derived validity coefficients associated with different assessment tools and strategies. These are very general estimates. They are intended only as guidelines for comparing the relative value of different assessment methods. They are not intended to be used as the basis for calculating detailed estimates of the impact of using assessments.[1]

**May only predict performance for a narrow range of job-relevant behaviors. For example, a knowledge and skills test assessing typing proficiency may only predict performance of technical tasks that require typing. Similarly, drug screens may only predict whether people will engage in counterproductive activities associated with drug use.

***These steps focuses on assessment scoring, and not the actual design of the assessment. They can be implemented to increase the effectiveness of any form of assessment assuming adequate data sets are available.

[1]Listed below are a few of the references used to develop the estimates in this table. But one should not expect to find a one-to-one correspondence between specific validation results reported in these studies and the estimates of percentage of performance variance predicted listed in the table. The estimates in the table are intended to provide a general sense of the relative predictive value of various assessment methods. They are not intended nor assumed to provide highly accurate estimates of the actual validity that will be obtained for any specific assessment application, given the range of variables that influence the results of individual validation studies (e.g., the nature of job performance, quality of the performance criteria, design of the assessments, characteristics of the candidate pool).

Ackerman, P.I., & Kanfer, R. (1993). Integrating laboratory and field study for improving selection: Development of a battery for predicting air traffic controller success. *Journal of Applied Psychology, 78.*

Hough, L.M., & Ones, D.A. (2001). The structure, measurement, validity, and use of personality variables in industrial, work, and organizational psychology. In N. Anderson, D.S. Ones, H.K. Sinangil, & C. Viswesvaran (Eds.), *Handbook of industrial, work and organizational psychology* (pp. 233–267). London: Sage.

Hunter, J.E., & Hunter, R.F. (1984). Validity and utility of alternative predictors of job performance. *Psychological Bulletin, 96,* 72–98.

Robertson, I.T., & Kindner, A. (1993). Personality and job competencies: The criterion-related validity of some personality variables. *Journal of Occupational and Organizational Psychology, 66,* 225–244.

Schmidt, F.L., & Hunter, J.E. (1998). The validity and utility of selection methods in personnel psychology: Practical and theoretical implications of 85 years of research findings. *Psychological Bulletin, 124,* 262–274.

Sternberg, R.J., Wagner, R.K., Williams, W.M., & Horvath, J.A. (1995). Testing common sense. *American Psychologists,* pp. 912–927.

Tett, R.P. Jackson, D.N., & Rothstein, M.R. (1991). Personality measures as predictors of job performance: A meta-analytic review. *Personnel Psychology, 44,* 703–742.

example, structured interviews (Method 4) are estimated to predict 5 to 10 percent of employee performance variance in a job. Self-report personality measures (Method 5) are also estimated to predict 5 to 10 percent of employee performance variance. Using both structured interviews and personality measures together is likely to predict more performance variance than using either method by itself. But there is likely to be overlap in the kinds of information structured interviews and personality measures provide about candidates. In other words, the information provided by these two methods is somewhat redundant. Consequently, their combined use would probably not predict a full 20 percent of the performance variance in a job, although the two methods used together are likely to predict more performance variance than either method used by itself.

Methods 9 and 13 are techniques used to enhance the effectiveness of other assessment methods. They are not assessment methods themselves. For example, localized scoring (Method 9) is a way of more effectively interpreting the information collected by assessment methods such as personality measures, knowledge tests, and ability tests (Methods 5, 6, and 7). Implementing localized scoring requires using some other assessment method to actually collect information from candidates. Because Methods 9 and 13 reflect ways of interpreting assessment data rather than collecting it, their impact is represented as a relative increase in performance variance predicted over and above what companies can achieve using other assessment methods by themselves.

The remainder of this chapter discusses the assessment methods in Table 7.1 in greater detail. Reviewing the strengths and limitations of each method will help you determine what assessment solutions are likely to make the most sense for hiring situations you may be examining. If you are only hiring one or two people, you may only want to implement the first few methods. If you are building an assessment process to hire thousands of people, then it may make sense to implement almost every method in the table.

THE OPERATIONAL IMPACT OF ASSESSMENTS

The primary purpose of using assessments is to improve company performance through increasing the accuracy of staffing decisions. But the degree to which companies will see operational improvements through using assessments depends on a variety of factors other than the assessments themselves. These factors include things such as applicant quality, hiring ratios, and hiring manager compliance (that is, do hiring managers actually use the assessments to guide their staffing decisions?). Four factors in particular tend to have considerable influence on whether changing assessment practices translates into bottom-line financial gains: hiring volumes, quality of applicant flow, staffing practices, and employee retention.

Hiring Volumes

The value of a staffing assessment is only realized to the degree that a company uses the assessment to hire new employees. The rate at which this happens is a function of both workforce growth and employee turnover. For example, a company with 10 percent annual turnover that implements general knowledge, skills, and ability tests (Step 6 in Table 7.1) might wait ten years before seeing the full 15 to 25 percent improvement in employee performance due to the use of these assessments.

Figure 7.1 illustrates how one might expect workforce quality to change over time after assessments are implemented. Early use of assessments

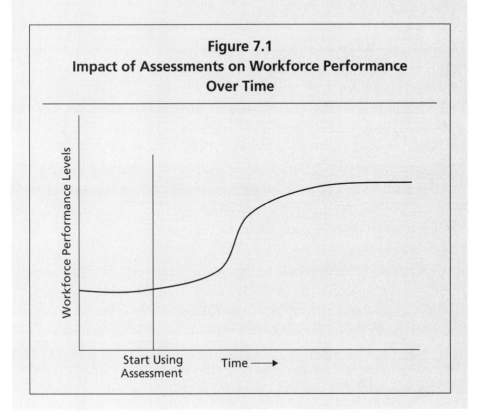

Figure 7.1
Impact of Assessments on Workforce Performance Over Time

Workforce Performance Levels

Start Using Assessment

Time ⟶

leads to relatively little change because the company has not hired enough people to have a significant impact on the performance of the workforce. As assessments begin to have more and more influence on the nature of the workforce over time, there are increasing levels of positive change. Eventually, the workforce becomes fully transformed through the use of assessments. At this point, changes in workforce quality slowly taper off, with overall workforce performance remaining at a higher level of effectiveness.

Quality of Applicant Flow

The impact of assessments is limited by the quality and number of applicants being evaluated by the hiring manager. Assessments can help hiring managers choose the best applicants of those available, but they cannot improve the number or overall quality of the pool of available applicants. Doing this requires companies to develop recruiting techniques that encourage the best-quality applicants to apply for job openings.

Staffing Practices

Assessments do not hire people; people hire people. Hiring decisions are ultimately made by hiring managers or recruiters. Assessments provide useful information to help people make the best hiring decisions possible, but assessments only work if they are being used appropriately. This includes ensuring that the assessments are being effectively administered to candidates and that hiring managers, recruiters, and other hiring decision makers are accurately interpreting the information provided by the assessments. Assessments only work if hiring decision makers use them consistently and appropriately.

Employee Retention

The impact of assessments is limited by a company's ability to retain and fully leverage the capabilities of the employees they hire. Implementing assessments can lead to hiring people who are better suited to their jobs, but who are also systematically different from employees hired prior to the use of assessments. Because many people tend to prefer working with people who are similar to them,[2] initial use of assessments may lead to increased turnover in the short term as the company seeks to assimilate new employees whose interests and skills are different from previous hires. Companies may also need time to adjust existing management styles and work cultures to fully retain and leverage the skills of these new people. For example, one way to reduce workforce turnover is to use assessments to hire people who value job stability and long-term co-worker relationships. Companies experiencing high levels of turnover may initially find it hard to retain these people because the existing culture does not provide the very thing these people value: a stable co-worker population. As the company replaces its workforce with employees who prefer higher levels of job stability, slowly its work environment will shift from a high-turnover culture to a culture of retention.

Assessments have the power to fundamentally transform the performance of a company's workforce. They do this through systematically helping to hire employees whose attributes match and support the business needs of the organization. Such changes can have a massive effect on bottom-line financial outcomes, but time is needed for this transformation to take place. Furthermore, improving workforce quality is not merely a matter of staffing. It is equally a matter of ensuring that the company's management practices and organizational structure support the talents of these newly hired employees.

METHOD 1. NO STANDARDIZED ASSESSMENT: START AT THE BOTTOM AND WORK UP

Any company that hires people uses some type of assessment method. The alternative would be simply selecting candidates at random. The first step in designing a staffing assessment system is to look at existing staffing processes to see whether they provide useful information for predicting employee performance. Be critical in this review. Remember that even lengthy interviews and assessment exercises with candidates may collect little useful predictive information if these interviews and exercises do not follow a clear structure and have not been designed and validated against appropriate performance criteria.[3] It is usually best to build on current staffing methods if possible, but do not retain current methods if they are ineffective or inefficient.

METHOD 2. SELF-REPORT PRE-SCREENING QUESTIONNAIRES: THE VALUE OF STRUCTURE

There is little sense in implementing assessments unless they will be used in a consistent, well-structured manner. This requires documenting and following a systematic process for collecting and reviewing information from candidates. Staffing technology systems can be a big help for creating these processes. In addition to increasing administrative efficiency, staffing technology enforces a standardized approach to applicant screening. This results in creating staffing processes that are both faster and more systematic.

Most staffing technology systems provide some support for the use of pre-screening questionnaires. These questionnaires are a good starting point for introducing the concept of assessments in general. The value of pre-screening questionnaires is readily understood by most hiring managers and candidates. This is particularly true when they are compared to more complex assessments such as personality measures and ability tests. But you still need to be careful when deploying automated staffing systems with pre-screening questionnaires lest you create processes that systematically screen out the wrong people.[4] As one staffing manager described it, using pre-screening questionnaires is kind of like using a chainsaw. They are relatively easy to use, and once you get a little practice with them they can have a massive impact in terms of increased efficiency. But if you are careless and use them incorrectly, they can quickly do some serious harm.

METHOD 3. APPLICANT INVESTIGATIONS: AVOIDING CATASTROPHIC HIRING MISTAKES

The wrong employees can be a company's greatest liabilities. Applicant investigations such as background checks and drug tests are a relatively easy way to reduce the risk of making catastrophic staffing mistakes such as hiring people who lack legally mandated certifications, who engage in highly counterproductive behaviors such as drug use or large-scale theft, or who show a proclivity toward workplace violence. The downside of investigations is that they add cost and time to the staffing process and may lead to the loss of some candidates who find applicant investigations to be inappropriate or invasive (see sidebar, "When to Use Drug Screens"). Also, while investigations can help avoid catastrophically bad hires, they have little value for predicting whether candidates will demonstrate superior job performance.

Companies should restrict invasive applicant investigations such as drug tests and certain kinds of background checks to positions for which they have clear relevance. There are several reasons for this. The first is simply one of cost savings. Drug screening and more in-depth background checks can be expensive and difficult to implement, yet may only eliminate a very small percentage of the applicant population. This makes them among the most expensive types of assessments relative to their actual influence on hiring decisions. Second, many candidates find drug screening and extensive background checks to be an overly invasive violation of their personal privacy. Third, albeit somewhat rare, there may be some instances in which drug screening or background checks could actually negatively impact hiring practices. For example, an HR director of a retail sporting goods chain once explained that his company conducts background investigations on all candidates because the company wants to make sure applicants are who they say they are. In contrast, the company limits the use of drug screens to certain positions for which drug use poses a considerable threat to workplace safety or security. The choice to limit drug tests was done largely because, as he put it, "Drug use really isn't an issue for many of our sales associate positions. Plus drug screens would eliminate many of the candidates who make the best snowboard sales people." This company was not sanctioning drug use, but simply acknowledging that a candidate's previous drug use was relevant for some jobs, but largely irrelevant for others.

METHOD 4. STRUCTURED INTERVIEWS: MAXIMIZING TIME SPENT WITH CANDIDATES

Virtually all companies conduct some type of employment interview before hiring candidates. Because of their prevalence, considerable research has been done exploring the effectiveness of different types of hiring interviews.[5] The basic findings of this research follow:

- *Unstructured interviews work very poorly, if at all.* Interviews that do not follow a well-defined agenda and set of questions tend to have limited value for predicting job performance. The hiring manager or recruiter will often spend most of the interview talking, while the candidate merely sits and listens instead of responding to questions. The candidates who probably do the best in unstructured interviews are those who are smart enough to not interrupt the interviewer while he or she is talking and who smile and agree with whatever the interviewer says.

- *Structured interviews work reasonably well.* Structured interviews follow a set agenda with pre-defined questions. They are far more effective than unstructured interviews at predicting job performance.[6] Structured interviews are most effective when interviewers are trained on how to use rating scales listing things to listen for when evaluating candidates' responses. Even relatively inexperienced college students who used structured interviewing techniques were more accurate at evaluating the skills of job candidates than highly experienced hiring managers who used unstructured techniques.[7]

- *Behavioral-based structured interviews tend to work the best.* The most effective structured interviews use behavioral-based questions that ask candidates to describe things they have done in the past that relate to various challenges and tasks they will have to perform on the job.[8] For example, candidates applying for a customer service job might be asked to "Tell me about a time you had to calm down an angry or irate person." The interviewer then uses something called a "behavioral-anchored rating scale" (BARS) to evaluate the candidate's response. BARS lists specific things to listen for in the candidate's response to the interview questions that are indicative of effective or ineffective performance.

Because virtually all companies conduct some form of hiring interview, the implementation of structured interviewing techniques is usually one of the easier ways to leverage assessments to improve the staffing process. While making the change to structured interviews does require some level of training, hiring managers often welcome these changes because they make the interviewing process both easier and more effective.

METHOD 5. BROAD SELF-REPORT AND SITUATIONAL JUDGMENT MEASURES: ASKING CANDIDATES FOR GREATER LEVELS OF SELF-DESCRIPTION

Implementing the use of self-report measures that assess job-relevant aspects of a candidate's personality, motives, and experiences is a good next step after structured interviews for several reasons. First, these assessments can be automated and provide a good complement to the manual, time-intensive nature of interviews. Second, compared to other automated assessments such as ability and skill tests, self-report measures tend to be easier to administer, are usually perceived more positively by applicants, and pose less risk of adverse impact.

The assessments referenced in this particular method are limited to readily available "off-the-shelf" measures of broad personality traits such as emotional stability, dependability, adaptability, agreeableness, and self-confidence. These assessments take advantage of the fact that there are certain kinds of candidate attributes that are relevant to the performance of almost all jobs (see sidebar, "The Benefits of Being Smart, Reliable, and Confident"). This method may also include pre-configured assessments designed to predict specific types of performance in broad classes of jobs, for example, personality measures designed specifically to predict sales performance. This includes self-report integrity tests designed to identify applicants who are likely to engage in highly counterproductive behaviors such as theft, poor attendance, and adversarial treatment of customers and co-workers.

Because the broad assessment measures used in this method are not configured specifically for one job or company, there is a risk that they may oversimplify the relationship between candidate attributes and performance.[9] For example, many off-the-shelf sales assessments assume that risk taking, outgoing, talkative applicants always make the best sales people. This is true in many settings, but there are jobs in which effective sales is associated with more reserved, observant, and consultative behaviors, as opposed to the aggressive, outwardly persuasive style associated with the "stereotypical" sales person. Broad, off-the-shelf assessments may also fail to measure candidate characteristics that are critical for performance in a particular company or specific job. For example, having a general sense of understanding and tolerance toward other cultures is related to success in foreign job assignments.[10] Such a specialized trait is unlikely to be adequately addressed by a broader, more general measure of personality.

Broad measures may also overemphasize certain relevant, but less critical candidate attributes. This can result in screening out candidates who might actually make effective employees. For example, many integrity tests assess traits associated with risk taking and independence that are predictive of theft and failing to follow rules. But these traits may also be positively related to potentially desirable behaviors such as acting decisively or taking initiative in the face of uncertainty. Using integrity tests to evaluate candidates for jobs for which these latter behaviors are highly valuable could lead to screening out a disproportionately high number of potentially good candidates for the wrong reasons.

It is possible to control for some of these problems through the use of the localized scoring described in Method 7. However, completely avoiding these problems requires creating more tailored self-report measures described in Method 10.

THE BENEFITS OF BEING SMART, RELIABLE, AND CONFIDENT

Years of personnel selection research suggest that a few candidate attributes appear to be relevant to performance in virtually all jobs. While these attributes are not always the most important candidate characteristics for job success, candidates who lack them tend to encounter performance problems. These attributes include:

- *Being smart.* People who score higher on general ability or "intelligence" tests tend to be more effective at learning new tasks, solving problems, and mastering new jobs. Performance in any new job requires some amount of learning, and performance of many jobs depends largely on people's ability to quickly learn new tasks or solve difficult problems over time.[11] Consequently, applicant scores on general ability tests are almost always positively related to performance, regardless of the job.

- *Being reliable.* Success in any job depends in part on fulfilling others' requests and "doing what you are told." As a result, candidate levels of conscientiousness and reliability usually show some association with job performance. People who score low on personality measures assessing general dependability and conscientious are less likely to follow work rules and tend to show higher levels of absenteeism, turnover, and counterproductive behavior.[12] These are behaviors that influence performance in most jobs.

- *Being confident.* People who score higher on measures assessing resilience and self-confidence tend to be better at coping with challenging work demands.[13] Because performance of all jobs requires some ability to cope with frustrations, setbacks, and stress, there are few jobs for which a significant lack of confidence is likely to be viewed as a desirable employee attribute.

Research suggests that people who significantly lack any of these three attributes are more likely to encounter performance problems at work. This is because virtually all jobs require some level of learning, problem solving, rule following, and ability to cope with challenges.

This does not mean people have to be extremely smart, reliable, or confident to be successful. In fact, there are times when being extremely smart, reliable, or confident may switch from being strengths to weaknesses. For example, people can be overly confident. In addition, other attributes may be more critical for success in certain jobs. For example, physical ability could be more important than mental ability for some manual labor jobs. Nevertheless, one would be hard-pressed to find any job for which having extremely low levels of ability, reliability, or confidence has no detrimental effect on job performance. Candidates with serious limitations in any of these three areas are likely to struggle with certain aspects of performance in most jobs.

METHOD 6. BROAD KNOWLEDGE AND SKILLS TESTS: TESTING BASIC JOB REQUIREMENTS

This method introduces tests that measure general types of knowledge and skills that influence performance across broad classes of jobs, for example, tests measuring candidates' reading or math skills, comprehension of different languages, ability to use common software packages such as word processors or spreadsheets, or familiarity with technical knowledge in specialty areas such as information technology or accounting. Off-the-shelf tests of many common types of knowledge and skills are readily available to companies via the Internet. Companies staffing jobs that require certain general types of skills and knowledge can benefit from incorporating these tests into their staffing processes. These tests are particularly useful if many applicants lack fundamental skills and knowledge required for the positions they are seeking. Another advantage of these assessments is that candidates and hiring managers can easily see their relevance to the job and tend to be positively disposed toward their use.

The main limitation of these tests is that they are only relevant to jobs in which performance is heavily influenced by differences in employees' knowledge and skills. For example, a typing test will only be useful if differences between high- and low-performing employees largely reflect differences in typing skill. If most employees and job applicants type well enough to sufficiently perform the job, then a typing test will provide little value for distinguishing between good and bad candidates. These tests are also only useful if the knowledge and skills they assess are critical for job performance. For example, typing speed may have some impact on the performance of mechanical engineers, but it may not be enough to justify eliminating highly skilled engineering candidates simply because they do not type well. Last, in many cases the knowledge and skills measured by these types of tests are things that could be learned on the job. In cases in which there is a scarcity of qualified candidates, it may make more sense to teach people what they need to know once they are on the job, rather than seeking to hire people who already possess the knowledge and skills needed to perform the work.

A possible operational challenge to using knowledge and skills tests is the potential requirement to administer them in a "proctored" setting. This is a setting in which candidates are monitored to ensure they are not cheating or having someone else complete the assessment for them, for example, having candidates complete the test on-site at a testing center where they can be watched by a test administrator. Proctored testing is not always a requirement for using knowledge and skills tests, but some companies or assessment vendors may require it to control for concerns related to test security and applicant faking. If proctored testing is required, it will significantly increase the logistical challenges and costs associated with using knowledge and skills tests.

METHOD 7. BROAD ABILITY TESTS: GETTING A GENERAL SENSE OF CANDIDATES' ABILITY TO LEARN AND SOLVE PROBLEMS

This method introduces the use of broad ability tests that measure mental capabilities related to reasoning, critical thinking, and logical problem solving. There are many types of broad ability tests readily available on the market under names such as intelligence tests, critical thinking tests, problem-solving tests, and reasoning tests.

Scores on most broad ability tests partially reflect an attribute called "general ability."[14] General ability predicts how quickly and effectively people are able to process unfamiliar information and solve novel problems.[15] Tests of general ability are arguably the single most effective type of assessment for predicting job performance. This is because virtually all jobs require some level of learning and problem solving. Assessing general ability is particularly useful for predicting performance in jobs that require rapidly learning new concepts and solving complex problems.

There are two major challenges to using broad ability tests. First, these tests almost always show adverse impact against certain EEOC-protected groups. The reasons for the adverse impact of ability tests are complex and have yet to be fully understood[16] (see sidebar, "Demographic Group Differences in Assessment Scores"). Although broad ability tests tend to be very predictive of job performance, their adverse impact is often cause enough for companies not to use them. A second reason why companies may be reluctant to use broad ability tests is because applicants tend to dislike them.[17] Ability tests can be quite mentally challenging, and many use highly abstract problems with relatively low face validity (see the sidebar in Chapter Four, "Face Validity Versus Criteria Validity: The Case of the Raven"). Candidates often perceive them to be difficult to complete and may not understand how they relate to the position they are applying for.

There is extensive evidence demonstrating the validity, job relevance, and legal defensibility of ability measures, despite problems they may have in terms of adverse impact and negative applicant reactions.[18] Companies staffing jobs that require rapidly learning new information, quickly processing complex data, and making decisions under time pressure should consider including ability tests as a key part of their assessment process. But companies using ability tests should also take particular care to conduct job analysis and validation studies that clearly document the job relevance of these assessments in case their use is legally challenged based on grounds of adverse impact.

DEMOGRAPHIC GROUP DIFFERENCES IN ASSESSMENT SCORES

One of the more hotly debated topics in the field of psychology is whether demographic groups differ systematically on various psychological attributes. For example, are societal assumptions that men are better at mechanical tasks and women are better at caring and nurturing tasks reflections of cultural stereotypes, or are they indicative of innate psychological differences between men and women? The answers to these sorts of questions have important implications for evaluating whether certain staffing assessments and hiring methods fairly or unfairly favor candidates from certain demographic groups.

If there truly are differences between demographic groups on job-relevant attributes, then we would expect certain assessments to systematically favor applicants from demographic groups that have more of these attributes. For example, due to human genetics, on average men are physically stronger than women. As a result, it is reasonable to expect that male applicants will tend to do better than female applicants on a physical skill assessment that predicts performance of job tasks that require lifting heavy weights. Furthermore, if such an assessment is used to select candidates, then over time its use will lead to hiring significantly more male applicants than female applicants.

Most people accept that differences exist between demographic groups for visible physical attributes like strength, height, or general body size. For example, Asians as a group tend to be shorter than African Americans. People are far more skeptical of the existence of demographic differences for less tangible attributes such as reasoning ability, emotional resilience, or spatial orientation and direction finding.

Of all the differences that people have suggested may exist between demographic groups, perhaps none has received more time and attention than differences between EEO-protected ethnic groups on measures of general ability. Decades of research have shown that on average whites and Asians tend to score significantly higher on general ability tests than Hispanics and African Americans do. A range of factors appear to contribute to these differences, including culture, socioeconomic status, and genetics. But which of these factors is the main contributor to the differences in ability test scores is far from certain and may never be conclusively answered.

Any company considering the use of ability tests for personnel selection should consider the impact that these tests may have on applicants from certain demographic groups. At the same time, companies should recognize that ability tests are among the most effective tools for predicting job performance, particularly for jobs that emphasize rapid processing of complex and novel information and solving unfamiliar problems. These two things create something of a dilemma for staffing practitioners. On one hand, companies want to avoid using assessments that systematically screen out greater proportions of applicants from certain demographic groups. On the other hand, companies want to maximize the accuracy of their staffing decisions. Resolving this dilemma requires making a choice between the business value of maximizing staffing accuracy versus the business risks associated with having a potentially less diverse employee population.

It is important to emphasize that differences in ability test scores between demographic groups are slight in comparison to the overall differences in scores across all applicants. In other words, there is considerable overlap in ability test scores across demographic groups. The scores of many white applicants on a broad ability test will be well below the scores achieved by many black applicants. The differences in ability test scores that exist between demographic groups only become noticeable when one aggregates data across large numbers of people. What this means at a practical level is that knowing someone's demographic status does not allow you to accurately predict his or her ability test score.

METHOD 8. INTEGRATING BROAD SELF-REPORT MEASURES, KNOWLEDGE AND SKILLS TESTS, AND ABILITY TESTS: PREDICTING MAXIMAL AND TYPICAL PERFORMANCE

This method focuses on integrating the three types of assessments used in Methods 5, 6, and 7. This method uses two complementary kinds of assessments to more fully predict different aspects of job performance. The result is an assessment method that provides a more complete picture of candidate potential.

The knowledge and skills tests and broad ability tests discussed in Methods 6 and 7 present candidates with objective questions that are scored as logically or factually correct or incorrect. These types of assessments are sometimes referred to as measures of "maximal performance."

Assessments that focus on maximal performance are useful for predicting performance in tasks that require solving complex problems using logical reasoning, drawing on specific types of knowledge, and rapidly processing information under time pressure (for example, fixing machinery, developing new tools and technology).

The self-report measures of personality, motives, and interests discussed in Method 5 ask candidates subjective questions about preferences, attitudes, or beliefs that usually do not have a single factually correct answer. These types of assessments are often referred to as measures of "typical performance." Assessments that focus on typical performance are useful for predicting performance on tasks that depend more on volition than ability (for example, showing up to work on time, smiling at customers, staying calm during arguments).[19]

There are considerable advantages to implementing assessment methods that include measures of both typical and maximal performance. By including both kinds of assessments, companies are better able to predict the full range of employee behaviors that influence job performance. Another advantage of combining these types of assessments is that use of the self-report assessments described in Method 5 can reduce the level of adverse impact that often occurs when using the knowledge, skills, and ability tests described in Methods 6 and 7.[20]

METHOD 9. LOCALIZED SCORING: ACCURATELY INTERPRETING CANDIDATE RESPONSES

This method focuses on techniques for more effectively scoring and interpreting many of the assessments described in earlier methods. Assessments such as personality measures, pre-screening questionnaires, and knowledge, skill, and ability tests provide quantitative data that is scored using mathematical formulas to estimate a candidate's performance potential. The accuracy of these formulas can be significantly improved using localized scoring methods that draw on company- or job-specific data to strengthen the relationships between assessment results and actual job performance.

When you evaluate a candidate based on an assessment score, you are assuming there is a relationship between that score and actual job performance. However, until you do some form of local scoring, you can never be certain that this assumption is true. For example, imagine I told you a candidate applying to be a bus driver in your city took an ability test and received a score of 317. Does this tell you whether this person is likely to be a good bus driver? Your answer should be "no" because you have no way of knowing whether a score of 317 tells you anything about the person's likely performance as a bus driver. What if I told you that the test was called the "Bus Driver Performance Index"? Does the test now give you insight into whether to hire this person as a bus driver? Your answer should still be "no." Just because a test is given a name that seems job-relevant does not mean it actually predicts job performance. How about if I told you the test had been shown to be valid predictor of bus driver performance? Your answer should still be "no" because you don't know whether a score of 317 is high or low.

Now what if I told you that this test was given to a group of two hundred bus drivers currently working in your city. The bus drivers who scored above 300 on the test had 50 percent fewer accidents on the job than drivers who scored below 300. Now would you be comfortable using this test to help guide the decision whether to hire this person as a bus driver? Your answer is probably moving toward "yes" because you have data that gives some sense of what an assessment score of 317 on this test means in terms of likely performance as a bus driver. This is the kind of data that is provided by local scoring.

Assessment results are only meaningful if they provide information that allows us to accurately predict whether some candidates are likely to be more or less effective than other candidates who might be hired. Local scoring helps make assessment results more meaningful by comparing a candidate's assessment scores against data gathered from other candidates or employees who took the same assessment. This is most often done using two types of scoring methods: norming and criteria validation and optimization.

Norming

Norming is a statistical process that compares a candidate's assessment scores against scores received by other people who have taken the same assessment. Norming enables us to say things like "This candidate's score places her at the 90th percentile compared to other candidates applying for the same or similar jobs." These comparisons are often referred to as "norms." Norms are calculated for different comparison groups or "populations" of people. For example, one might norm a candidate's assessment scores using a comparison group consisting of existing employees. This would tell us how well the candidate performed on the assessment relative to existing employees who completed the same assessment. This is often expressed in statements such as "The candidate's score put him at the 65th percentile when normed against current employees."

It is important that norms used to evaluate candidates be based on an appropriate comparison group. Many assessment companies offer general norms that compare candidate scores against the scores of everyone who has ever taken the assessment, regardless of these people's jobs or employment status. General norms can be useful when trying to rank candidates at a very high level, but are often difficult to interpret with regard to specific jobs or positions. For example, imagine that a candidate applying for an administrative assistant position in a hospital was asked to take a reading test as part of the selection process. The candidate's reading score placed her at the 45th percentile relative to a general pool of candidates applying for a wide variety of jobs across hundreds of organizations. This might seem to be useful information at first. However, we do not know whether being at the 45th percentile reflects a high enough level of reading for this particular position. Being an administrative assistant at a hospital might require working with complex documents. A candidate at the 45th percentile relative to the general population might struggle to read these documents. But what if the job does not require reading highly complex documents? Then being at the 45th percentile may reflect a reading level that is higher than what the administrative assistant job requires. Until some effort is made to establish what general norms mean at the local level, attempts to interpret them require a lot of guesswork. This is why it is beneficial to calculate local norms using data from candidates or employees applying or working in jobs that are similar to the one being staffed.

The more unique the job or applicant population, the more important it is to base norms on groups of people whose characteristics are relevant to the position being staffed. This can be done by gathering assessment data from a sample of current employees or by using data from other candidates applying for the same or similar jobs. Many assessment vendors offer different job-specific norms computed from data collected from candidates applying for similar jobs in other organizations. For example, a vendor might be able to provide norms computed on entry-level retail job candidates, candidates applying for nursing jobs, and so forth.

A limitation of norms is that they only indicate how a candidate performed on an assessment relative to other applicants or employees. Norms do not necessarily provide predictive information about a candidate's likely job performance. Just because someone scores in the 90th percentile does not necessarily mean she is more likely to perform better than a candidate who scored at the 20th percentile. Such a statement would only be true if additional validation data had been collected showing that higher assessment scores are indicative of superior performance. Do not simply accept statements that "Candidates with high normative scores make better employees." Ask for validation evidence backing up such claims. Ideally, this will include criteria validation data. But for some assessments such as knowledge and skills tests, content validation evidence may be adequate.

Criteria Validation and Optimization

Criteria validation and optimization involves using statistical techniques to change how assessments are scored in order to improve their ability to predict job performance. Criteria validation mathematically demonstrates relationships between assessment scores and performance data. Optimization uses the results of criteria validation studies to change how assessments are scored to better predict job performance. Because optimization in not possible without conducting some form of criteria validation, criteria validation will be discussed first.

As discussed earlier in Chapter Four, criteria validation involves making mathematical comparisons among assessment data collected from applicants or employees with measures of job performance. Criteria validation helps answer the question, "What does a certain score on an assessment actually mean in terms of a candidate's likely performance?" Criteria validation data also provides very strong evidence of job relevance should the legality of an assessment ever be challenged.

Optimization uses data from criteria validation studies to change how an assessment is scored so it more effectively predicts performance in a specific job. For example, imagine that a company implemented a personality assessment to predict performance in customer service jobs. This personality assessment measures two traits: "agreeableness," defined as the tendency to smile and get along with others, and "orderliness," defined as the tendency to keep things well-organized and pay attention to details. Through criteria validation, the company discovered that customer ratings of employee service performance are more closely related to orderliness than to agreeableness. Customers place more value on having employees keep track of their requests than on having employees smile and treat them in a pleasant manner. While agreeableness might still influence job performance, it has less influence than orderliness. Consequently, the company might optimize the assessment to emphasize orderliness more than agreeableness when calculating a candidate's overall assessment score.

Criteria validation and optimization uses data to increase the relationship between assessment scores and employee performance. In contrast, norming just looks at how candidates' assessment scores compare to those of other groups of candidates or employees. Criteria validation and optimization is always preferable to norming for improving assessment accuracy. But far more resources and data are required to conduct a criteria validation study than to calculate assessment norms. While not ideal, norming is an acceptable way to do localized scoring for an assessment, provided there is some validation evidence that candidates with higher norm scores are likely to outperform candidates with lower norm scores.

Companies should be cautious about using one localized scoring method referred to as "employee profiling." Employee profiling involves collecting assessment data from current high-performing employees and then using it to establish an ideal assessment score or profile. Candidates' assessment scores are contrasted against this profile to see whether they "look like" successful employees. Profiling is a faulty way to score an assessment because it does not indicate what differentiates high performers from low performers (see sidebar "Profiling and the Dangers of Cloning High-Performing Employees"). Profiling just looks at what current high performers happen to have in common. It does not provide evidence showing whether any of these common attributes are actually relevant to performance. Employee profiling can potentially work to improve staffing decisions, but it can also be very misleading and may lead to hiring candidates based on characteristics that have little to do with actual performance.

PROFILING AND THE DANGERS OF CLONING HIGH-PERFORMING EMPLOYEES

Profiling is a localized scoring technique that involves comparing candidates' assessment scores with the scores that high-performing employees received on the same assessment. Some assessment vendors use profiling as a means to "validate" their tests, and they may even refer to the process as validating. However, profiling is different from validating because it does not actually look at relationships between assessment scores and measures of job performance. This makes profiling a much weaker practice than validating. Vendors that practice profiling only focus on how high-performing employees scored on the assessment, and may not ever collect assessment data from poor performers. As a result, no comparison is made to determine how the assessment scores of low performers differ from those of high performers.

Assessment companies that score their assessments using profiling often claim to be "cloning" the star people in a company's workforce. Such blind duplication of employee characteristics is not necessarily a good thing. Just because high performers share a trait does not necessarily mean that the trait is desirable. Companies that focus on hiring candidates who "look like" current high-performing employees may be selecting applicants based on both negative as well as positive employee attributes. For example, many sales managers will readily admit that their highest performing sales people are often the hardest to manage, given their fiercely individualistic and competitive nature. Having a sales team comprised entirely of high-performing but highly competitive people could be problematic because they tend not to collaborate well with others.

Because employee profiling does not make distinctions between desirable and undesirable high-performer attributes, it is a very risky way to select candidates. It may also systematically decrease the diversity of a company's workforce, since candidates are screened to look like the current employee population. It can be contrasted against criteria validation and optimization methods that focus on screening candidates based solely on traits that have been shown to have strong relationships to actual performance. Unlike the profiling approach, which groups characteristics of current employees together and assumes they must all be desirable, the criteria validation approach limits selection to characteristics that directly influence performance while allowing variation around all other characteristics.

METHOD 10. CONTEXT-SPECIFIC SELF-REPORT MEASURES: ASKING CANDIDATES TO DESCRIBE THEMSELVES IN GREATER DETAIL

This method involves replacing or augmenting the broad self-report assessments discussed in Method 5 with more fine-tuned measures that hone in on specific employee attributes that drive performance in a particular job or work environment.[21] The value of context-specific assessments lies in creating stronger relationships between assessment content and the specific behaviors that drive success in a job.

To illustrate how context-specific assessments work, consider the following personality questions:

Indicate whether you agree with the following statements as accurate descriptions of you:

1. I am very good at most of the things I do.

2. I am very good at expressing my ideas to others.

3. I am very good at making formal presentations to large groups of people.

These questions provide a contrast between the kind of content used in broad personality assessments and more context-specific assessments. The first question, "I am very good at most of the things I do" taps into general self-confidence and self-esteem. This is the kind of question one often finds on broad personality measures. This question may predict how candidates respond to challenging situations and requests in general. Conversely, it may also reflect negative candidate characteristics such as narcissism. The second question, "I am very good at expressing my ideas to others" is slightly more contextual. It gets at a person's confidence in his or her speaking skills, as opposed to broad confidence overall. It may predict behaviors related to how one performs in a group setting that require interacting with others. The third question, "I am very good at making formal presentations to large groups of people" is highly contextual. It would typically not be found on a broad self-report measure, but it might appear on a contextual measure focused on jobs that require making formal presentations. In addition to reflecting aspects of general self-confidence, this question is likely to tap into a person's previous experience and training making large presentations. It could be effective at predicting behaviors related to formal speaking. In fact, because it is more closely matched to actual speaking behavior, it may provide considerable value for predicting public speaking performance over the other more general questions. But it might be less useful for predicting other behaviors related to social confidence that do not involve public speaking, for example, some successful public speakers are actually somewhat shy and humble when off stage. They might agree with this question, but disagree with the other two questions.

By including context-specific self-report measures that more precisely match assessment content to a particular job or work setting, companies can substantially increase assessment effectiveness. These measures may also appear to be more job-relevant and may be more favorably received by applicants. Context-specific assessments are also often shorter than more generic, broad assessments because they are tailored to only measure specific things that drive success in a particular job. They can be very useful when staffing jobs that require employees to display unique types of behaviors or work in highly distinctive environments. Context-specific assessments can also give companies greater competitive staffing advantage, because they are frequently proprietary and cannot be resold to competitors. In contrast, most broad "off-the-shelf" assessments can be purchased by any company.

The main disadvantage of context-specific measures is that they can take significant resources to develop and may only be valid for a limited range of jobs and/or work settings. Development of context-specific assessments requires conducting a thorough job analysis to determine the unique characteristic of the job that influence performance. It may also require development of new assessment content, which can be a fairly labor-intensive process. Last, some form of local norming or criteria validation study is likely to be required to establish scoring for the assessment.

METHOD 11. CONTEXT-SPECIFIC KNOWLEDGE, SKILLS, AND ABILITY TESTS: SEEING WHAT A CANDIDATE CAN ACTUALLY DO

This method focuses on the use of context-specific knowledge, skills, and ability tests that require candidates to interpret information and perform tasks that are very similar to things employees actually do on the job. These tests can be contrasted with the broad tests described in previous methods that assess more general knowledge and problem-solving skills. Context-specific knowledge, skills, and ability tests are often called "work samples." They require candidates to perform activities that are almost identical to actual tasks performed in the job, for example, assessing candidates' truck-driving skills by having them drive a truck through an obstacle course, or assessing candidates' computer-programming skills by requiring them to write a portion of computer code.

Because they involve performing tasks that are highly similar or even identical to tasks done in the actual job, context-specific knowledge, skills, and ability tests are possibly the single most predictive type of assessment. However, they may only be effective at predicting those aspects of the job that they simulate. For example, having candidates drive trucks will tell you a lot about their truck-driving skills, but may not provide any insight into whether they are likely to show up to work on time. Nor will knowing how a candidate performs on a task that involves writing computer code give you much insight into whether he or she is likely to get along with co-workers.

Context-specific knowledge, skills, and ability tests can be very useful for staffing jobs in which performance depends on carrying out well-defined technical tasks or activities that require job-specific knowledge or skills. These assessments are particularly valuable for jobs that require performing highly unique or specialized tasks (for example, air traffic controllers), or utilizing in-depth subject-matter knowledge and skills (for example, computer programming). Context-specific knowledge, skills, and ability tests also tend to be favorably viewed by applicants because they are so similar to the job itself.

The main problem with these tests is that they can be expensive to design, time-consuming to administer, and may become quickly outdated if the nature of a job changes over time. Another potential limitation of these tests is that they may show adverse impact against certain EEOC-protected groups if they require solving complex problems using logical reasoning or critically processing novel information. The more specialized your job, the more you may want to consider using context-specific tests. But remember that these tests often cost a lot to develop and may rapidly lose their job relevance if significant changes are made to the technology and/or work processes used in the job.

METHOD 12. INTEGRATING CONTEXT-SPECIFIC SELF-REPORT MEASURES AND KNOWLEDGE, SKILLS, AND ABILITY TESTS: PREDICTING HIGHLY SPECIFIC TYPES OF MAXIMAL AND TYPICAL PERFORMANCE

When we covered Method 8, we discussed the value of integrating broad tests of knowledge, skills, and ability with broad measures of personality. Method 12 focuses on the value of integrating context-specific versions of these same types of assessments. Context-specific knowledge, skills, and ability tests are effective for predicting people's maximum performance in job situations that require carrying out specific tasks for which success depends both on what they know and what they can do. In contrast, context-specific self-report measures provide insight into people's typical performance in more unstructured settings in which their performance depends more on what they choose to do. Taken together, these two types of assessments provide extensive and highly detailed insight into how candidates are likely to perform in a range of job-relevant situations.

METHOD 13. ADVANCED, NON-LINEAR SCORING: "TURBO-CHARGING" ASSESSMENT RESULTS

When covering Method 9, we discussed the value of using localized scoring to strengthen relationships between assessment results and job performance measures. The localized scoring methods described in Method 9 typically use statistical techniques that rely on something called linear, mathematical models. The methods described here are similar to localized scoring as described in

Method 9, but focus on the use of statistical techniques that rely on non-linear mathematical models.[22]

Non-linear mathematical models allow for the discovery and utilization of complex interactions between candidate characteristics and job performance. These more complex relationships tend to be overlooked by linear models (see sidebar, "Non-Linear Job Performance: More Is Not Always Better"). By more precisely measuring and modeling the candidate characteristics that influence job performance, non-linear scoring methods can substantially increase the overall effectiveness of assessment solutions.[23]

Any form of assessment that provides quantitative data could potentially be improved through the use of non-linear scoring models. However, developing non-linear scoring models requires access to relatively large datasets (for example, assessment and performance data from one thousand or more employees). Due to these data requirements, use of non-linear modeling methods is not feasible for many assessment applications. Fairly intensive statistical analyses are also required to develop non-linear scoring algorithms. But given their potential value, companies staffing very large numbers of positions should definitely explore the possible use of non-linear scoring.

NON-LINEAR JOB PERFORMANCE: MORE IS NOT ALWAYS BETTER

Most assessments are scored using mathematical models that assume that candidate attributes are linearly related to job performance. These linear models assume that the more of an attribute a candidate has, the more likely he or she is to be effective in the job. Most assessment scoring algorithms also assume that candidate attributes are additive in nature. Additive models assume that if two candidate characteristics individually show positive relationships to performance, then being high in both characteristics is always better than being high in one and low in the other. In sum, the linear and additive scoring models used by most assessments treat candidate attributes as though "more is always better."

The main advantage of linear, additive scoring models has to do with the data required to build them. It is possible to build stable, reliable linear, additive scoring models with data from as few as one hundred employees. These models can be quite effective for predicting performance in most job situations, and the datasets required to build them are much smaller than the datasets needed to build reliable scoring models that do not assume linear or additive relationships between employee characteristics and performance.

Linear, additive models do have two major limitations that can constrain their effectiveness. First, linear models do not account for the possibility that some applicant characteristics switch from being positively related to performance to being detrimental if they go above a certain level. For example, self-confidence is positively related to performance in a lot of jobs that require dealing with risk and uncertainty, but people with too much self-confidence may become reckless. Most linear models are unlikely to pick up on this shift, and will continue to favor the more confident candidate no matter how over-confident he or she may be.

Most linear, additive scoring models also ignore the possibility that applicant characteristics may interact or moderate one another. The value of being high in one characteristic may depend in part on whether one is high or low in some other characteristic. For example, "fear of failure" is often negatively related to performance because it is associated with a reluctance to take on challenging tasks. However, people can have high self-confidence and also be high in fear of failure. Such people can make very effective employees because their belief in their ability to succeed is tempered by a sense of concern over potentially making mistakes. People with this combination of characteristics may be more effective than more risk-taking individuals who are high in self-confidence but low in fear of failure.

The core problem with linear, additive scoring models is that they over-simplify relationships between employee characteristics and employee performance. The results achieved by high-performing employees often do not come from simply doing more of the same things average employees are doing. High-performing employees often achieve superior results by doing things differently than average-performing employees do. These more complex relationships can only be captured using non-linear scoring models.

Some of the advantages of non-linear scoring are illustrated in Figure 7.2. This figure indicates the relationship between sales performance in a retail store and two candidate attributes called "social leadership" and

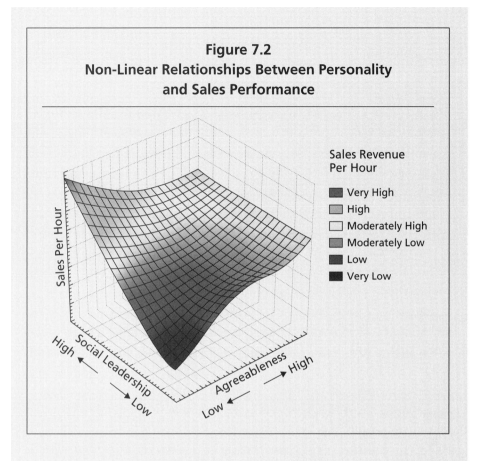

Figure 7.2
Non-Linear Relationships Between Personality and Sales Performance

Sales Revenue Per Hour

- ■ Very High
- ■ High
- □ Moderately High
- ■ Moderately Low
- ■ Low
- ■ Very Low

Sales Per Hour

Social Leadership — High — Low

Agreeableness — Low — High

"agreeableness." Both attributes were assessed using a self-report personality measure. Social leadership reflects a person's tendency to take the lead in conversations and discussions (for example, "I am often the first person to speak up in group meetings"). Agreeableness reflects a person's emphasis on maintaining harmonious, pleasant relationships with others (for example, "I always act polite, even to people I do not like"). Both attributes show positive linear relationships to sales performance. Socially confident employees are more likely to start conversations with customers and as a result sell more product. Agreeable employees tend to treat customers in a way that makes them feel welcome in the store and as a result also sell more product.

As expected, the worst sales people are low in social confidence and low in agreeableness. Conversely, many effective sales people are high in social confidence and high in agreeableness. But the best sales people in this particular store are actually high in social confidence but low in agreeableness. Being low in agreeableness does not mean these people are unfriendly toward customers. They simply are not very interested in spending time engaging in pleasant conversations. They want to sell product. They will proactively start conversations with a customer to see whether there is an opportunity for a sale. If there is an opportunity, they will pursue the conversation toward closing the sale. But if there is no sales opportunity, they cut the conversation short and move on to the next customer. This type of behavior is highly effective given the short, highly transactional nature of sales in this particular store. This unique type of behavior would also almost certainly be overlooked by assessments that relied solely on linear, additive scoring.

Developing statistically reliable non-linear assessment scoring models similar to the one illustrated in Figure 7.2 often requires datasets with assessment and performance data from one thousand employees or more. Improvements in staffing technology are making it increasingly feasible for companies to collect such large datasets. These systems collect assessment data from candidates during the staffing process and then automatically link this data with job performance and tenure data gathered on employees after they are hired. Referred to as "closed-loop validation" methods, these systems allow companies with large hiring volumes to quickly amass the datasets needed to utilize non-linear assessment scoring. The result is to transform staffing into a data-driven, continuous improvement process that captures the complex, non-linear relationships that exist between candidate attributes and subsequent job performance.

CONCLUDING REMARKS: DETERMINING WHAT ASSESSMENT METHODS TO USE

The thirteen methods outlined in Table 7.1 illustrate multiple ways that assessments can be deployed to support staffing. The methods range from simple standardization of the hiring process to development of highly tailored assessment content and non-linear scoring models. Which methods make the most sense for any given staffing situation will depend on variables such as the number of positions being filled, the complexity of the positions, and the impact these positions have on the overall success of the organization. When staffing jobs with lower hiring volumes, less complexity, or less organizational impact, then the simpler, easier-to-deploy techniques described in Methods 1 through 9 may suffice. The more complex techniques described in Methods 10 through 13 should be considered for jobs that have larger staffing volumes, greater job complexity, and more significant impacts on business outcomes.

The most important thing to take away from Table 7.1 and what you have read in this chapter is that assessment methods are available to support the needs of virtually any staffing situation. Many of the methods described in Table 7.1 can be implemented with relatively little cost or operational impact. While the predictive accuracy of these simpler methods might be considered "sub-optimal" when compared to other more complex methods, they are far better than hiring candidates using no assessment method at all.

Notes

1. Angoff, W. (1983). Validity: An evolving concept (pp. 19–32). In H. Wainer & H. Brown (Eds.), *Test validity*. Mahwah, NJ: Lawrence Earlbaum Associates.
2. Edwards, J.R. (1991). Person-job fit: A conceptual integration, literature review, and methodological critique. In C.L. Cooper & I.T. Robertson (Eds.), *International review of industrial and organizational psychology* (Vol. 6; pp. 283–357). Hoboken, NJ: John Wiley & Sons.
   Liao, H., Joshi, A., & Chuang, A. (2004). Sticking out like a sore thumb: Employee dissimilarity and deviance at work. *Personnel Psychology, 57,* 969–1000.
3. Campion, M.A., Pursell, E.D., & Brown, B.K. (1988). Structured interviewing: Raising the psychometric properties of the employment interview. *Personnel Psychology,* pp. 25–41.
4. Handler, C., & Hunt, S.T. (2003). *Do online applicant pre-screening tools really work?* Electronic Recruiting Exchange. www.ere.net/articles/db/46DCF7A42B0441A7BDD9054D2D529C71.asp
5. Harris, M.M. (1989). Reconsidering the employment interview: A review of recent literature and suggestions for future research. *Personnel Psychology, 42,* 691–726.
6. Campion, M.A., Pursell, E.D., & Brown, B.K. (1988). Structured interviewing: Raising the psychometric properties of the employment interview. *Personnel Psychology,* pp. 25–41.
7. Maurer, S.D. (2002). A practitioner-based analysis of interviewer job expertise and scale format as contextual factors in situational interviews. *Personnel Psychology, 55,* 307–327.
8. Janz, T., Hellervik, L., & Gilmore, D.C. (1986). *Behavioral description interviewing.* Boston, MA: Allyn & Bacon.

9. Ashton, M.C. (1998). Personality and job performance: The importance of narrow traits. *Journal of Organizational Behavior, 19,* 289–303.

10. Spreitzer, G.M., McCall, M.W. Jr., & Mahoney, J.D. (1997). Early identification of international executive potential. *Journal of Applied Psychology, 82,* 6–29.

11. Hunter, J.E. (1986). Cognitive ability, cognitive aptitudes, job knowledge, and job performance. *Journal of Vocational Behavior, 29,* 340–362.

12. Barrick, M.R., & Mount, M.K. (1991). The big five personality dimensions and job performance: A meta-analysis. *Personnel Psychology, 44,* 1–26.

13. Judge, T.A., Erez, A., Bono, J.E., & Thoreson, C.J. (2003). The core self-evaluations scale: Development of a measure. *Personnel Psychology, 56,* 303–331.

14. Carroll, J.B. (1993). *Human cognitive abilities.* New York: Cambridge University Press.

15. Humphreys, L.G. (1979). The construct of general intelligence. *Intelligence, 3,* 105–120.

16. Hunt, E. (1995). The role of intelligence in modern society. *American Scientist, 83,* 356–368.

17. Murphy, K.R., Cronin, B.E., & Tam, A.P. (2003). Controversy and consensus regarding the use of cognitive ability testing in organizations. *Journal of Applied Psychology, 88,* 660–671.

18. Gottfredson, L.S. (1994). The science and politics of race-norming. *American Psychologist, 11,* 955–963.

19. Ackerman, P.L. (1993). Intelligence, attention, and learning: Maximal and typical performance. In D.K. Detterman (Ed.), *Current topics in human intelligence: Vol. 4, Theories of Intelligence.* Norwood, NJ: Ablex.

20. Pulakos, E.D., & Schmitt, N. (1996). An evaluation of two strategies for reducing adverse impact and their effects on criterion related validity. *Human Performance, 9,* 241–258.

21. Paunonen, S.V., & Nicol, A.A.A.M. (2001). The personality hierarchy and the prediction of work behaviors. In B. Roberts & R. Hogan (Eds.), *Personality psychology in the workplace.* Washington, DC: American Psychological Association.

22. Collins, J.M., & Clark, M.R. (1993). An application of the theory of neural computation to the prediction of workplace behavior: An illustration and assessment of network analysis. *Personnel Psychology, 46,* 503–524.

23. Scarborough, D., & Somers, M.J. (2006). *Neural networks in organizational research: Applying pattern recognition to the analysis of organizational behavior.* Washington, DC: American Psychological Association.

Incorporating Staffing Assessments into the Hiring Process

The previous chapters discussed various types of staffing assessments, how they work and how to evaluate their effectiveness, and the strengths and limitations of different assessment methods. This chapter addresses how to integrate assessments into a company's staffing processes. The chapter is broken into three sections. The first section reviews general principles that should guide the design of any staffing assessment process. The next two sections describe how these principles can be applied to develop integrated staffing assessment processes for hourly and salaried jobs.

PRINCIPLES OF STAFFING ASSESSMENT PROCESS DESIGN

Designing a staffing assessment process requires answering two basic questions: (1) Which assessments should be used to evaluate candidates? and (2) When should candidates take these assessments? The answers to these questions will depend on a variety of operational factors, including:

- The nature of the job being staffed (simple jobs with few requirements versus complex jobs with extensive requirements).

- The hiring volume (hiring one person or thousands).

- The location of applicants (centrally located versus distributed across multiple sites).

- The staffing skills of the people using the assessments (untrained hiring managers versus professional recruiters).

- The cost of the assessments and the resources available to pay for those costs (some assessment have fairly low fixed costs, while others may cost $100 or more per use).

Given the number of factors involved, there is no single best way to use assessments. But there are four core principles that should always be considered when designing any staffing assessment process: (1) establishing multiple assessment hurdles, (2) ensuring similar treatment of all applicants, (3) giving hiring managers ultimate responsibility over who to hire, and (4) creating a conversation to establish a two-way flow of information with candidates.

Principle 1. Establish Multiple Assessment Hurdles

Many staffing assessment processes use several kinds of assessments. This makes it possible to evaluate a wide range of candidate attributes and more fully predict different aspects of job performance. Candidates applying for a single job may be asked to answer a pre-screening questionnaire, take a knowledge or skills test, respond to a self-report personality assessment, complete a timed ability test, participate in a structured interview, and submit to a background investigation. Candidates would probably react negatively if they were asked to complete so many assessments in one sitting. Giving all these assessments to every candidate who applied would also require a lot of time and probably cost a lot of money. The simplest way to avoid these problems is to give assessments at different places in the staffing process. Candidates must pass certain assessments early in the process before they are asked to take additional assessments later in the process. This method is commonly referred to as a "multiple hurdle" selection process.

The order assessments are administered in during a multiple hurdle process is very important. Assessments administered earlier in the process will be given to more candidates. They will be administered more frequently and will probably screen out the largest number of candidates. Assessments used early in the process may also be one of the first things candidates experience when applying for a job and could make a significant impression on applicants' overall attitudes toward the hiring organization. Given these issues, assessments used early in the staffing process should ideally be short, inexpensive, informative, and relatively engaging to applicants. Longer, more expensive, or more invasive assessments should be used later in the process.

Pre-screening questionnaires, short culture fit or personality measures, and highly engaging job simulations can be effectively used as the first hurdle in a selection process. More lengthy or less engaging assessments such as long self-report personality measures and ability tests should usually be used later in the process. Time-consuming assessments such as in-depth structured interviews and potentially invasive assessments such as drug and background checks tend to be best used toward the end of the staffing process as some of the last hurdles before the final selection decision.

It is usually best to score assessments used early in the process in a manner designed to "screen out" applicants who clearly don't meet the requirements of the job. This scoring focuses on removing candidates who lack basic job qualifications. It can be contrasted to scoring methods that focus on "selecting in" candidates by identifying a few top applicants with the greatest overall potential for success. The reason for focusing on screening out candidates is because assessments used as first hurdles in a selection process tend to be relatively short and often have much less predictive accuracy than longer, more in-depth assessments used later in the process. Over-relying on these shorter assessments to identify the best candidates may result in removing large numbers of potentially successful candidates. An exception to this might be made for companies that have an overwhelming number of highly qualified applicants. But always keep in mind that there is a big difference between simply screening out candidates and actually screening out the right candidates.

Principle 2. Ensure Similar Treatment of Applicants

Assessment is fundamentally about effective measurement, and effective measurement depends on standardization. From a staffing perspective, this means making sure all candidates go through the same steps in the hiring process in the same order. Assessment results must also be interpreted using the same criteria across all candidates. Failing to follow consistent processes leads to unsystematic measurement. This can make even the best assessments ineffective. Treating applicants inconsistently also creates legal risks if applicants from different demographic groups are treated differently from each other.

There are two exceptions that might be made to the principle of ensuring similar treatment of applicants. These exceptions do not actually violate this principle because they are applied in a systematic, standardized way across applicants. The first exception has to do with determining whether applicants from certain hiring pools should be given the same assessments as other applicants. For example, should current employees applying for a new job within the company (internal candidates) be required to complete the same assessments as external candidates applying from outside the company? A similar case could occur for candidates applying from a school or technical program for which they may already have been assessed and screened based on certain job-relevant attributes. In such cases, it may make sense to exempt certain applicants from having to complete some assessments, given the availability of historical information about their previous job performance and qualifications. Alternatively, these candidates might complete the same assessments, but the assessment results would be interpreted differently in a manner that takes into account sources of information about their potential that are simply not available for other candidates.

Another possible exception to using the same assessments with all candidates may occur when assessments given early in the staffing process are used to decide whether further assessments should be given to certain candidates. For example, candidates whose responses to a qualifications questionnaire raise concerns about their math ability might be singled out to take a math knowledge test. While such branching assessment methods seem appealing, in general they are not a good idea. There are two reasons for this. First, giving certain assessments to some candidates but not to others based on prior assessment results can pose significant logistical challenges. Second, requiring some candidates to complete an assessment that other candidates do not have to take may raise concerns that all applicants are not being treated fairly and consistently.

Other than the two exceptions noted here, applicants should always be given the same assessments in the same order until they are either removed from the hiring process, offered a position, or select out on their own. One advantage of staffing technology systems is their ability to enforce this sort of standardization. These systems can be set up so that they require hiring managers and/or recruiters to have candidates complete necessary assessments before they can advance the candidate to the next step in the hiring process.

Principle 3. Give Hiring Managers Ultimate Responsibility Over Whom to Hire

It is critical that staffing processes clearly reinforce that hiring managers have ultimate control and responsibility over who is hired. This does not mean that hiring managers should be allowed to hire whomever they please. But it does mean that hiring managers should never be placed in the position of having to hire candidates they do not feel are right for the job.

There are at least two reasons why it is critical to give hiring managers the final say over who is hired:

1. *Hiring managers must feel ownership for selection decisions.* If hiring managers feel that they are forced to hire candidates, they are likely to feel resentment toward the staffing process. If they have no sense of ownership toward hiring decisions, they may make little effort to help candidates succeed after they are hired. This can result in a self-fulfilling prophecy whereby new employees are set up for failure as a result of having to work for managers who never wanted to hire them in the first place.

2. *A hiring manager's intuition is meaningful.* Many criticisms have been made in this book about the accuracy of people's subjective evaluations of candidates. But even though our intuition is often flawed, it is not without value. Many times we are able to "feel" things intuitively that we may not recognize rationally.[1] Although our intuition is often wrong, it can also be very right. Hiring managers should never be told to ignore their intuition about candidates. If a hiring manager feels a candidate is "not right," this should trigger further discussion and investigation into why the hiring manager feels this way.

This principal focuses on giving hiring managers ultimate authority over whether *not* to hire a candidate. It does not mean giving hiring managers authority to hire whomever they please. To the contrary, companies should be very assertive in defining hiring standards that managers must comply with. For example, just because a hiring manager wants to offer a job to a personal friend does not mean he or she should be able to. All candidates should be required to meet the same hiring criteria, regardless of how the hiring manager may feel about them.

Principle 4. Create a Conversation with Candidates

Staffing is not a one-way process of companies evaluating candidates. At the same time that a company is evaluating a candidate, the candidate is evaluating the company. The best candidates tend to have multiple job opportunities. If candidates dislike a company's staffing process, they are less likely to accept employment offers from that company.

The best way to create a staffing process that candidates will enjoy is to treat it like a conversation. Approach the process as a two-way information exchange between the company and the candidate about possible job opportunities. Take steps to ensure the staffing process does not give candidates the feeling of going through an interrogation during which they answer a lot of questions while receiving little or no information in return. The following are three techniques for creating this sense of conversation with candidates:

- *Create Personal Touch Points.* These are different points built into the staffing process that give candidates a chance to talk with a person about the job, the company, and the hiring process. These can involve conversations with hiring managers, recruiters, current job incumbents, or any other people who can help build a personal connection with the candidate. This is by far and away the most valuable method for changing the staffing process from a cold, informal evaluation to a friendly conversation about career options.

- *Provide Realistic Job Previews.* Realistic job previews (RJPs) provide candidates with information that gives them a sense of the tasks involved in the job, its work environment, and the general company culture.[2] RJPs can be conducted by providing literature or videos about the job, having employees talk to candidates, and taking candidates on tours of the work environment. Many assessments can also help to provide RJP information. Job simulations, qualifications questions, and knowledge and skill tests all provide some insight into job tasks and work challenges. These assessments have the unique advantage of gathering selection data from candidates while simultaneously providing candidates with information about the nature of the job.

- *Offer Recruiting Information.* The staffing process should constantly expose candidates to information explicitly designed to sell them on reasons why they should work for the company. At different steps candidates should be given information about the benefits of working for the company, the company's mission, history, and culture, and potential career opportunities within the organization. It is possible to incorporate this type of information on the same web pages that are used to administer online assessments. Some of this information can be incorporated into assessments themselves, for example, structuring interviews to include a portion of time for candidates to ask questions about what it's like to work for the company and training interviewers how to answer these questions to put the company in the best possible light.

Integrating these three techniques into a company's staffing processes helps to provide a greater sense of conversation between the candidate and the company. Each step in the process should be intentionally designed to provide the candidate with a little more information about the job while also requiring the candidates to provide a little more assessment information about themselves. This exchange continues back and forth until a final hiring decision is reached.

The four principles described here should be carefully followed when designing any assessment process, but this does not mean that all staffing assessment processes should look the same. Two assessment processes can use much different assessment methods and still adhere to the basic principles of multiple hurdles, similar treatment of applicants, giving hiring managers ultimate authority over hiring decisions, and creating a conversation with candidates. This is illustrated in the next two sections in this chapter by looking at staffing assessment processes for two common hiring situations: staffing high-volume, entry-level positions and staffing professional positions. Although the operating environments and assessment requirements for professional versus entry-level staffing are quite different, the basic principles underlying the staffing assessment process design are the same.

DESIGNING STAFFING PROCESSES FOR ENTRY-LEVEL JOBS

"Entry-level" jobs are positions that require little or no previous experience or specialized training. The majority of hiring done in industries such as retail, food service, manufacturing, and call centers is done to fill hourly, entry-level jobs. Several important considerations must be taken into account when designing staffing processes for entry-level jobs. These include:

- *Very high staffing volumes.* It is not uncommon for large companies to have 10,000 or more employees performing entry-level jobs. Entry-level jobs also tend to have relatively high levels of turnover that require companies to constantly hire to keep these positions filled.

- *Limited staffing support.* Hiring for entry-level jobs is often done by store or unit managers working in remote geographic locations. These hiring managers frequently have little access to staffing resources, training materials, or human resource personnel to help them with making hiring decisions.

- *On-site hiring.* Many applicants for entry-level jobs walk into the place of employment with the hope and intention of being hired on the spot. They may not tolerate hiring processes that require them to complete multiple assessments over several days.

- *Few job requirements.* By definition, entry-level jobs do not require candidates to have a lot of previous education or experience. Everything candidates need to know to perform these jobs is typically provided to them through training and on-the-job instruction. Because the jobs do not require previously acquired knowledge and skills, predicting job performance usually depends more on assessing what candidates can and want to do based on their motives, personality, general abilities, and interests, as opposed to assessing what they have done based on previous education or work experience.

Table 8.1 describes an assessment process designed to support staffing for entry-level jobs. This process utilizes six different kinds of assessments: pre-screening questions, personality measures, ability tests, knowledge and skills tests, structured interviews, and background investigations. The assessments are delivered in three phases or "hurdles." The first hurdle involves administering pre-screening questions and personality measures through an integrated electronic application that candidates complete either on-site at the work location or off-site through the Internet. Candidates who pass the electronic application are invited to complete a second hurdle consisting of a structured interview conducted on-site with the hiring manager. Because the electronic application generates assessment scores within a matter of seconds, the interview can be conducted immediately after the candidate finishes the application. This is important because qualified hourly candidates who walk into a work site to apply for a job may never return if they leave without receiving some sort of provisional employment offer. A background investigation is then done for candidates who pass the behavioral interview. Candidates who pass this third and last hurdle are officially offered a position. Each of these hurdles will be discussed in more detail.

Table 8.1
Example of an Entry-Level Staffing Process

Step/Hurdle	Actions	Assessment Tools
Pre-Hire		

1. Electronic application administered on-site or off-site	On-site or web-based system electronically collects job application information and assessment data from candidates. The system automatically screens out candidates who do not meet the minimum requirements for the position. The application takes approximately thirty to forty minutes and consists of the following steps.
	• Introduction
	• Registration/contact information
	• Job opportunities
	• Pre-screening questions
	  • Legal requirements
	  • Job requirements
	  • Experience and education
	• Candidate work interests and requirements
	• Ability, knowledge, skills tests
	• Work styles/personality assessment
	• Background check information collection
	• Next steps
		Pre-screening questionnaire Personality measure Ability test Knowledge and skills test

2. Structured interview	Hiring manager conducts thirty-to forty-five-minute interview on-site with applicants who pass the assessments in the electronic application.	Behavioral-based interview
3. Background investigation	Conduct a background investigation with high-potential candidates prior to making a final offer of employment.	Background investigation

Final Hiring Decision Made by Hiring Manager

Entry-Level Assessment Hurdle 1. Electronic Application

The assessment process starts with an electronic application. Automating the application is necessary to manage the high volume of candidates associated with entry-level positions. Electronic applications make it easier for candidates to apply for jobs, protect hiring managers from spending time with candidates who are not appropriate for the job, and allow companies to efficiently monitor the staffing process.

The electronic application is set up so that candidates have the option of applying both on-site at the work location or remotely over the Internet. The ability to apply on-site is particularly important for entry-level jobs. Most entry-level employees live close to their work, and a substantial number of entry-level applicants will apply at the worksite if given the option.[3] Companies that do not give entry-level candidates the option of applying on-site may lose significant numbers of candidates to other companies that accept applications at the workplace. There is also evidence that allowing candidates to apply on-site can significantly reduce the time needed to fill vacant positions.[4]

Because the electronic application is the first component of the selection process, it has the greatest impact on candidate flow and screening. Consequently, it must be very carefully designed. At a minimum, the application must:

- *Collect necessary candidate application information in an appropriate format.* Attention must be given to ensure that the necessary data is collected during the application to screen and process job candidates. This information may include things such as personal contact information, assessment data, information required for potential background or credit checks, EEO information, and other applicant information that may be required by law. The application must record the data in a way that allows it to be easily analyzed, reported, and utilized to support staffing decisions. The application should also minimize the use of free text questions, because they are difficult to score automatically. Including free text questions in assessments can also increase a company's legal exposure if candidates include information in the answer that is of a legally sensitive nature (for example, disclosing that they have children or suffer from a disability).

- *Securely store candidate information.* Much of the data collected in a job application is highly sensitive.[5] Data security is critical. There may also be legal requirements on how long certain types of data must be kept by the hiring company.

- *Be easy to use.* The application must provide candidates with an intuitive, interactive experience that facilitates their ability to apply for positions. Depending on the candidate population, it may also be critical to design the application so it can be used by individuals with low to moderate literacy levels or limited computer skills.

- *Provide a positive applicant experience.* The application must provide candidates with a positive experience that serves to strengthen the company's employer brand. The application content should be designed to appear job-relevant and be presented in a way that is intuitively logical to candidates. It should emphasize the concept of information exchange instead of mere data collection. (See the sidebar, "Creating an Integrated Electronic Entry-Level Job Application" for more discussion on this point.)

After applicants complete the electronic application, an initial estimate of their suitability for the job is automatically computed. Applicant responses to questions about work requirements, employment history, personality, ability, knowledge, and interest in the job are scored in seconds to provide the hiring manager with an overall hiring recommendation. Hiring managers can then review the application results to identify the candidates they want to interview.

CREATING AN INTEGRATED ELECTRONIC ENTRY-LEVEL JOB APPLICATION

The staffing process for entry-level jobs often requires that candidates apply for a job and complete initial assessments at the same time. Integrating assessments into the job application makes it possible for hiring managers to review candidates "on the spot" after they apply. But it also significantly lengthens the application and may pose a challenge to creating a job application process that candidates will view as reasonable, fair, and efficient. The following are two strategies for overcoming this challenge.

First, to the extent possible, restrict the content of the application to multiple-choice questions. Using multiple-choice questions reduces the time required to complete applications, lowers legal risks by preventing applicants from entering legally sensitive or otherwise inappropriate information into the application, and eliminates the problem of collecting textual data that either no one reads or that is read and misinterpreted.

Second, the content of the application should be divided into meaningful, coherent sections reflecting different steps in the hiring "conversation." The sections should be designed so that candidates understand why the information in each section is being collected, its relevance to the job, and its value for ensuring that the candidates are appropriately matched to a position that fits their skills and interests. Here are examples of what these sections might look like and how they might be perceived by candidates:

- *Section 1. Introduction.* This section welcomes the candidate and encourages him or her to apply. It provides a brief explanation of the online process, why it is used, how long it will take, and the information needed to complete the application (for example, address, phone number, Social Security number, names of references). The section may also inform the candidates that they can apply either at the workplace or online. From a candidate's perspective, this section might be seen as conceptually saying, "Welcome. Thanks for being interested in working with us. Here's how the application process works."

- *Section 2. Registration/Contact Information.* This section allows the candidate to create a user account so he or she can submit a job application. To create the account, the candidate must enter name, address, phone number, or other form of unique identifying information. From a candidate's perspective, this section might be seen as conceptually saying, "How can we get in touch with you about potential opportunities?"

- *Section 3. Job Postings.* This section allows the candidate to search through available jobs. The list could be limited to jobs the candidate can apply for at a particular work location or could indicate jobs that the candidate can apply for at other locations. From a candidate's perspective, this section might be seen as conceptually saying, "What type of job do you want?"

- *Section 4. Pre-Screening Questions.* This section consists of three subsections, each addressing different types of applicant qualifications:
    Legal Requirements. This section addresses information that is legally required to be included as part of the application process. It may include state and federally legislated legal employment

disclaimers as well as legal questions pertaining to job requirements such as age limits, licensures, or certifications. If relevant, EEO information (that is, candidate gender and race information) should also be collected at this phase as soon as the candidate expresses an interest in a specific position.[6] From a candidate's perspective, this section might be seen as conceptually saying, "We have to ask this stuff—it's the law."

Job Requirements. This section provides the candidate with a list of key job duties and requirements, including any relevant information required by the Americans with Disabilities Act (ADA). The candidate may be asked if he or she has prior experience performing certain tasks. Questions about job duties and requirements can also be used to provide candidates with a realistic job preview of some of the things they will have to do if hired into the position. This section may also ask candidates whether they are willing to complete background investigations or drug tests required for the position. From a candidate's perspective, this section might be seen as conceptually saying, "These are some of the requirements for performing this job. Are you willing to meet these requirements?"

Experience and Education. This section gathers information about previous experience that can be used to predict performance. This typically includes questions about previous work and school experience, but may also include questions about hobbies and previous achievements relevant to the job. This may include questions about whether candidates have worked with the company previously, their familiarity with company products and services, and whether they know anyone who works for the company. Reference information may also be collected here. From a candidate's perspective, this section might be seen as conceptually saying, "What things have you done in the past that might be related to the job you are applying for? What other accomplishments have you achieved and who might we contact to learn more about your past performance?"

- *Section 5. Candidate Work Interests.* This section asks candidates about their requirements or interests regarding work. This typically includes things such as schedule availability and pay expectations. It may also include job or culture fit assessments designed to predict organizational commitment and retention. From a candidate's perspective, this section might be seen as conceptually saying, "What do you want or require from a job or employer?"

- *Section 6. Work Samples.* This section is used to administer ability and knowledge tests to applicants, assuming such tests are job-relevant. The tests ideally contain content that reflects tasks and situations found on the job so they can be presented as realistic job previews and not just tests. From a candidate's perspective, this section might be seen as conceptually saying, "These are some of things you'd be doing in this job."

- *Section 7. Work Styles.* This section consists of self-report question-naires such as personality measures designed to evaluate whether the candidates' interests, motives, and work styles align with the demands of the job. From a candidate's perspective, this section might be seen as conceptually saying, "Tell us more about yourself at a general level. How do you approach work? What are your work interests, habits, and expectations?"

- *Section 8. Background Investigation Information.* This section collects information needed to conduct background investigations, assuming these are included as part of the assessment process. Note: the investigations may not necessarily happen at this point, but collecting the information now allows background investigations to be conducted more easily later in the hiring process if required. From a candidate's perspective, this section might be seen as conceptually saying, "This is additional information we need to process your application."

- *Section 9. Next Steps.* This section informs candidates how their application will be processed and what they can expect as things move forward. It might include questions asking candidates about their reactions to the application process and how they learned about the job opportunity. From a candidate's perspective, this section might be seen as conceptually saying, "Thanks for applying. This is what happens next."

An additional option when building this type of integrated assessment is to set it up as a series of "mini-hurdles" that assess candidates as they work through the application. In this approach, the application stops when candidates fail to meet some key criteria. For example, candidates who indicate in Section 5 that they are unwilling to complete a mandatory background check may not be allowed to continue through any more of the sections.

Hourly Assessment Hurdle 2. Behavioral Interview

Most electronic applications can be scored in seconds after they are completed. This allows hiring managers to interview qualified applicants "on the spot," if desired. Alternatively, hiring managers may choose to review electronic applications periodically each day or week and arrange interviews with the candidates who show the highest potential based on their application results.

Because unqualified candidates are screened out before meeting with the hiring managers, hiring managers can devote more time to interviewing high-potential candidates. This allows them to make effective use of structured interview techniques such as behavioral interviews. Some electronic application systems may also suggest specific areas of information to probe during interviews based on the candidate's responses to different application questions (for example, gaps in employment history, being fired from a previous job). While most of the time during the interview should be focused on evaluating the candidate, some time should also be allotted to recruiting the candidate on the benefits of working for the company.

Hourly Assessment Hurdle 3. Background Investigation

The final step in the assessment process is to conduct a background investigation on the candidates identified as potential hires. This final check reduces the risk of making potentially catastrophic hiring mistakes (for example, hiring someone who is not legally eligible for the job). The background investigation can be launched automatically using candidate information gathered earlier during the electronic application.

The assessment process described in Table 7.1 supports multiple operational and strategic staffing goals. These include:

- *Accuracy.* Integrating several types of assessments into the selection process improves the accuracy of hiring decisions.
- *Efficiency.* Using multiple hurdles to screen out unqualified or inappropriate candidates serves to protect the hiring manager's time. This gives hiring

managers more time to spend interviewing and recruiting candidates with the greatest potential for success.

- *Speed.* Automating the assessment process reduces the administrative time needed to screen, select, and hire candidates. The total time spent by hiring managers to evaluate and hire candidates ranges from none for unqualified candidates screened out early in the process to approximately one hour for candidates who are interviewed and subsequently hired.

- *Consistency.* Standardizing the employment application and selection process helps ensure staffing is done using appropriate, legally defensible, and optimally effective methods.

- *Improved Candidate Experience.* Integrating the assessments into the application provides candidates with a seamless and efficient application experience (for more discussion of the candidate experience, see the sidebar, "Entry-Level Staffing Assessment: The Candidate's Perspective"). Applicants may also find it easier to apply electronically via the web, rather than having to come on-site and fill out a paper application. Last, by paying careful attention to the content of the assessments and how they are presented, candidates are more likely to view the staffing process as fair, job-relevant, and informative.

ENTRY-LEVEL STAFFING ASSESSMENT: THE CANDIDATE'S PERSPECTIVE

It is useful to consider what staffing assessment processes look like from the candidate's perspective. Remember, companies are not just evaluating candidates during the selection process. Candidates are also evaluating the company. Here is a summary of what the process described in Table 8.1 might look like from a candidate's point of view.

Imagine you are employed in an entry-level retail job, but are dissatisfied with your current position and would like to work elsewhere. You have heard good things about another retail company and decide to see whether they have any job opportunities you might be qualified for.

After finishing a shift at your current job, you go to one of the other retail company's stores located close to your home. You ask a clerk about applying for a job and she directs you to a small computer kiosk located near the front of the store. You sit down at the kiosk and read a screen that thanks you for your interest in applying for a position at the company. The system states that the application process is fully automated, will take about forty-five minutes to complete, and will require you to have a variety of information about previous employers, as well as your Social Security number. The system states that you can also apply over the web by going to the company's career page. It's late in the day, and so you decide to go home and apply for the job using your home computer.

That evening, you go online and visit the company's website. The website screen is similar to the one on the kiosk at the store. After reviewing what information will be required for the application, you click "apply now" and begin completing the application. The first section in the application asks you to enter contact and identification information and create a user account. This will allow you to apply for multiple jobs in the company without re-entering your contact information each time.

After entering your contact information, you are taken to a screen where you can search for different jobs based on location and job type. You ask to see job opportunities located within five miles of your home. There is an opportunity at the store you visited earlier that day, so you decide to apply for that particular job. The next screen lists several legal requirements informing you of various rights as a job applicant. You scan through these and mark a box indicating that you have reviewed them. You are also asked to provide some voluntary information about your demographic status that the company collects for legal purposes. The application clearly indicates that this information will not influence your eligibility for the position in any way.

The next section of the application provides a more detailed description of the job duties. You are asked whether you are able and willing to perform different job tasks. These tasks give a fairly good sense of what the job will involve, and while not all the tasks are necessarily enjoyable (for example, having to lift fifty-pound boxes), they are things you are willing and able to do. The section also contains several multiple-choice questions asking about previous work experience and education. It does not take long to answer these questions, as you simply have to click on the most appropriate answers. After providing information about your work experience, you are taken to a screen that asks what you want from a job in terms of pay expectations and shift schedules.

The next two sections are somewhat new to you. The first section presents various situations you might encounter on the job and asks you to indicate what the best response is to each situation. Some of these questions require you to critically interpret portions of instruction manuals similar to ones you have used in other jobs and to perform mathematical calculations related to answering customer questions about product prices and discounts. These questions are hard, but they make sense given the kind of job you are applying for. The next section asks about your beliefs, interests, and preferences as they relate to work. The application informs you that the purpose of this section is to make sure that your interests align with the challenges, opportunities, and general environment associated with the position you're applying for. Both sections take a total of about twenty-five minutes to complete.

The next section indicates that all candidates must complete a background check prior to being hired and asks whether you are willing to consent to this check. After you say "Yes," you are asked to provide information needed to conduct the background check. You are then taken to a screen thanking you for completing the application and indicating that you will be contacted for any potential job opportunities within two weeks. The final part of the application asks a few questions about the general application experience.

A few days after you complete the application, you receive a phone call from the hiring manager at the store where you applied. She asks a few questions about your schedule to make sure the job is appropriate for you and then asks if you can come in the next day for an interview. You arrange a time and arrive at the store the next day. The hiring manager greets you, takes you on a quick tour of the store, and then brings you back to a quiet meeting room to conduct the interview. She tells you that the interview will consist of several questions about your previous work experiences, and that all candidates are asked these same questions to ensure everyone is treated consistently. The interview takes about thirty minutes. After the interview, the hiring manager says she will call you later on that day to update the status of your application. A few

> hours later, you receive a call from the hiring manager indicating that she would like you to start work as soon as possible. The only thing left is for her to conduct a final background check, which she can do using the information you already provided as part of the online application. The only other question is up to you: Do you want the job?

SAMPLE STAFFING ASSESSMENT PROCESS FOR PROFESSIONAL JOBS

The requirements for staffing professional jobs are significantly different from those for entry-level jobs. The following are a few of the major differences:

- Entry-level staffing often involves hiring hundreds or thousands of people a year for a few fairly well-defined positions requiring little if any specialized skills or qualifications. In contrast, professional staffing typically involves hiring smaller numbers of people for a wider variety of positions, many of which require highly specialized knowledge, experience, and skills.

- Entry-level candidates typically spend less than two hours meeting with perhaps one or two managers or HR personnel before being offered a position. Professional candidates often spend eight hours or more meeting with many different employees across the company before being hired.

- Selection decisions for entry-level jobs are frequently made by hiring managers with little formal training or experience in staffing. Selection decisions for professional positions often involve the use of highly trained recruiters and staffing professionals whose primary responsibility is to identify, screen, and assess job candidates.

Due to the differences between entry-level and professional hiring, staffing processes appropriate for entry-level jobs may not work well for professional jobs. But the basic guidelines and principles for designing effective assessment processes are the same for both kinds of jobs. Staffing processes for professional jobs, like those for entry-level jobs, should focus on standardizing how information is collected from applicants to maximize efficiency and use of data. The processes should integrate multiple forms of assessments to provide an accurate reading on candidate potential. The assessments should be delivered using a multiple-hurdle approach, with hiring managers having final authority over whether to hire someone. And emphasis should be placed on treating the staffing process as a "two-way conversation" between the applicant and the company.

Table 8.2 provides an overview of a staffing process for professional jobs that integrates multiple assessments in a manner that candidates are likely to find engaging and job-relevant. Various types of standardized staffing assessments are listed that might be used at each step in the process. Table 8.2 does not include staffing techniques related to recruiting candidates and socializing new employees that do not specifically depend on the use of assessments (for example, establishing employee referral networks, advertising job opportunities, creating employer brands, or conducting new employee orientation). These other techniques should be a part of the staffing process, but since they are not based around the use of assessments they are not discussed here.

Professional Hurdle 1. Sourcing

Step 1 identifies potentially qualified candidates using assessment tools that search and sort electronic copies of resumes that have been placed on the web, posted on electronic job boards, or submitted to career sites. Qualified candidates are then encouraged to apply for specific job openings. Assessments such as electronic recruiting agents and resume interpretation tools are specifically designed to support this step. While these assessments are useful, it is important to also use more traditional recruiting methods for generating candidates such as recruitment advertising and employee referrals. Remember that the value of assessments is entirely dependent on the overall quality and size of the candidate pool. If no qualified candidates apply in the first place, then the best selection method in the world will not improve the quality of hires.

Professional Hurdle 2. Screening Assessment

The purpose of this step is to screen out applicants who do not meet the basic requirements for a position (minimum experience or education, willingness to relocate, salary requirements, and so on). Pre-screening questionnaires are specifically designed to support this step. Depending on the number of interested applicants, it may make sense to also introduce assessments that take a more in-depth look at candidate interests, skills, and potential. But this step is early in the staffing process, so caution must be taken to avoid overwhelming candidates with

Table 8.2
Example of a Professional Staffing Process

Step/Hurdle	Action	Possible Assessment Tools
Pre-Hire		
1. Sourcing	Use career websites, job boards, and other tools to gather and review resumes from active and passive candidates.	Electronic recruiting agents Resume interpretation tools
2. Screening Assessment	Screen out candidates who do not meet the basic requirements for the position or whose career interests do not align with the opportunities provided by the job or the organization.	Pre-screening questionnaire Culture and environmental fit measure Knowledge and ability tests Personality measures
3. Phone Interviews	Screen out candidates who do not have the minimum skills and competencies needed to perform the job and actively recruit high-potential candidates.	Structured interviews
4. In-Depth Online Assessment	Select in candidates who show the highest potential for job success.	Knowledge and ability tests Personality measures Situational judgment tests Work samples
5. On-Site Interviews and Assessments	Select in candidates based on more in-depth assessments conducted on-site. Provide candidates with greater sense of job requirements and opportunities.	Structured interviews Job simulations
6. Verification	Ensure candidates have not falsified any aspects of their applications and meet key job requirements.	Background investigations Drug tests and/or physical ability tests (if relevant to the position)
Final Hiring Decision Made by Hiring Manager		
Post-Hire		
7. On-Boarding Feedback and Development	Provide newly hired employees with developmental feedback to help them more quickly get "up to speed" in their new roles.	Knowledge and ability tests Personality measures Situational judgment tests

lengthy assessments. It is best to restrict assessments at this stage to tools that are short, easy to complete, and/or highly engaging.

Professional Hurdle 3. Phone Interviews

Candidates who show the greatest match to the needs of the job are contacted by a recruiter and/or hiring manager to further gauge their potential. Short, structured interviews can be effectively applied at this step to confirm whether candidates possess core attributes needed for the position. These interviews should also be used to sell the benefits of the position to promising candidates. Some small amount of time should be used to explain the methods the company uses to select employees and why they are beneficial for both the company and the candidate.

Professional Hurdle 4. In-Depth Online Assessment

The difference between assessments used in this step and assessments used in Step 2 have to do with the length of the assessments and how they are used. The assessments used in Step 2 are likely to be fairly short and are used primarily to screen out candidates who do not meet certain minimum requirements. In contrast, the assessments used in Step 4 may be fairly long and are used to help select in candidates who show the greatest potential for job success.

The assessment tools used in Step 4 are likely to be more in-depth, expensive, and time-consuming than assessments used earlier in the staffing process. There are two reasons for this. First, there are fewer candidates at this step, which helps keep assessment costs low. Second, assuming that some level of recruiting took place earlier in the process, candidates at this step are likely to have more commitment to the job opportunity and thus more willingness to spend time completing assessment tools to ensure they are a good fit for the position. This second assumption will only be true if efforts have been made in previous steps to sell candidates on the job opportunity and to explain the rationale for using assessments as part of the staffing process.

Professional Hurdle 5. On-Site Interviews and Assessments

In this step, the results of the assessments used in Steps 2, 3, and 4 are reviewed to determine which candidates to invite on-site for more in-depth interviews and discussions. Typically, the on-site visit will include structured interviews with several people in the company. The on-site visit can also be used as an opportunity to have candidates engage in some more realistic job simulations or work sample exercises. It is important to intersperse the assessment activities in this step with other activities designed to provide the candidates with information about the job opportunity and entice them to accept an offer should one be made.

Professional Hurdle 6. Verification

It is recommended that hiring offers always be made contingent upon satisfactory results from background investigations and, if relevant, physical exams and/or drug screens. This hurdle provides a "safety check" to avoid catastrophic hires that can result from employing candidates who have hidden or falsified some aspect of their pasts. The assessments in this step are used later in the staffing process due to their cost, somewhat invasive nature, and legal requirements that may restrict their use until after an employment offer has been made.

Professional Hurdle 7. Post-Hire On-Boarding Feedback and Development

This step is not really a "hurdle," since it occurs after candidates have been hired. However, it should be seen as an extension of the hiring process. Many assessment tools, such as personality measures and knowledge tests, can provide developmental information that may help recently hired employees adjust to their new roles. Using assessments in this manner can facilitate new employees' efforts to "get up to speed" in their positions. If this step is taken, care must be used to ensure that the assessment information is presented to employees in an appropriate and helpful manner.

The staffing process in Table 8.2 is a multiple-hurdle assessment method that provides detailed information for making hiring decisions, while also providing candidates with a positive recruitment experience. A key feature of this process is the steady increase in the level of information exchange between the candidate and the company with each step. By the time Step 6 is reached, both the candidate and the company know a significant amount about each other. As a result, both the company and the candidate are better equipped to make the right decision about whether the job fits with the candidate's interests and capabilities. (For more information about what this process looks like from the candidate's perspective, read the sidebar, "Professional Staffing Assessment: The Candidate's Perspective.")

PROFESSIONAL STAFFING ASSESSMENT: THE CANDIDATE'S PERSPECTIVE

Candidates for many professional positions must possess a fairly extensive range of qualifications in order to be eligible for hire. As a result, the number of candidates eligible for professional positions is almost always much smaller than the number of candidates available for entry-level jobs. For this reason, it is important to carefully consider the candidate's perspective when designing a professional staffing assessment process. The process must be engaging to applicants and must avoid doing things that might cause qualified candidates to remove themselves from the applicant pool (this is often referred to as candidates "self-selecting" out of the process). These issues were carefully considered when designing the staffing process outlined in Table 8.2. The following is a description of how this process might be perceived by a candidate.

Imagine you were an experienced mechanical engineer working for a large company. One day you receive a phone call from a recruiter at another company asking to talk to you about a possible job opportunity. The recruiter says she found your resume while searching a database of resumes kept by a job board that you had visited a few years ago. Based on your resume, you possess some very specific skills that appear to match a position at her company. After talking with the recruiter about the position, you agree to apply. The recruiter tells you that the company follows a highly structured application process to ensure equal treatment across candidates. The process begins with an electronic application that takes about twenty minutes to complete.

The recruiter e-mails you the link to the company's career site, where you can apply for the position. You are asked to enter your basic contact information and to respond to a short series of questions about your work experience and technical background. The career site also contains information about the company's culture, mission, and history. Included are several video clips of other engineers who work for the company talking about why they chose to work there.

You are contacted by the recruiter a few days after you complete the application. She says your application meets all of the minimum requirements for the job and asks to schedule a call to see whether it makes sense for you to visit the company for a series of more in-depth meetings and interviews. The recruiter says she will be asking you some more questions about your work history, but also indicates that you should use the call as an opportunity to ask her more questions about the position. You schedule the call for the following week.

The recruiter starts the call by asking whether you have any more questions about the position. After answering your questions, she says she is going to ask you some questions about your work history. The recruiter explains that the company has put a lot of time into understanding what attributes make people successful in their particular culture and work environment. The company follows a very structured staffing process to make sure the people they hire will be successful. After all, she says, "It wouldn't be good for anyone to end up in this job if it doesn't truly suit your skills and interests." She then asks you five questions that explore some of your previous work experiences. After you answer the questions, she says that she will be contacting you shortly about possible next steps.

A few days later, you receive an e-mail from the recruiter indicating that the hiring manager wants to talk to you directly. You arrange a call and have an informal chat with the hiring manager about your interests, the job opportunity, and the match between his managerial style and your work preferences. At the end of the call, the hiring manager says he'd like you to fly out to meet with his team in person. In keeping with the company's staffing process, the day will consist of a structured series of meetings and interviews with various people. You will also be asked to comment on some different technical scenarios so they can get a better sense of "how you think" as an engineer.

The hiring manager indicates that prior to your trip you will be sent a link to a website containing several questionnaires. These questionnaires take about sixty to ninety minutes to complete. The manager explains that these measures provide the company with additional information and insight into your work preferences and problem-solving style. The company uses these measures because they have been shown statistically to predict job success. They also provide objective information that can be used to more fairly evaluate people based on data that does not depend solely on whether someone is a good interviewer. The manager stresses that the measures are not scored pass-fail, but do provide an important "piece in the puzzle" they consider when making hiring decisions. He concludes by saying, "Some of the questions are really hard and no one gets them all correct, me included. Don't beat yourself up if you're not sure about some of your answers."

You work with the recruiter to arrange for an on-site visit a few weeks later. Prior to the trip, the recruiter e-mails you a link to the website where you can complete the assessment measures. The first measure is fairly easy to complete. It consists of answering a bunch of questions about how you typically behave at work. The second measure presents you with several problems related to engineering. Some of these problems are really hard, but you remember what the manager said about not being too worried when you encounter a problem that you have difficulty answering.

When you arrive on-site at the company, you are given a schedule that switches between structured interviews with members of the manager's team and more informal meetings with your potential future co-workers. The meetings with your potential co-workers give you a chance to learn more about what it's like working at the company and being part of the hiring manager's work group. Throughout the day, you notice that every person is well prepared for the interviews and meetings. You also notice that you are never asked the same interview question twice.

Midway through the day, the recruiter presents you with a dossier of information describing a challenging scenario related to your technical area of expertise. She says you are to look through this information and present some ideas to the hiring manager and his team on how you might deal with this scenario. You find this task challenging, but also rewarding because it is exactly the kind of stuff that you would be doing should you be hired into this position. At the end of the day, you are tired but feel that the company has definitely gotten a good read on your skills, abilities, and interests. The day also provided you with a lot of information about what you would be doing at the company and what it is like to work there.

Both the hiring manager and recruiter call you the day after the trip to thank you for your time and to ask whether you have any lingering questions. You are told they will be getting back to you with next steps in a few days. Two days later the recruiter calls to make you a job offer. The offer, she indicates, is contingent on a final background check that they do as part of their "due diligence" before officially employing any new hires. You accept the offer, consent to the background check, and begin thinking about your upcoming career change.

CONCLUDING REMARKS: USING ASSESSMENTS

This chapter described general design principles for integrating assessments into a company's staffing process and provided examples illustrating how these principles can be used to build staffing processes for entry-level and professional jobs. But designing an assessment process is not just a matter of figuring out when to administer different assessments. It also requires addressing topics raised in earlier chapters, such as how to use job analysis to select and configure assessments, determining who will be responsible for administering assessments and interpreting assessment results, and establishing methods to monitor, validate, and optimize assessment results over time. All of these things must be considered to create a maximally effective hiring process. Implementing staffing assessments can be quite complex, requiring attention to a range of technical and operational details. It can become even more complicated if assessments will be used in multiple countries and must conform to different national laws and work with candidates who have different cultural expectations regarding the staffing process.

While using staffing assessments is not a trivial undertaking, it should not be viewed as an overly daunting task either. A company's initial foray into using assessments does not necessarily have to include all of the various assessment types and "hurdles" contained in the examples provided in this chapter. Simply implementing one or two selection hurdles using a few assessments like structured interviewing or pre-screening questionnaires can greatly improve the accuracy and efficiency of a company's staffing process. Additional hurdles incorporating other assessment types can be phased in over time, leading to a more manageable deployment process.

Thousands of companies have successfully integrated assessments into their staffing processes. The issues that impact the success of staffing assessment strategies are well understood by experienced assessment professionals. The key is to take advantage of this expertise. Companies should employ the assistance of someone with experience in assessment system design when implementing a staffing assessment process for the first time. In this sense, implementing staffing assessments might be likened to the process of building a house. The process can seem quite overwhelming if you are not familiar with it, but can go quite smoothly provided you ally yourself with competent and experienced professionals.

Notes

1. Gladwell, M. (2005). *Blink: The power of thinking without thinking.* New York: Little, Brown.
2. Meglino, B.M., Denisi, A.S., & Ravlin, E.C. (1993). Effects of previous job exposure and subsequent job status on the functioning of a realistic job preview. *Personnel Psychology, 46,* 803–822.
3. Kronos-Unicru. (2006). *Best practices for multi-channel applicant sourcing.* www.kronos.com/About/ApplicantSourcingWP.pdf
4. Kronos-Unicru. (2006). *Fastest hire in the west.* www.unicru.com/FileBin/Newsletters/04062_FastestHire.html
5. Adamowicz, J., & Hunt, S.T. (2005). *Responsibilities associated with the collection, storage, and use of online staffing data.* Paper presented at the 20th Annual Conference of the Society for Industrial and Organizational Psychology, Los Angeles, California.
6. For more information, see Office of the Federal Register, National Archives and Records Administration. (2005, October 7). 41-CFR Part 60–1: Obligation to solicit race and gender data for agency enforcement purposes: Final rule. *Federal Register, 70*(194).

chapter NINE

Conclusion

There are over six billion people in the world. Perhaps a quarter or more of these people are employed or seeking employment at any one time. Whether these people end up working in the right jobs will have a profound effect on their personal happiness, the health and well-being of their friends and family, the success of the companies that hire them, and the overall economic strength of the countries they live in. Unfortunately, a great many of the staffing decisions made every year lead to suboptimal staffing outcomes and outright job failures. Staffing assessments can and should be used to reduce the number of these hiring mistakes.

When appropriately designed and deployed, staffing assessments substantially improve the accuracy of hiring decisions. Because of the Internet, companies can easily access a variety of assessment tools to improve their odds of making good hires. In sum, many of the historical constraints that have led to bad hires are gone. It is now largely a matter of companies recognizing and taking advantage of the staffing assessment tools that are readily available to them.

Many hiring organizations and candidates express considerable skepticism toward the use of assessments. This skepticism often has good cause. History provides many examples of times when assessments have been improperly designed or incorrectly used in a manner that led to misreading people's true potential. But the fact that assessments can be misused and are not always perfect is beside the point. Extensive research data and numerous practical applications conclusively show that appropriate use of well-designed assessments does lead to better hiring decisions. The question we should be asking is not whether staffing assessments work, but how to get more companies to take advantage of the value these tools provide.

One of the challenges to the use of assessments lies in how many companies and candidates view the concept of assessments in general. People often see assessments as tests solely designed to uncover candidate weaknesses and keep people out of jobs. Assessments are seen as a "barrier" designed to eliminate candidates from the hiring process. While many assessment vendors do emphasize the ability of their tools to screen out bad candidates, this view is actually counter to the spirit that guided many early efforts to develop assessments. Much of this work was driven by a belief that people should be given opportunities based on objective evaluations of their personal skills, strengths, and talents.[1] Hiring decisions should be based on a person's potential, and not on less relevant factors such as demographic background, socioeconomic status, or family name. Assessments were seen as a way to reduce the damage caused by stereotypes and social stigmas that have historically influenced staffing decisions.[2] Many of the early developers of assessments did not see them as barriers to prevent hiring people, but as tools to provide candidates with hiring opportunities they might not otherwise be given if they were forced to rely on less objective staffing methods like personal contacts and unstructured interviews.*

The objective nature of assessments allows companies to more effectively place people into jobs where they are most likely to succeed. Assessments also help reduce the influence that people's subjective beliefs about personal appearance, background, or ethnic characteristics have on hiring decisions. When viewed from this perspective, assessments are not tools that prevent people from getting jobs. They are tools that help companies make better hiring decisions while helping candidates achieve career success. Two stories illustrating this aspect of assessments are provided in the sidebar "The Opportunity to Succeed."

The ultimate goal of this book is to help companies hire people who are more likely to succeed in their jobs. This goal can be achieved by having companies take greater advantage of the benefits of staffing assessment tools. When used appropriately, staffing assessments lead to better hiring decisions. Better hiring decisions result in

---

*This statement is only true for some of the early assessment developers. Controversy has surrounded assessments virtually since they began to receive widespread use in society. While some early assessment developers viewed them as tools to more accurately evaluate and learn about people, others viewed them largely as a source of data that might be used to justify and advance what most people would now consider to be racist beliefs.

happier, more productive workforces, more satisfied customers, increasingly profitable organizations, and ultimately a stronger economy and more stable world for all of us.

THE OPPORTUNITY TO SUCCEED

Because of their objective nature, assessments frequently call attention to candidate attributes that might otherwise be ignored, overlooked, or misinterpreted by more subjective and intrinsically biased human decision makers. The use of assessments can lead to providing job opportunities to candidates that they might never have been given using less accurate staffing methods. The following stories illustrate how assessments can change people's lives for the better through providing them with these sorts of career opportunities.

The first story is about the design of a self-report biodata measure created to predict tenure of employees hired to work on large river barges in the Midwest and Southern United States.[3] These positions require spending weeks at a time on barges floating up and down rivers in all kinds of inclement weather. The jobs were described as low paying, tedious, and lonely. The company commissioning this assessment was experiencing over 200 percent annual turnover. Turnover would have been even higher but people had to wait to quit until the barges returned to port.

Questions were raised about who would ever want this sort of job. But analysis of the assessment data did uncover one particular type of individual who appeared to do well as a barge worker. These were people who by their own admission found it hard to get along with others. In fact, there was a significant relationship between tenure as a barge worker and previous felony convictions. Some of the best and longest-tenured barge workers were people who do not particularly enjoy being around others, but who also realize this about themselves. This does not mean these employees were unable to get along with people, but simply that they were content in jobs that required spending days largely by themselves. Nor does it mean that barge workers tend to be anti-social or that being anti-social makes one a better barge worker. It does mean that the attributes that drive success as a barge worker are much different from the attributes associated with success in many other jobs that involve a higher level of social interaction.

This study showed that there are some jobs that are well-suited for people who may have historically been viewed as too anti-social and perhaps even unemployable for many other positions. Although this is only one example, it does give the sense that perhaps, when it comes to employment, there truly are opportunities for everyone. Assessments can be a valuable tool for helping candidates to find these opportunities.

The second story is about a young child growing up in a working-class family in an industrial city. This boy had no reason to expect that his life would be much different from his friends' and family's lives before him. After finishing high school, he expected he would find a manual labor job in one of the local factories or coal mines, and that would be the end of his education. All of this changed when he completed a series of ability assessments administered as part of a national educational testing program.

His assessment results suggested that he had a high level of natural ability for abstract reasoning and complex problem solving. Based almost entirely on the strength of these results, the boy was given the opportunity to enroll in a more academically advanced school. This led to being offered a scholarship to a university. From that point on, his life took a path that was well beyond what he had ever imagined possible growing up as "just another working class child from a lower-income family." Eventually, he became a world famous professor known for his contributions to the study and understanding of mental health.

Both of these stories are based on actual events. Some changes have been made in the interest of maintaining company and individual confidentiality. The stories illustrate ways assessments can contribute to the betterment of society. The story of the barge workers illustrates how assessments can provide job opportunities to people who might otherwise be dismissed as "unemployable." This story also shows how companies can leverage assessments to help staff even the most hard-to-fill positions. The story of the boy who went on to become a professor illustrates how assessment can help people overcome societal barriers and stigmas to achieve their full potential. It was not only the boy in the story who benefited from assessments. Hundreds of thousands of people have benefited from the contributions this person made to the science of mental health. These people also owe a small debt of gratitude to the individuals who decided to administer assessments to a group of working-class children in an industrial city to see whether they could uncover any intellectual "diamonds in the rough."

Notes

1. Hothersall, D. (1995). *History of psychology* (3rd ed.). New York: McGraw-Hill.
2. Lemann, N. (1995, September). The great sorting. *The Atlantic Monthly,* p. 84.
3. Hunt, S.T. (2002). On the virtues of staying "inside of the box": Does organizational citizenship behavior detract from performance in Taylorist jobs? *International Journal of Selection and Assessment, 10,* 1–8.

GLOSSARY OF COMMON ASSESSMENT TERMS

Italicized words within a definition represent terms that are defined elsewhere in this glossary. Definitions are based on what is considered to be common usage of terms. However, there is not always complete agreement in how assessment developers, researchers, and vendors use all these terms. In keeping with the non-technical nature of this book, definitions are limited to high-level descriptions of what a term represents. Minimal effort is made to describe the mathematical or theoretical aspects of terms that are associated with the scientific design of assessments. Similarly, this glossary only provides general descriptive information about legal terms pertaining to assessments. It is not intended to be used for formal legal guidance. Readers seeking such advice should consult their own legal counsel.

360-Degree Survey   A performance feedback survey designed primarily as a performance development tool. 360 surveys collect input from an employee's peers, supervisor, and direct reports regarding the employee's effectiveness in terms of critical work-related behaviors and *Competencies*. 360 surveys are sometimes used as measures of performance in *Criteria Validation* studies.

4/5ths Rule (also called 80/20 rule)   A guideline provided by the *EEOC* used to evaluate whether a selection process has *adverse impact* against certain groups of applicants. This states that a hiring process is under suspicion of displaying adverse impact if, on average, fewer than four applicants from a protected group are hired for every five non-protected applicants hired into the same position. For example, imagine a company hired 50 percent of all white applicants who applied for a position. If this company did not hire at least 40 percent of the applicants from a protected group who applied for this position (e.g., Hispanics, Asians, Blacks), then it would be considered to be in violation of the 4/5ths guideline. This is because 40 percent divided by 50 percent is equal to 4/5ths. An assessment that violates the 4/5ths rule may still be legal provided it is shown to be clearly *job relevant*.

Ability/Abilities   Refers to mental capabilities and skills that influence performance of specific job tasks. Many abilities are influenced by genetics, but learning and experience do significantly increase performance levels with regard to most types of ability. Examples of common work-related abilities include *Verbal Ability, Numerical Ability, Spatial Ability,* and *General Cognitive Ability.*

Ability Tests   Tests that have been specifically designed to measure work-related *Abilities.* These are often referred to as cognitive ability tests, critical thinking tests, problem-solving tests, reasoning tests, or *Intelligence Tests.*

Achievement Test   A test that measures acquired knowledge or skills, usually as the result of previous instruction and education. For example, a test measuring a person's knowledge of a foreign language or a test measuring familiarity and understanding of accounting rules and regulations. Achievement tests are often contrasted with *Aptitude Tests,* which are designed to measure individual characteristics that depend more on innate traits and abilities, as opposed to prior learning and experience.

Active vs. Passive Candidates   Distinction made between candidates who are actively looking for work and those who may be interested in job opportunities, but who are not currently actively seeking a job. For example, a person who is currently unemployed and looking for work would be an active candidate. In contrast, a person who is already employed and is not actively looking for a new job but whose attributes make him or her a good candidate for a position a company is seeking to fill would be considered a passive candidate.

Adverse Impact   A situation in which the use of a specific staffing assessment tool results in members of a legally *Protected Class* being selected at a rate that is not proportional to the rate at which members of the majority are being selected. Statistically speaking, a selection method is usually said to have adverse impact if members of the minority group are selected at anything less than *4/5th* the rate of those in the majority group. Adverse Impact is not necessarily illegal if it can be proven that the staffing assessments in question are clearly and directly related to job performance. Despite this, Adverse Impact is a major obstacle to workforce *Diversity* and should be avoided whenever possible.

Alternate Forms   Two or more forms of a test that are similar in nature (i.e., intended to measure the same thing and have similar difficulty levels but using different test items) and intended to be used for the same purpose. Alternate Forms of assessments are often created as a way to protect test security so that not all applicants receive the exact same tests. Alternate Forms are also created when an assessment is translated into another language.

For example, if an assessment was created in English and then translated into Spanish, then the Spanish version is viewed as an alternate form of the English version of the assessment. Considerable care must be taken to ensure that alternative forms of assessments share similar *Psychometric* characteristics. Alternate forms are also known as parallel forms or equivalent forms.

Alpha/Alpha Coefficient   See *Reliability.*

Americans with Disabilities Act (ADA)   Legislation passed by the U.S. government that protects the employment rights of individuals with mental and physical disabilities. The ADA places significant restrictions on the kinds of information that can be collected by assessments during the hiring process. The ADA and *Civil Rights Act of 1964* are considered to be the two most influential pieces of legislation affecting the use of assessments.

Applicant   Generally speaking, a person who has expressed interest in gaining employment in a specific job or organization. The *EEO* has provided more specific guidelines that can be used to determine whether someone is an applicant or not because it has implications for how companies calculate *Adverse Impact* statistics.

Applicant Pool   The population of people who have identified themselves as applicants for a potential job. The goal of *Sourcing* is to increase the number and quality of people in a company's applicant pool for different job openings. The goal of *Selection* is to identify and hire those individuals in the applicant pool who have the greatest chance of being successful employees.

Aptitude Test   Assessments designed to measures a person's underlying potential for performing certain kinds of tasks. Most assessments labeled as Aptitude Tests represent different types of *Ability Tests* or *Personality Measures.* Aptitude tests are often contrasted against *Achievement Tests,* which focus more on learned skills and knowledge gained through prior education and experience.

Assessment   Any test, procedure, question, or exercise used to measure an individual's employment-related qualifications or characteristics (i.e., skills, knowledge, aptitudes). The information collected is used to influence or guide subsequent staffing or personnel decisions.

Assessment Administration System/Assessment Platform   An electronic, usually online system that allows staffing professionals to configure and administer staffing assessments. These systems allow users to accomplish tasks such as scheduling candidates for assessments, attaching links to assessments to *Job Postings,* tracking a candidate's progress in the selection process, and sorting and searching assessment results.

Assessment Center   Not a physical place but rather a set of activities meant to provide an assessment of an individual's key work-related attitudes, behaviors, competencies, and abilities. These things are usually measured by activities that include *Ability Tests, Personality Measures, In-Basket Exercises, Structured Interviews,* and *Work Samples.* Assessment centers tend to be very expensive and most commonly used for assessing the developmental needs of current employees at managerial levels and above. When assessment centers are used for employee selection purposes, they are usually used only for filling high-level leadership positions for which there are few candidates.

Assessment Delivery Systems The system used to deliver assessment content to a candidate. Many assessment delivery systems are web-based. Assessments can also be delivered via paper, phone (*IVR*), in person, *Kiosks*, or wireless devices.

Assessment Vendor Any organization that makes staffing assessments available for sale to members of the general public or to qualified testing experts.

Attribute (Candidate or Employee) Term used to refer to characteristics possessed by individuals that influence their *Fit* with different jobs. Assessments work by measuring attributes that either influence job performance or that are requirements for employment. Assessments can be used to measure a range of attributes including experience, education, credentials, knowledge, skills, abilities, interests, personality traits, and physical capabilities.

ATS (Applicant Tracking System) An applicant tracking system (ATS) is a software application designed to automate a company's staffing process. Systems may provide support for a wide range of staffing activities, including *Workforce Scheduling,* creating *Job Requisitions,* placing *Job Postings* on the web, communicating with candidates and hiring managers, receiving and processing *Job Applications,* screening and scheduling candidates, and enrolling newly hired employees into a company's payroll or *HRIS.* ATS's are sometimes referred to as *Candidate Management Systems.*

Average Length of Service Data indicating the average amount of time employees remain in jobs or organizations after they have been hired. Average Length of Service is commonly used as a *Criterion* for *Validating* assessments designed to increase *Retention.*

Background Investigations A term that describes assessment methods that are used to uncover and/or verify a variety of different types of information about a job candidate. Background Investigations are important because they can help organizations to avoid making *Catastrophic Hires* and can help reduce the risk of employee theft and other *Counterproductive Work Behaviors.* Background investigations usually consist of *Credit Checks, Criminal Record Checks,* verification of employment and educational information, and checks of motor vehicle records.

BARS (Behaviorally Anchored Rating Scales) Rating method typically used with *Structured Interviews* or *Performance Ratings* to facilitate collection of accurate evaluations of a candidate or employee's attributes or behavior. BARS provide behavioral definitions associated with different rating values used to evaluate a person's attributes or performance. For example, customer service ratings might indicate that an employee should receive a 1 if he or she "avoids talking to customers," a 2 if he "asks customers if they have any questions," and a 3 if she "proactively engages customers in conversations about products and services and asks whether they have any specific questions." By associating specific, observable behaviors with different ratings, BARS help reduce subjectivity across raters when making evaluations.

Basic Skills Test Assessments of competencies in "basic skills" that are widely required in training and employment settings (e.g., reading, writing, simple mathematics).

Behavioral Assessments Assessments for which the results are interpreted based on insight they provide into the likely future job behaviors of candidates. Typical behavioral assessments include *Talent Measures* such as ability tests, personality measures, and situational judgment measures. See also *Direct Assessments*.

Behavioral Interview/Behaviorally Based Interview A type of *Structured Interview* in which candidates are asked questions about work-related behaviors they have displayed in the past. The rationale behind this interviewing method is that past behaviors are often the best predictor of future behaviors. Behavioral Interviews are most often created by collecting *Critical Incidents* from job incumbents that describe how employees have either effectively or ineffectively responded to specific situations related to different *Competencies*. This information is then used to create questions and *Behavioral Anchored Rating Scales* that can be used to evaluate each question.

BFOQ (Bona Fide Occupational Qualification) A candidate characteristic that can provide a legitimate reason for excluding a person from consideration for a job, even if it results in creating adverse impact. For instance, being a male is likely to be a BFOQ for the job of men's room attendant since being male is a key job requirement.

Big Five Personality Traits See *Five Factor Personality Model*.

Biodata A *Self-Report Measure* that evaluates an applicant's suitability for a job based on past experiences. Biodata can be used to assess aspects of a candidate's *Personality, Knowledge, Ability, Skills,* or *Interests*.

Branching A form of assessment design wherein the content of the assessment changes depending on how candidates respond to different assessment questions. For example, candidates might be asked a general question about whether they had knowledge of a certain type of software. Those candidates who answered "yes" would then be asked more specific questions about the software, while candidates who answered "no" would be directed to the next phase of the assessment. Branching is an efficient form of assessment design. However, it can be difficult to develop effective branching assessments, and as a result branching is found in relatively few assessment systems. *Computer Adaptive Testing* represents a highly sophisticated form of assessment branching technology.

Broad Assessment An assessment designed to measure very general, high-level attributes of a candidate that are assumed to influence performance across a wide range of jobs. Assessments that are designed to measure things such as *General Ability* and the *Five Factor Model* personality traits are examples of broad assessments.

Call Center Assessment An assessment *Simulation* that collects information from candidates by having them talk with a live call center representative. Candidates typically access these systems using an 800 number. Candidate data is usually collected either by having the call center representative ask specific interview or test questions or by conducting job *Simulation* exercises (e.g., having the call center representative pretend to be an angry customer to see how the candidate manages the situation).

Candidate   An individual being considered for possible employment in a job or organization. The terms Candidate and *Applicant* tend to be used somewhat interchangeably, but technically, a candidate is someone the company is considering hiring, while an *Applicant* is someone who has expressed interest in being hired. As a result, not all candidates are necessarily *Applicants* and vice versa (see for example, *Passive Candidates*).

Candidate Management System   See also *Applicant Tracking System (ATS)*. An application that allows staffing professionals to manage information obtained from job applicants and use this information for administrative purposes. While these systems perform many of the same functions as an *ATS,* they often have much more limited functionality. A common difference between candidate management systems and ATSs is whether they are set up to transfer data to an organization's *HRIS*. ATSs almost always provide this functionality, while many candidate management systems do not.

Candidate Pool   A group of applicants being considered for potential employment in a job or organization. See also *Applicant Pool.*

Candidate Profiles   Information that summarizes an individual's suitability for a job relative to specific job requirements. Candidate Profiles often contain a graphical representation of a candidate's traits and compare them to the ideal range of these traits in terms of effective job performance. Many Candidate Profiles also contain detailed narrative information about a candidate's strengths and weaknesses relative to job performance requirements.

Career Portal/Career Site   The careers section of a corporation's website. There is a wide range of functions and services associated with these portals. Portals often include detailed information about a company's values, information, and testimonials from current employees, tools to help search and apply for jobs, and links to assessments used to evaluate job candidates.

Career Interest Inventory   An assessment that focuses on helping people identify careers that match their interests. These assessments are useful for helping recent graduates or persons contemplating a career change to understand the type of work that is of intrinsic interest to them. These inventories are usually used for outplacement and career development and are not commonly used for employee selection.

Catastrophic Hire   A staffing decision that results in the hiring of an employee who later does something that significantly damages a company's profitability, reputation, and/or morale. The results of a Catastrophic Hire include things such as workplace violence, sexual assault, fraudulent insurance claims, damage to company property, or large-scale theft.

Civil Rights Act of 1964   A key piece of legislation that places severe restrictions on the use of selection methods and assessments that may *adversely impact* candidates from certain demographic groups. This act led to the creation of the U.S. Government *Equal Employment Opportunity Commission (EEOC).*

Client Norming   See *Local Norming*.

Classical Test Theory   A collection of statistical methods used to guide the design of most *Behavioral Assessments*. Assessments designed based on *Classical Test Theory* are often compared to assessments that utilize more complex *Psychometric* methods such as *Computer Adaptive Testing* and *Neural Networks*.

Closed-Loop Validation/Closed-Loop Optimization   *Criteria Validation* and assessment scoring methods that use data collected from employees after they are hired to optimize the relationships between pre-hire assessment data and post-hire performance criteria.

Cognitive Abilities   Unique mental skills and capabilities associated with solving problems and processing data. Examples include the ability to make decisions under time pressure, ability to solve problems through the use of logic and reasoning, and the ability to track multiple types of information simultaneously (multi-tasking).

Compensatory Scoring   An approach to personnel assessment that allows high scores in one or more areas to be counterbalanced with low scores in another area. Also known as "Additive Scoring." Compensatory Scoring is simple to develop and is therefore widely used. However, it creates a risk that a candidate may be hired despite having significant limitation in a certain area. For example, a compensatory scoring method based on assessments of math skills and customer service skills might result in hiring a person with very strong math skills, even though he lacked customer service skills. See also *Non-Compensatory Scoring*.

Competency/Competencies   The term Competency is often used in a variety of different ways. However, the most common definition defines a competency as a set of behaviors that influence organizational performance. For example, "building relationships" and "planning and organizing" are competencies that influence performance in many jobs.

Competency Model   A set of *Competencies* that have been shown through *Job Analysis* to be necessary to successful performance within a specific job or *Job Family*.

Competency-Based Assessments   Assessments designed around the behaviors found in a competency model instead of around more "psychological" attributes such as *Personality Traits* or *Abilities*. Competency-based assessments often integrate multiple types of assessment methodologies in order to predict the various behaviors defined by the competencies.

Competency-Based Reports   Much like a *Candidate Profile*, these are reports that describe a candidate's suitability for a specific job based on the likelihood that he or she will display the *Competencies* that influence performance for that job.

Computer Adaptive Testing (CAT)   A sophisticated method of assessment *Branching* that provides a highly efficient means to measure candidate attributes. CAT assessments are relatively difficult to develop and are almost exclusively used to measure *Knowledge, Skills, and Ability,* although theoretically CAT could be used to measure other traits such as *Personality* and *Motives.* CAT uses *Item Response Theory* to create tests wherein the questions people are asked change based on their performance on previous questions. For example, if you answer a question correctly you are given a more difficult question, but if you answer the question incorrectly then you are given an easier question. The Branching processes actually used by CAT assessments are usually much more complex than this simple illustration.

Concurrent Validation/Concurrent Validity   A type of *Criteria Validation* study in which current employees are asked to take a staffing assessment. The employees' scores on the assessment are then *Correlated* with measures of their job performance to explore the strength of the relationship between assessment scores and job performance.

Construct Validation/Construct Validity   A validation process that examines whether an assessment accurately measures the underlying candidate attributes it is designed to measure (e.g., determining whether an assessment designed to assess emotional stability truly does assess emotional stability). The demonstration of construct validity requires the collection of several types of evidence that reflect the relationships among the assessment, other types of assessments, and measures of different types of job performance. Construct validation is of considerable interest to assessment developers and scientists who wish to understand how employee attributes relate to job performance. It is typically of less interest to business leaders, who simply wish to hire more effective employees and are less concerned about the theoretical reasons that explain why they are more effective. Such leaders tend to focus far more on *Content Validity* and *Criteria Validity.*

Content Validation/Content Validity   Process for demonstrating the relevance of an assessment instrument by rationally demonstrating that performance of the job is related to attributes the assessment measures or to behaviors that the instrument has been shown to predict. Content validation is a legally defensible method for establishing job relevance of an assessment tool provided that it is done using rigorous *Job Analysis* techniques.

Correlation/Correlation Coefficient   Correlation refers to the degree to which changes in one variable are associated with changes in another (e.g., whether changes in assessment scores are associated with changes in job performance). A Correlation Coefficient is a statistic that indicates the degree to which two mathematical variables relate to each other (e.g., the relationship between an assessment score and a measure of job performance, or the relationship between two different assessment scores). Correlation coefficients can range from -1 to 1. A positive correlation means that as one variable goes up, the other also tends to increase. A negative correlation means that as one variable goes up, the other tends to go down. 0 indicates no relationship. A correlation of 1 indicates a direct positive relationship between the two variables such that as one goes up, the other always goes up by the same relative amount. Correlations at or near 1 are unrealistic in an assessment setting. Most effective assessments show correlations with job performance in the range from .10 to .50, depending on the kinds of assessments and measures of job performance being used. Correlation does not imply causation. For example, a high test score may be indicative of high performance, but the test score itself does not actually cause high job performance. The correlation between the test score and performance is actually caused by some underlying candidate attributes that influence both a person's score on the test and his or her performance on the job.

Cost per Hire   The amount of money that must be spent to make each hiring decision. It can be computed using this simple formula: Cost per Hire = Recruiting Costs/ Number of Positions Filled.

Counterproductive Work Behavior   Work-related behaviors that are damaging to the employer. The term usually refers to highly incompetent or intentionally damaging behaviors such as theft, fraud, absenteeism, violence, sexual harassment, or on-the-job substance abuse that negatively affect organizational performance.

Covert Integrity Test   A personality-based assessment designed to predict whether an applicant will engage in *Counterproductive Work Behaviors.* Covert tests disguise the fact that they are assessing a candidate's propensity to engage in these types of behaviors. This is in contrast to *Overt Integrity Tests* that do not try to disguise the fact that they are measuring these things.

Credit Check   An assessment that evaluates candidates based on an evaluation of their financial credit history.

Criminal Record Check   An assessment that evaluates candidates based on an investigation of their criminal history (e.g., prior convictions for criminal offenses).

Criterion/Criteria   A measure of job performance used to calculate the *Criteria Validity* of a staffing assessment. Criteria are usually considered to fall into two categories: subjective criteria such as supervisor ratings of performance and objective criteria such as tenure, attendance, or productivity. Assuming they are appropriately collected (see *Performance Ratings*), subjective criteria usually provide the best information about the actual employee behaviors that are predicted by assessments, and as such tend to be more useful for understanding the accuracy of an assessment for predicting employee performance. In contrast, objective criteria tend to be tied more closely to financial outcomes associated with better employee selection, and as a result are often more useful for understanding the financial *Utility* gained by using an assessment.

Criteria Validity/Criteria Validation Study   A statistical technique used to demonstrate how well a staffing assessment predicts job performance. This technique usually involves the correlation of assessment scores of applicants (*Predictive Validation Study*) or existing employees (*Concurrent Validation Study*) with subjective *Criteria,* such as supervisory measures of job performance gathered using a *Performance Rating Form,* or objective criteria, such as attendance, sales productivity, or tenure. Criteria validity provides very strong evidence of an assessment instrument's *Job Relevance.*

Cronbach's Alpha   See *Reliability.*

Custom Interview Guides   A set of interview questions and associated rating scales that are created based on the results of data collected earlier in the staffing assessment process.

Some online staffing assessment systems have functionality that generates a set of interview questions aimed at providing staffing personnel with the opportunity to probe potential weak areas identified by earlier assessments. Thus, each interview guide (e.g., set of interview questions) is customized to help gather information needed to gain a more complete understanding of each particular candidate's potential strengths and weaknesses.

Customized Assessments   Unlike *Off-the-Shelf Assessments,* Customized Assessments are created for a specific job in a specific company. Customized assessments are typically more valid and, in some cases, shorter than off-the-shelf tests. Customizing an assessment usually involves creating a tailored *Competency Model* and assessment scoring algorithm based on a company-specific *Job Analysis* and *Validation* study. See also *Tailored Assessments.*

Culture/Culture Fit   The match between the values and interests of an individual and the general work environment, norms, and career opportunities found in a company or functional work area of that company. While culture fit does not always predict an applicant's ability to perform a job, it can be used to effectively predict less tangible attitudinal outcomes such as job satisfaction, organizational commitment, and turnover.

Culture and Work Environment Fit Inventories   Assessments created to measure cultural fit between an applicant and an employer. Many of these are based on the use of scales that measure personality, work values, and work preferences.

Cut-Off Score/Cut Score   The minimum score on a staffing assessment measure (or combination of measures) that will allow an applicant to move on in the selection process. Many assessments provide descriptive information about candidates, but do not provide strict cut-off scores. Use of cut scores is usually associated with assessments designed to support *High Volume Staffing* or assessments that measure minimum qualifications (see *Knock-Out Questions*). There are many variables that must be considered when setting a cut-off score including the size and quality of the *Applicant Pool,* the number of openings that must be filled, and the quality of the hires desired by the organization. Where a cut-off score is set can also influence whether an assessment displays *Adverse Impact.*

Dashboard Reporting   A feature found in many *Assessment Platforms* that provides hiring decision makers with comprehensive assessment information about multiple applicants. Most dashboard systems utilize layered reporting in which high-level information about multiple candidates is presented in initial screens that provide access to other screens containing more detailed information about specific candidates.

Direct Assessments   Assessments wherein the results are interpreted directly, regardless of their actual association with future job performance behaviors. Assessments commonly used as Direct Assessments include drug screens, qualifications questionnaires, and background investigations. See also *Behavioral Assessments.*

Diversity   A term used to refer to the demographic, ethnic, and cultural makeup of a company's workforce or applicant population. Most companies strive to have the diversity of their workforce reflect the diversity of their community and customers. Staffing assessments that display *Adverse Impact* can decrease a company's diversity and may be illegal if they are not *Job Relevant*.

DOT (*Dictionary of Occupational Titles*)   A comprehensive listing of different types of jobs and career categories found in the U.S. economy. The DOT was created and maintained by the U.S. government. It has been replaced by a new listing of jobs created by the U.S. government called the *O*Net*.

Drug Screen   Refers to a variety of assessment methods that chemically test for the presence of specific drugs in a person's metabolism. See also *Urinalysis*.

Dustbowl Empiricism   A somewhat negative reference toward assessment development techniques that do not pay much attention to *Construct Validity*. The term dates back to the 1930s when several significant assessments were developed by researchers working in the Midwest who relied heavily on *Empirical Methods*.

EEO/Equal Employment Opportunity   The concept that individuals should have equal treatment in all employment-related situations. The term EEO usually refers to legal requirements and guidelines such as those provided by the U.S. government's *Equal Employment Opportunity Commission (EEOC)*.

EEOC/Equal Employment Opportunity Commission   The U.S. government agency responsible for enforcing the *Civil Rights Acts of 1964*, the *Americans with Disabilities Act (ADA)*, and other key pieces of *EEO*-related legislation.

Electronic Recruiting Agents   Web-based applications that allow users to use *Key Word Searches* to automatically scan the web to find resumes of candidates who are qualified for a specific position. Used by recruiters to identify and retrieve information that they can use to make contact with viable job applicants.

Empirical Methods   Refers to approaches to assessment development that focus on using data-intensive methods to develop and score assessments based on maximizing their predictive accuracy, with less emphasis on understanding why they work. An assessment developer who focused solely on empirical methods would only be concerned with *Criteria Validity* and would have little to no interest in *Construct* or *Face Validity*. Empirical methods are a critical part of effective assessment design, but an over-reliance on them can raise criticisms that people may be misled by potential errors in the data and that more attention should be given to understanding what *Attributes* the assessment is actually measuring.

Empirical Validation/Empirical Validity   See also *Criteria Validation*. Refers to various statistical methods for establishing the relationship between an assessment instrument and performance of a specific job. Empirical Validation requires having individuals complete the assessment instrument and then comparing their scores on the instrument to measures of their job performance. Empirical Validation is often considered to provide the strongest evidence for the legal defensibility of an assessment instrument. It also provides the data needed to optimize the scoring of assessments to maximize their predictive accuracy.

Employee Profiling   A method for establishing scoring guidelines for an assessment that relies solely on collecting assessment data from current employees in the organization. The purpose of employee profiling is to identify the characteristics of high-performing employees and then select candidates based on the degree to which they match this profile. A limitation of employee profiling is that it assumes that any characteristics that are shared by current employees are both job-relevant and desirable, which is a highly questionable assumption. By focusing on selecting candidates who "look like" current employees, this method can result in needlessly reducing workforce *Diversity*.

Employment/Employer Brand   The message an organization sends to candidates regarding what the company is like as an employer. Creating effective employment brands is a major component of candidate *Recruiting*. Staffing assessment tools also affect employer brand. If candidates perceive assessments as unpleasant or non-job-relevant, they are likely to be less favorably disposed toward the company as a potential employer.

Face Validity   Reflects the degree to which the content of an assessment tool looks like the actual tasks performed on the job. Assessments with high face validity are not necessarily more effective than other assessments, but they will appear to be more job-relevant. Applicants and hiring managers tend to prefer using measures with high face validity because they "look like things you actually do on the job."

Faking   See *Response Distortion*.

Fit   Term used to refer to the match between the *Attributes* of a candidate and the requirements of a job or organization. See also *Culture Fit*.

Five Factor Personality Model   A widely used model for describing personality that has been shown to relate to performance for a range of jobs. Also called the Big 5, this model contains five broad traits of personality commonly referred to as conscientiousness, extraversion, openness to new experiences, neuroticism, and agreeableness. Of these, conscientious is most often related to job performance. There is considerable debate over the adequacy of the five factor model. However, it has had a major influence on the development of personality assessments, and many personality-based staffing assessments are said to measure one or more of the five factor traits.

General Ability/General Cognitive Ability   General Ability is a broad *Attribute* that reflects how quick and accurate a person is at processing information and solving problems that require the use of logic and reasoning. It is sometimes referred to as "g" and is often considered to be the same thing as general intelligence or IQ. Research has demonstrated that assessments of general intelligence are among the single most effective predictors of performance across a wide range of jobs, particularly those that require rapidly learning new information and solving difficult mental problems.

Hard Skills   Hard Skills is an informal term that refers to specific technical abilities or solid factual knowledge required to do a job. It is sometimes said to reflect "what you know" as opposed to "how you use it," which is more a reflection of *Soft Skills*. For example, the ability to replace a flat tire might be considered to be a "hard skill" for an auto mechanic, while the ability to interact and build effective relationships with auto owners might be considered to be a "soft skill."

High-Volume Staffing   Staffing positions for which there are many openings to fill and many applicants applying for those openings. Entry-level customer service, retail, food service, and call center representative positions are examples of positions that often have high staffing volumes.

Hiring Recommendation   A specific recommendation made by an assessment to help staffing personnel make decisions based on the match between a candidate's assessment results and job performance requirements. Many assessments only provide information about candidates and do not provide specific hiring recommendations. Assessments that do provide hiring recommendations often express them in very simple terms such as "hire" or "do not hire" or by assigning candidates codes such as red for do not hire, yellow for hire with caution, and green for no hiring concerns. See also *Cut-Off Scores.*

HRIS (Human Resource Information System)   Software systems designed to support management of human resource data (e.g., payroll, job title, employee contact information).

Impression Management   See *Response Distortion.*

In-Basket Exercise   A type of *Simulation* that requires candidates to read through materials such as e-mails, client correspondence, financial reports, and memos similar to things that they might receive on the job. The candidate is then asked to formulate strategies, write documents, or take other actions in response to the information and questions contained in the materials. In-basket exercises are typically used for higher-level management and professional jobs. They are usually scored manually, but can also be automated.

Incremental Validity   Refers to the degree to which adding a new assessment to the hiring process will increase the *Validity* of employee selection decisions. If using an additional assessment significantly increases the size of the overall *Validity Coefficient* of a selection process, then this new assessment is said to provide incremental validity over the other assessments in the process. For example, if use of both a personality measure and an ability test more accurately predicted performance than use of either assessment by itself, then these two assessments would be said to provide incremental validity over each other.

Incumbents   A term used to refer to existing employees in a job. For example, a *Concurrent Validation* study requires collecting assessment and performance data from job incumbents.

Integrity Tests   *Self-Report* assessments designed to predict an applicant's propensity to engage in *Counterproductive Work Behaviors.* There are two major types of integrity test, *Covert* and *Overt.* Covert tests disguise the things they are measuring, while overt do not.

Interviews   Assessments whereby candidates are evaluated based on how they answer questions posed to them by a person. Most interviews utilize open-ended questions. See also *Structured Interview, Behavioral Interview,* and *Situational Interview.*

IQ (Intelligence Quotient)   See *General Ability.*

Intelligence Tests   Term often used to refer to *Ability Tests* designed to measure *General Ability.*

Interests   *Attributes* associated with what a person wants to do or the work environment he or she wants to work in. See also *Motivational Fit, Values, Career Interest Inventory,* and *Culture Fit.*

Item   An individual question found on a staffing assessment measure. Most staffing assessments are composed of groups of several items.

Item Response Theory (IRT)   A collection of statistical methods used to guide the design and scoring of assessments. Item Response Theory is primarily used with *Ability* and *Knowledge Tests.* See also *Computer Adaptive Testing.*

IVR (Interactive Voice Recognition) Assessment   Assessments that collect information from candidates using an automated telephone system. Candidates typically access these systems using an 800 number. Candidates answer questions either by using the telephone keypad or by speaking to a computer designed to recognize specific voice responses.

Job Analysis   A systematic process for describing the behaviors that influence performance in a job. The results of Job Analysis can be used to guide development of assessment instruments, as well as to demonstrate the job relevance of existing assessment instruments. Job analysis typically involves spending time observing employees performing the job, interviewing subject-matter experts, and collecting data from job incumbents and supervisors using structured questionnaires or focus groups. Conducting job analysis is a critical step for establishing the job relevance and legal defensibility of an assessment instrument.

Job Application   A paper form or online process used to collect information from individuals interested in being considered as candidates for a specific job. Applications typically collect information such as a candidate's name, address, and work interests. They are often required to include material informing candidates of their legal rights and may also collect information relevant to *EEO* legislation. Job Applications do not necessarily include any assessment content, although many applications do incorporate assessments such as *Pre-Screening Questionnaires* and *Personality Measures.*

Job Board   A website or part of a website that allows job seekers to view available jobs posted by a variety of organizations. Once applicants have identified a job that they are interested in applying for, the Job Board provides them with a way to send job-related information such as a resume to the employer. Some job boards may also ask candidates to complete assessments as part of the application process. Many job boards also have a variety of additional services to help job seekers manage their careers and their ongoing job search process.

Job Family   A grouping of jobs sharing similar characteristics (e.g., a typist, a receptionist, and an administrative assistant could all fall under the clerical job family). Often a single assessment or set of assessments can be effectively applied to help guide selection decisions for all jobs contained within a single job family.

Job Profiling   A method for comparing different jobs to determine whether an assessment tool that predicts performance for one job can be used with another job. It typically involves evaluating job similarity by having subject-matter experts answer a series of questions about whether certain types of tasks are performed in a job, and then comparing this to a similar task profile created for another job. Job Profiling can be used to establish the job relevance and legal defensibility of an assessment tool, although it is not as thorough a method as *Job Analysis*.

Job Posting   A notice advertising a job to candidates. Job Postings can be placed in a wide range of locations, including online on a company's *Career Site* or on a *Job Board*, or as print ads run in newspapers, or placed in store windows.

Job Relevance   Term used to describe whether the *Attributes* measured by an assessment truly influence job performance and/or reflect actual *Job Requirements*. A key factor in evaluating the legal defensibility of an assessment is demonstrating its job relevance.

Job Requirement   See *Requirements*.

Job Requisition   An internal document used in organizations to indicate a hiring need. Most companies do not start recruiting for a job until a Job Requisition has been formally approved.

Job Simulations/Work Samples   An assessment method that requires applicants to perform job tasks that simulate tasks and working conditions found on the actual job, for instance, call center simulations that require applicants to use computer screens similar to those used on the job to enter data from callers and access information needed to answer customer inquiries.

Key Word/Key Word Search   A method of searching resumes or job posting databases that requires the entry of a specific word or string of words. For instance, if searching for an accounting job, a visitor to a job board might enter the Key Word "accounting" into the search field. Some *Candidate Management Systems* and *ATSs* provide companies with highly sophisticated Key Word Search methods for evaluating the quality of applicant resumes.

Kiosks   A technology device that allows applicants to apply for jobs on-site in a company's store, lobby, or other hiring location. Kiosks offer a way for applicants who literally "walked in the door" to apply. They also help with recruiting applicants who might otherwise not have Internet access.

Knockout Questions   Specific questions on an assessment instrument that are used as independent criteria for qualifying or removing candidates for consideration for a position during the *Pre-Screening* phase of the hiring process. For example, a question asking candidates if they can provide eligibility of their right to work in the United States might be used as a Knockout Question. A company might decide that if candidates do not answer "yes" to this question they will no longer be considered for the position, regardless of how they performed on the rest of the assessment. Knockout questions should be used very conservatively and only to assess very clearly defined, highly objective *Requirements.*

Knowledge   A body of information (conceptual, factual, or procedural) that can be applied directly to the performance of specific job-related tasks. For example, knowledge of the Java computer programming language is a type of knowledge relevant to performing certain information technology jobs.

Knowledge and Skills Tests   Tests of skills or job-specific knowledge. Examples include tests to assess a person's ability to use certain software programs or to evaluate the person's understanding of specific technical terminology related to his or her profession (e.g., accounting tests).

KSAOs   KSAO stands for Knowledge, Skills, Abilities, and Other requirements. The phrase KSAO is often used to describe the *Attributes* identified through a *Job Analysis* as being critical for job performance. Information about a job's KSAOs can be used for a wide variety of HR functions, including selection, training and development, performance management, and compensation.

Legally Defensible/Legal Defensibility (as applied to assessments)   Providing sufficient evidence to demonstrate job relevance and appropriate nature of an assessment instrument according to relevant government laws, regulations, and guidelines. See also *Americans with Disabilities Act, Civil Rights Act,* and *EEOC.*

Local Norming   A process whereby the scores of an organization's existing applicants (or in some cases, employees) are analyzed to establish scoring *Norms* for assessments. Local Norming allows a company to identify how candidates' assessment scores compare to the scores of other applicants applying for the same type of job and/or at the same organization. Local Norming is done to maximize the predictive utility of the assessments while maintaining optimal applicant flow. There may be some risks to local norming if it is used as a method for *Employee Profiling.*

Local Scoring   Establishing scoring algorithms for an assessment that are based on an organization's specific employee or candidate population. Creating Local Scoring tends to increase the effectiveness and validity of assessment instruments. It is often a benefit that comes from conducting a *Local Validation* study.

Local Validation   Refers to a *Criteria Validation* study conducted for a specific company or job to statistically compare employee or applicant scores on an assessment instrument with measures of their job performance and/or tenure. Local Validation provides the strongest evidence of the job relevance for an assessment instrument and can be used for *Optimization* of assessment content or scoring based on the unique characteristics of a specific job or organization.

Meta-Analysis   A statistical technique used to demonstrate that an assessment instrument reliably predicts performance across a broad range of jobs. Meta-Analytic data is often used to support the use of *Validity Generalization.*

Motivational Fit   Degree to which a person's interest and preference for working in certain types of jobs and environments match the characteristics and environment associated with a specific position or organization. Motivational Fit is similar to *Culture Fit,* but focuses on a person's match with a specific job, as opposed to his or her match with the broader organization or work group.

Multiple Hurdles   An approach that requires a candidate to pass a series of assessments in order to progress in the selection process. Multiple hurdle assessment processes involve administering assessments at different places in the staffing process. Candidates must pass certain assessments early in the process before they are asked to take additional assessments later in the process, for example, requiring the candidates to pass a *Pre-Screening Questionnaire* before they are allowed to participate in a *Structured Interview.*

Neural Network/Neural Net   Short for "Artificial Neural Network," this refers to a class of statistical methods used to develop scoring algorithms for assessments. The strength of neural nets is their ability to identify and model complex, non-linear patterns and relationships within large data sets. Their main limitations are that they cannot be reliably used with small data sets, they often provide little insight into the reasons why they work, and it may be unclear how well their validity will generalize across different jobs (see *Empirical Methods*).

Non-Compensatory Scoring   A method for making *Hiring Recommendations* based on multiple assessments that works by setting an independent *Cut Score* for each assessment. Candidates are only recommended if their scores are above minimum scores set for each of the assessments. Non-Compensatory Scoring helps to avoid some of the problems associated with *Compensatory Scoring.*

Norms   Databases that can be used to calculate average scores on an assessment for a particular group of candidates or employees. Norms are often used to guide decisions about how to interpret assessment scores. For example, norms would be required to determine whether a candidate's assessment score is above the 50th percentile relative to other candidates applying for similar jobs. Norms can change substantially across different applicant groups, and there is often considerable value in using *Client Norming* to guide selection decisions.

Norm Groups   A group of individuals whose assessment scores are used to calculate *Norms* for an assessment. This process is often called "norming" an assessment. Norm Groups might consist of existing employees, candidates applying for a particular job in an organization, or groups of people all applying for the same type of jobs across several organizations.

Numerical Ability   The ability to interpret numbers, complete mathematical tasks, and identify and understand relationships in numerical data. Numerical Ability is considered to reflect a combination of *General Reasoning Ability* and experience and education related to working with different types of numerical data and using different types of mathematics. There are different aspects of numerical ability reflecting different types of numerical tasks.

Off-the-Shelf Assessments   Assessment tools that can be purchased and implemented with little to no customization. These are typically less expensive than *Tailored Assessments* and can be quickly deployed. Off-the-shelf measures may not be as valid or efficient as *Tailored Assessments* because they are often *Broad Assessments* designed to predict general aspects of performance, rather than focusing on the specific *Attributes* and behaviors that drive success in a particular job.

O*NET (Occupational Information Network)   A comprehensive listing of information about different types of jobs found in the U.S. economy. The O*NET was created by the U.S. government and is now being used instead of the older set of jobs contained in the *DOT.*

Optimization   Processes used to adjust the content or scoring of assessments to maximize the accuracy and effectiveness of the assessment for staffing a specific job or family of jobs. *Local Validation* studies and *Local Norming* can both be used as Optimization methods.

Overt Integrity Test   An *Integrity Test* that asks direct questions regarding *Counterproductive Work Behaviors.* This is in contrast to *Covert Integrity Tests* that mask their true intent.

Parallel Forms   See *Alternate Forms.*

Passive Candidate   See *Active vs. Passive Candidates.*

Percentile Score   A scoring metric that uses *Norms* to indicate how an individual scored on an assessment relative to other test-takers within a relevant applicant pool. For example, if an individual's score is at the 65th percentile, then 65 percent of test-takers in the *Norm Group* scored at or below that individual's score.

Performance Driver   Employee behaviors or attributes that influence superior job performance, as opposed to simply meeting minimum *Requirements.*

Performance Rating Form/Criteria Ratings   A form that is used in a *Criteria Validation* study to measure employee performance. Performance rating forms are typically used by managers or supervisors to rate the performance of subordinates based on a set of specific job-related criteria. The ratings made using these forms are then correlated with an employee's test scores in order to provide statistical evidence of the relationship between the test and job performance. Collecting accurate performance ratings requires use of well-designed forms, clearly communicating to raters that the ratings will only be used for assessment validation and will not be shared with the people being rated or any others in the organization, and providing raters with detailed instruction on how to appropriately measure and evaluate employee behavior.

Performance Variance   Indicates the difference in financial value associated with high- versus low-performing employees. It can be thought of as the difference between the "value of a great hire" and the "cost of a bad hire." The higher the Performance Variance in a job, the more value there is in hiring the best possible candidates for that job. Performance variance is a function of both the value of good performance and the cost of bad performance.

Personnel Selection   The process used to determine whether to make a job offer to a candidate.

Personality/Personality Traits   Attributes that reflect a person's behavioral tendencies, habits, and preferences. Personality is often referred to as a reflection of a person's "typical performance" over time, as opposed to *Abilities* that are said to reflect a person's "maximal performance" when working on specific, mentally or physically challenging tasks for a relatively limited amount of time. See also *Soft Skills* (which primarily reflect personality and *Interests*) and *Hard Skills* (which primarily reflect *Knowledge* and *Abilities*).

Personality Measures   Assessments that measure *Personality Traits*. To avoid the clinical connotations associated with the term "personality," many staffing assessment vendors call their Personality Measures by other names such as "workstyle assessments" or "talent measures."

Point-of-Sales Data   Frequently used to measure performance of employees working in retail settings, Point-of-Sales Data measures how much revenue or product is being attributed to a specific employee. Point-of-Sales Data is collected automatically by cash registers or other sales-tracking technology located in stores. Point-of-Sales Data is a commonly used as *Criteria* for validating assessments used to select retail employees.

Post-Hire Development and Training Systems   Systems created to help new employees adapt to the job and reach maximum performance as quickly as possible. Typically involves providing employees with some form of developmental feedback on their strengths and weaknesses related to the new job. It may also include materials and tasks designed to help orient new employees to the organization and build social relationships with their new co-workers.

Predictor   Any assessment tool that gathers information from applicants in order to predict their subsequent job performance. *Criteria Validation* studies involve statistically comparing Predictor measures (assessments) with *Criteria* measures.

Predictive Validation/Predictive Validity   A *Criterion Related Validation Study* in which applicants are given an assessment during the hiring process to see how well the scores on the assessment predict future job performance or tenure. At some point after the applicants have been hired (usually six months to a year), the applicants' scores on the staffing assessment are correlated with job performance criteria. This is the ideal method for conducting a *Criteria Validation* study. However, because it takes several months or years to complete, it is rarely used. *Concurrent Validation* studies are typically conducted instead.

Pre-Screening   The evaluation of candidate qualifications early on in the staffing process. Pre-Screening is typically used early in the hiring process to rank and/or remove applicants based on their *Requirements* and *Qualifications*. This frees up resources to be focused on gathering more in-depth information from qualified applicants.

Pre-Screening Questionnaire   An assessment tool that asks candidates to answer a set of pre-defined questions about *Requirements and Qualifications*. The term "pre-screening" is used to describe these questionnaires because they are commonly used to eliminate unqualified candidates early on in the selection process.

Proctored   Refers to the administration of assessments in a supervised, controlled setting (e.g., on the job site or at a specific testing center). The purpose of Proctored assessments is to increase assessment security, maintain control over access to assessment content, and ensure that the people completing the assessments are actually the same as the people applying for the job (i.e., to avoid having candidates employ others to complete an assessment for them).

Protected Group/Protected Class   Refers to the groups of individuals protected by *EEO* legislation. The classifications for protected status include race, gender, religion, color, national origin, age, disability, and veteran status. Employers may not refuse to hire or discharge anyone on the basis of the protected classifications unless the decision is based on a clearly defined *BFOQ*.

Psychometrics   Statistical processes and metrics that are used during the construction of assessments. The quality of an assessment can be evaluated based on its psychometric properties. Various psychometric techniques can be used during assessment development to help ensure the assessment's *Reliability* and *Validity*.

Qualified Candidate   A candidate who meets the minimum requirements to be eligible for a position. Regulations set forth by the *EEOC* require that companies track the demographic characteristics of qualified candidates to document potential *Adverse Impact* of selection methods. Specific information is available from the U.S. government that is intended to legally define when a candidate is considered to be a "Qualified Candidate."

Qualifications   Specific candidate characteristics or attributes that influence their eligibility for a job. Common qualifications include previous work experience, educational background, and job-relevant skills and knowledge. See also *Requirements*.

Qualifications Screens   See *Pre-Screening*.

Raw Score   The score a candidate receives on an assessment before it is *Normed* or otherwise transformed. The value of assessment Raw Scores depend solely on how the assessment is designed. For example, the Raw Score on an assessment with ten questions might range from 1 to 10, while the Raw Score on an assessment with thirty items might range from 1 to 30. This means that a 10 on the first assessment would be a perfect score, but a 10 on the second assessment would amount to less than half the total possible points. It is not possible to directly compare Raw Scores from two different assessments unless they are designed exactly alike. Because of this problem with Raw Scores, most assessment *Scoring Algorithms* transform Raw Scores into values that can be compared across different types of assessments such as *Z-Scores, Sten Scores,* or *Percentile Scores*.

Red Flag Response   A response to an *Item* on an assessment instrument that is felt to be highly indicative of a potential candidate weakness. For example, a candidate who marked "yes" in response to a *Pre-Screening Question* asking if he or she had ever been fired from a job might be marked as a Red Flag Response so that hiring managers could more thoroughly explore the reasons why the candidate was fired.

Reliability   Reliability provides a sense of how much differences in assessment scores are due to stable differences between candidates, and how much of these differences are due purely to error of measurement (i.e., chance). There are two broad types of Reliability: internal consistency and test-retest reliability. Internal consistency, sometimes referred to as "alpha" reliability, refers to the degree to which an assessment measures well-defined attributes. If an assessment has low internal consistency, then it is difficult to determine exactly what it is measuring. Test-retest Reliability refers to the extent to which an assessment is consistent when administered to the same individuals on different occasions. Reliability is typically reported in the form of "reliability coefficients" that range from 0 to 1. *Reliability Coefficients* for most well-designed assessments are above .6. Note, it is important not to confuse *Reliability Coefficients* with *Validity Coefficients*.

Reliability Coefficient   See *Reliability*.

Reporting Tools   Tools that allow clients to interpret and use the data collected via an assessment system. Information typically provided by Reporting Tools includes summaries of applicant scores on different assessment tools, number of applicants completing different assessments, passing rates broken down by different applicant characteristics, or *EEO* statistics.

Requirements   Characteristics applicants must possess to be considered for employment in a job. Common Requirements includes minimum levels of previous job experience or education, licensure or citizenship requirements, and willingness to perform specific job tasks (e.g., willingness to work certain shift schedules). Requirements differ from *Qualifications* in the sense that candidates either do or do not meet a job's requirements, but may differ by degrees in terms of the level of *Qualifications* they have for a job. See also *Bona Fide Occupational Requirements (BFOQ)*.

Requisition   See *Job Requisition*.

Response Distortion   Refers to situations in which candidates intentionally modify their responses to an assessment, usually as part of an effort to make them look more desirable for the job. *Self-Report Measures* and *Interviews* that rely on candidates to be open and honest about their preferences, experiences, and capabilities are particularly susceptible to Response Distortion. While a sizeable number of candidates probably engage in some level of Response Distortion, the impact it has on assessment scores and validity is questionable. It can also be controlled to some degree through effective assessment design.

Resume Capture   A technological feature found in many *Candidate Management* and *Applicant Tracking Systems* that allows candidates to upload electronic copies of their resumes into company databases as part of the job application process.

Resume Evaluation Software   A technological feature found in many *Candidate Management* and *Applicant Tracking Systems* that uses *Key Word Search* engines to search through databases containing electronic copies of resumes and evaluate them based on the fit between the text in the resume and the requirements of a job.

Retention   Refers to the length of time employees remain with a company or organization after they have been hired. Many assessments are designed to help increase employee retention. Retention is most effectively measured using statistics that reflect *Average Length of Service.*

ROI (Return on Investment)   Term referring to the financial value associated with the use of an assessment or any other type of organizational action or intervention. ROI is calculated by dividing the dollar value gained by the intervention by the costs associated with the intervention. See also *Utility Analysis.*

Scoring Algorithm   The mathematical formulas used to evaluate a candidate's responses to an assessment tool. Scoring Algorithms can be as simple as summing the number of answers a candidate answers correctly to create an overall score. They can also be as complex as using *Neural Networks* to interpret candidate responses. The data gathered by an assessment will only predict performance if it is interpreted using an appropriate scoring algorithm.

Screening   Used to refer to assessment processes that are designed to remove applicants who do not meet minimum *Requirements* or who lack key job *Qualifications* from the *Candidate Pool.* Screening methods focus on removing candidates who do not fit the job, in contrast to *Selection* methods, which focus on identifying those candidates with the greatest potential for job success. Screening typically occurs early in the hiring process, while *Selection* occurs later in the process.

Selection   Used to refer to assessment processes that are designed to identify applicants in a *Candidate Pool* that possess *Attributes* that suggest they have a high potential of job success. Selection may also include the step of making a job offer to applicants who are considered eligible for hire. Selection methods can be contrasted with *Screening* methods that focus on removing candidates who do not fit the job.

Selection Ratio   Statistic indicating the number of applicants who pass an assessment compared to the number of applicants who complete it. For example, if ten applicants completed an assessment but only five were considered to have passed the assessment, then the Selection Ratio of the assessment would be 50 percent (5 divided by 10 = .50). Selection Ratio depends directly on the *Cut Score* used with an assessment. Although it is not always the case, often the lower the selection ratio is for an assessment, the more likely the assessment is to display *Adverse Impact.*

Self-Report Measures   Assessments that ask applicants to describe themselves by indicating their interests, preferences, beliefs, and history. Examples of self-report questions include things such as asking candidates whether they agree with statements such as "I prefer to work alone," asking candidates about previous life experiences ("Have you ever quit a job?"), or asking them to evaluate their capabilities ("How skilled are you as a project manager?"). Many forms of assessments are Self-Report Measures, including *Personality Measures, Biodata* measures, and *Pre-Screening Questionnaires.* The phrase "self-report measures" is typically used to describe assessments that use multiple-choice questions to collect information from candidates, although technically some types of *Interviews* might also be considered a type of self-report measure.

Self-Select   Term used to describe when candidates voluntarily remove themselves from a job's *Applicant Pool.* Self-selection can be good or bad, depending on the potential of the candidate. One of the benefits of *Realistic Job Previews* is that they can cause candidates who would be a poor fit for a job to self-select out of the staffing process before they are hired. Conversely, one of the problems with using assessments that have poor *Applicant Reactions* is that they may lead to highly qualified candidates self-selecting out of the staffing process before the company has a chance to make a job offer.

Shrink/Shrinkage   Term used to refer to lost inventory or money associated with theft of company property and resources by employees. Shrink statistics may be used in a *Criteria Validation* study to evaluate the impact of an assessment.

Simulations/Job Simulations   Assessment tools that measure candidate skills by having them respond to a variety of situations designed to simulate actual job tasks. Simulations vary from low fidelity paper and pencil descriptions of different job scenarios, to high-fidelity simulations that use actual people to act out the roles of hypothetical customers or co-workers.

Situational Interview   A type of interview that asks candidates to discuss how they might respond in a specific work-related situation. An example is an interviewer asking a candidate "What would you do if you were faced by an irate customer?" These questions differ from *Behavioral Interviews* because behavioral interviews focus on asking questions about specific behaviors that have already occurred, while Situational Interviews focus on presenting hypothetical work-related situations.

Skills   Refers to a person's competence applying knowledge and/or physical capabilities to perform a particular task or closely related set of tasks. Proficiency in a skill usually depends on "natural" talents and abilities as well as experience and practice.

Subject-Matter Expert (SME)   Term used to refer to people who possess in-depth information about the nature of a job, work environment, or employee performance. SMEs play a critical role in providing the information needed to perform a *Job Analysis* or to collect *Performance Ratings* for a *Criteria Validation* study. Typical SMEs involved in these sorts of studies include human resource personnel, hiring managers, and current employees.

Socially Desirable Responding   See *Response Distortion.*

Soft Skills   Soft Skills is an informal term used to describe personal, interpersonal, and attitudinal behaviors that influence job performance. Frequently contrasted with *Hard Skills* that are associated with technical knowledge and performance (e.g., what a person knows), soft skills describe aspects of job performance that reflect how people interact with others and manage themselves when faced with challenges and problems.

Sourcing   The act of finding candidates to apply for a job opening. Sourcing can be active or passive. In active Sourcing recruiters call people in other organizations or search databases and job boards to try to locate qualified candidates. Passive Sourcing involves using resources such as print advertisements, career pages, or job boards to help applicants find out about available job openings and compel them to apply. See also *Active vs. Passive Candidates*.

Spatial Ability   The ability to manipulate mental representations of physical objects and orient oneself in physical space. There are many different aspects of Spatial Ability, including the ability to find one's way using a map, the ability to maintain a sense of orientation and awareness about the things found in one's immediate physical environment, the ability to estimate size and movement of physical objects, and the ability to manipulate mental representations of objects and shapes. Spatial Ability can influence performance in occupations such as airplane pilot, air traffic controller, carpenter, or baseball player.

Staffing   The process of acquiring, deploying, and retaining a workforce of sufficient quantity and quality to create positive impacts on the organization's effectiveness usually emphasizes the processes used to hire new employees into an organization.

Staffing Assessment   Any tool or system that systematically collects and interprets information from job candidates for the purpose of aiding hiring decisions.

Staffing Metrics   Statistical information that provides information about aspects of the staffing process. Some important Staffing Metrics include things such as time to fill positions, selection ratios, assessment validity, and costs per hire.

Stand-Alone Assessment   An assessment or *Assessment Platform* that is designed to function on its own, without being integrated with other assessments or technology platforms.

Sten Score   A transformation of an assessment *Raw Score* similar to a *Z-score*. Sten Scores recalculate assessment scores so that they have an average of 5.5, with most scores ranging between 1 and 10.

Streaming Criteria   *Validation* method whereby performance or tenure data is collected from newly hired employees on an ongoing basis and then fed back into an assessment system as a way to evaluate and improve the effectiveness of assessment tools. The use of Streaming Criteria creates a performance feedback loop that allows an assessment system to be constantly monitored and increased over time. Few assessment vendors currently offer this capability as a standard part of their solutions. However, given its benefits, the use of streaming criteria is likely to increase over the coming years. See also *Closed-Loop Validation*.

Structured Interview   A set of procedures that are used to ensure standardization in the interview process. Structured Interviews involve a set of standardized questions that are asked to all applicants. Applicant responses to these questions are scored using structured rating scales such as *BARS* that provide the ability to demonstrate the relevance of each answer to specific dimensions of job performance. Structured Interviews provide significantly higher levels of validity than do traditional, unstructured interviews. The two most common types of Structured Interviews are *Behavioral Interviews* and *Situational Interviews*.

Success Profile   A poorly defined term that is variably used to refer to *Competency Models, Candidate Profiles,* or *Employee Profiles.*

Talent Measures   *Behavioral assessments* designed to assess enduring candidate attributes related to personality, ability, motives, and/or values. Talent Measures can be thought of as assessments that measure what a person "can do," as opposed to measuring what he or she "has done" or "wants to do." If appropriately designed, talent measures are frequently among the most valid forms of staffing assessments. Talent measures tend to fall into two categories: ability measures that predict "maximal performance" when a candidate is applying his or her full energy and attention toward a specific, well-defined task, and personality or work style measures that predict "typical performance," reflecting how candidates choose to behave when engaged in general activities at work.

Tailored Assessments   Assessment instruments that are designed or customized to predict behaviors that influence performance in a specific job or organization. The customization associated with creating Tailored Assessments can range from building content from scratch to making minor modifications to how the instrument is scored. Tailored assessments are typically more efficient and effective predictors of performance than are more generic *Off-the-Shelf* assessments because they are designed around unique job demands. However, they usually require more time and resources to develop and deploy.

Technology Platform   The technology system used to deliver, score, and manage staffing assessments. Technology Platforms range from simple systems in which tests are e-mailed to applicants to extremely complex systems that incorporate a variety of advanced scoring and candidate management features. See also *Assessment Platform, Candidate Management Systems,* and *Applicant Tracking Systems.*

Tenure   The amount of time someone has spent in a specific job or organization. See also *Average Length of Service* and *Retention.*

Test   Another term for *Assessment.* The term "test" is usually applied when assessments are used to place people into categories as being eligible or ineligible for a job. This is in contrast to assessments that are used to provide descriptive information about candidates, but do not actually classify them as being qualified or unqualified for a job.

Title VII   A key portion of the *Civil Rights Act of 1964* that pertains directly to employee selection.

Transportability   Refers to the degree to which an assessment designed for one job can be shown to be relevant for another job. Transportability is typically based on a combination of *Content Validation* and *Meta-Analytic* evidence. See also *Validity Generalization.*

Turnover   Refers to the percentage of employees who leave a job or organization within a set amount of time. For example, annual turnover in a job is calculated by dividing the number of employees who left the job in a given year by the total number of employees in the job that same year. Turnover is typically divided into two categories: voluntary turnover reflecting employees who choose to quit a job for various reasons and involuntary turnover reflecting employees who were fired or otherwise let go from their jobs. Turnover statistics are often used as *Criteria* for evaluating the impact of assessments on employee *Retention*. However, for statistical reasons, *Average Length of Service* is considered to be a more superior measure of *Retention* than turnover.

Uniform Guidelines on Employee Selection   A set of guidelines and regulations issued by the *EEOC* that describe how to create legally compliant and defensible staffing practices.

Urinalysis/UA   An assessment used to test for past drug use by chemically analyzing a person's urine.

Utility Analysis   Financial methods used to identify the costs, benefits, and *ROI* associated with staffing activities. Utility Analyses help demonstrate the value added by staffing assessment systems by estimating past or projected financial gains captured from using a specific assessment or assessment process.

Validation   The process of establishing the validity of a personnel selection assessment. See also *Validity*.

Validity   The extent to which an assessment truly measures what it is purported to measure. Validity indicates the degree of accuracy of predictions or inferences based on assessment results. There are four primary types of Validity. Each views assessment accuracy from a somewhat different perspective. (See *Content Validity, Construct Validity, Criteria Validity,* and *Face Validity*.)

Validity Coefficient   An index calculated through *Criteria Validation* studies that represents the relationship between *Predictor* and *Criterion* scores. The usefulness of a predictor (i.e., staffing assessment measure) is determined on the basis of the magnitude of its validity coefficient. The Validity Coefficient is actually a *Correlation Coefficient* between *Predictor* and *Criteria* measures used in a *Concurrent* or *Predictive* validity study. Validity coefficients range from 0 (no relationship between predictor and criterion) and 1.0 (perfect relationship between predictor and criterion). Based on the author's experience, in most operational settings a validity coefficient below .10 suggests that a staffing assessment has little usefulness in predicting performance; validity coefficients of between .10 and .20 suggest a staffing assessment has moderate usefulness in predicting job performance; and validity coefficients above .20 suggest that a staffing assessment has high usefulness in predicting performance. However, the overall utility of an assessment does not solely depend on its validity. It also depends on the number of employees being hired, the performance variance of the job, and the size and quality of the candidate pool.

Validity Generalization   Validity Generalization refers to statistical processes used to examine results across multiple *Criteria Validation* studies to evaluate whether there appear to be stable relationships between *Predictors* and *Criteria* that generalize across different work environments and job situations. If the analysis reveals that a constant relationship is present across all situations, then its validity is said to be "generalizable" across these situations (e.g., showing that assessments measuring a certain personality trait reliably predict performance across a variety of sales jobs, no matter what the job or the industry). Validity Generalization arguments are used to support the concept of "transporting" validity evidence across multiple jobs. This means using the results of *Criteria Validation* studies conducted for an assessment in previous jobs as a basis for using the same assessment for new jobs that are considered to be similar in nature to those included in the original studies. (See also *Meta-Analysis.*)

Validation   The process of establishing the validity of a staffing assessment. (See also *Validity.*)

Values   Interests and beliefs that influence what one chooses to do. In an assessment setting, values typically refer to preferences about the kind of work people want to do and the organizational environment they want to work in. Values are often used in assessments designed to predict *Culture Fit* and *Motivational Fit.*

Verbal Ability   The ability to process written and verbal information, write clearly, and interpret and understand written information.

Web Assessment/Web-Based Assessment   Assessments delivered via the Internet.

Work Environment   The place where a job is performed.

Work Environment Fit   The match between a person's interests, skills, and preferences and characteristics of the work environment. Similar to *Motivational Fit.*

Work Samples   *Job Simulation* assessments that require applicants to perform tasks highly similar or identical to tasks actually performed on the job.

Work Style   A term used to describe personality and work values that influence job performance. See *Personality Measures.*

Workforce Analytics   Tools and processes used to evaluate the financial impact that staffing and workforce management actions have on company performance. Data for Workforce Analytics are often provided by *Candidate Management* and *Applicant Tracking Systems* that collect information across multiple candidates, positions, and assessments. Workforce Analytics data is often used to examine the *Utility* and *Validity* of different staffing assessment methods and practices.

Workforce Forecasting   Processes and methods used to forecast future staffing and hiring needs.

Z-Score   A statistical transformation of an assessment score that facilitates comparisons of results gathered from different kinds of assessments or from different applicant pools. Also called "standard scores," Z-Scores are calculated using a type of *Norming* technique that translates scores from any assessment to a standard scale with an average score of 0. Most Z-scores range from approximately -2 to 2.

INDEX

A

Abilities. *See* Candidate attributes

The Academy of Management Journal, 142

Accuracy issue: criticism regarding assessment accuracy, 142–144; effects of faking on, 146–149; "Why Assessments Are More Accurate Than People," 144–146

Action-oriented competencies, 126*t*

Americans with Disabilities Act (ADA), 154–155, 221

Anderson, M., 11–14

Applicant faking: assessment scores affected by, 148–149; failed efforts of, 147–148; low level of, 147; as not the same as lying, 147; research on assessment accuracy and, 146–149; self-awareness versus, 148

Applicants: data faked by, 147–149; drug screens of, 41, 42*fig*, 185; ensuring similar treatment of all, 211–212; investigating, 43*t*, 44*t*, 184–185, 185; professional level job screening of, 228, 230; quality and number of, 182. *See also* Candidates; Hiring process

Assessment accuracy, 94–95

Assessment centers, 49*t*–50*t*, 70

"Assessment Length and Assessment Accuracy," 168–169

Assessment. *See* Staffing assessment

Assessment tools. *See* Staffing assessment tools

Assessment validity. *See* Validity

B

Background investigation information, 222, 223–224

"Baseball and Staffing Assessment," 138–139

Behavioral assessments: direct versus, 72–75; interviewing approach to, 13, 46*t*, 54–55, 186, 223

Behavioral-anchored rating scale (BARS), 186

Behavioral-based questions, 46*t*, 54–55

Behavioral-based structured interviews, 46*t*, 54–55, 186, 223

Binet, A., 158–159

Biodata inventories, 47*t*, 63–64

"A Brief History of Staffing Assessments," 158–159

Brown, M., 1–3

C

Candidate attributes: being smart, reliable, confident, 84, 188–189; competency library on, 125, 126*t*;

271

Hiring decisions: assessments for reducing mistakes in, 237–239; Hurricane Katrina example of poor, 1–3; importance of, 3–4; increasing assessment validity to maximize accuracy of, 175, 176–180; responsibilities for, 213. *See also* Staffing assessments

Hiring managers: assessments for reducing mistakes by, 237–239; decisions by, 1–4, 175, 176–180; giving ultimate responsibility to, 213

Hiring process: assessments as adding too much time to, 167–169; designing assessment for entry-level, 215–227; designing assessment for professional level, 227–235; Internet technology using assessments and, 16*fig*; Internet technology without assessments using, 14–15*fig*, 16; legal issues to consider in, 152–157; "A Place for Everyone," 238, 239–241; prior to Internet staffing technology, 14–15*fig*. *See also* Applicants; Employees; Hiring process

"How to Take a Staffing Assessment: A Message to Candidates," 163, 164–167

Hurricane Katrina, 1–3

I

Integrity and reliability tests, 47*t*, 62–63
Intellectual competencies, 126*t*
Intelligence quota (IQ), 84, 188
Internal consistency method, 85
International Journal of Selection and Assessment, 142
Internet staffing technology: staffing process prior to, 14–15*fig*; staffing process using assessments and, 16*fig*; staffing process without assessments using, 14–15*fig*, 16
Interpersonal competencies, 126*t*

Interviews: behavioral-based questions used in, 46*t*, 54–55; motivational questions used in, 45*t*, 54; on-site assessments and, 230–231; phone, 230; situational questions used in, 45*t*, 54; structured and unstructured, 45*t*, 52–53, 55, 185–186. *See also* Staffing assessment tools

Investigations: assessment through, 184–185; collecting background information, 222, 223–224; credit reports, 44*t*, 51; criminal record checks, 43*t*, 51; general information about, 51–52; reference checking, 43*t*, 51; Social Security verification, 43*t*, 51

J

Jackson, M., 10
Job analysis: content validity established through, 90–91; defining/describing critical employee behaviors through, 120, 124–128; job relevance documented by, 155. *See also* Jobs
Job Analysis and Competency Modeling, 125–126
Job performance: attending to the changing nature of, 127; balancing different types of, 126–127; distinguishing between maximal and typical, 127–128; genetic components of, 22–24, 26; identifying key outcomes of, 119–120, 121–124; impact of assessments over time on, 181*fig*–182; limitations of, 115; linking assessment processes to, 138–139; non-linear relationships between personality and sales, 205*fig*; performance variance of, 28–30; validity coefficient predicting, 27–28. *See also* Jobs
Job performance data: ensuring accurate, 113–114; performance benchmarks as part of, 114–115

Job performance measurements: using right level of performance in, 111–112; statistically predictable, 112–113

Job performance predictions: assessment accuracy of, 142–146; assessment process used for, 119–139; context-specific measures for, 202; difficulties in measuring, 111–115; emotional intelligence fad for, 129–130; how assessments develop, 81*fig*–83; psychometrics used for, 82, 83–86. *See also* Candidates

Job relevance, 154

Job simulations: high-fidelity, 49*t*–50*t*, 70; low-fidelity, 49*t*, 69–70

Job-performance-centric mindset, 131

Jobs: competency modeling for, 125–126; designing assessments for entry-level, 215–227; designing assessments for professional level, 227–235; providing candidates with requirements of, 220–221; providing realistic previews of, 214; staffing the ones that no one wants, 123–124. *See also* Job analysis; Job performance

Journal of Applied Psychology, 142

Journal of Organizational Behavior, 142

Journal of Personality and Social Psychology, 142

K

Knowledge, skill, and ability tests: for ability to learn/solve problems, 190–193; on basic job requirements, 189–190; context-specific, 201–202; "Demographic Group Differences in Assessment Scores," 191–193; general information on, 65–66; integrating context-specific self-reported and, 202; integrating measures of broad, 193–194; past learning achievement

measured by, 49*t*, 67–68; problem-solving aptitude measured by, 48*t*, 66–67

L

Legal issues: 4/5ths (or 80 percent) guidelines to assess risk, 153; job relevance, 154; legal risks of staffing assessments, 152–153; prohibited information, 154–157

Low base rate, 112

Low performance variance, 112

Low reliability performance measures, 112–113

Low-fidelity job simulations, 49*t*, 69–70

M

Maximal job performance, 127–128

Minority populations, 153, 192

Moneyball: (Lewis), 138, 139

Motivation measures, 82, 83–86

Motivational questions, 45*t*, 54

N

"No One is Good at Everything," 121, 122–123

Non-linear scoring: described, 202–203; "Non-Linear Job Performance: More Is Not Always Better," 203–206; relationships between personality and sales performance, 205*fig*

Norming, 195–197

Nunnally, J. C., 86

O

Oakland A's, 138

"Off-the-shelf" assessments, 200

Offensiveness issue: as criticism of assessments, 160–164; "How to Take a Staffing Assessment: A Message to Candidates," 163, 164–167

Staffing assessment design principles: 1: establish multiple assessment hurdles, 210–211; 2: ensure similar treatment of applicants, 211–212; 3: giving hiring managers ultimate hiring responsibility, 213; 4: creating conversation with candidates, 214–215

Staffing assessment effectiveness: choosing what assessments to use to ensure, 109–111, 120, 128–136; determined through validity, 86–109; maximizing cost savings and, 175–176; two basic requirements for, 80

Staffing assessment measurements: "Demographic Group Differences in Assessment Scores," 191–193; diagram showing types of, 20*fig*; genetic components of job performance, 22–24, 26; Raven's Progressive Matrix, 88–90, 89*fig*; what candidates can do, 21–22; of what candidates have done, 20–21; what candidates want to do, 24–25. *See also* Candidate attributes; Self-report measures

Staffing assessment methods: 1: no standardized assessments, 183; 2: self-report pre-screening questionnaires, 184; 3: applicant investigations, 184–185; 4: structured interviews, 185–186; 5: broad self-report and situational judgment measures, 47*t*, 49*t*, 56–65, 69–70, 184, 186–189; 6: broad knowledge and skills tests, 48*t*, 49*t*, 65–68, 189–190; 7: broad ability tests, 190–193; 8: integrating broad, knowledge, skills, and ability tests to predict performance, 193–194; 9: localized scoring to accurately interpret candidate responses, 194–199; 10: context-specific self-report measures, 199–201; 11: context-specific knowledge, skills, and ability tests, 201–202; 12: integrating context-specific

self-report, knowledge, skills, and ability tests, 202; 13: advanced, non-linear scoring, 202–206; balancing two competing objectives when designing, 175–176; determining which one to use, 206–207; incrementally improving accuracy/efficiency of hiring decision, 176–180; "The Operational Impact of Assessments," 177, 180–183. *See also* Staffing assessment selection

Staffing assessment process: four general steps in, 119–120; linking job performance and, 138–139; step 1: identify key performance outcomes, 119–120, 121–124; step 2: use job analysis to define/describe critical employee behaviors, 120, 124–128; step 3: choose an effective assessment, 120, 128–136; step 4: appropriately collecting and interpreting assessment data, 120d, 136–139

Staffing assessment selection: job-performance-centric mindset during, 129, 131; operational requirements considered during, 134–136; questions to ask during process of, 129; systematic process to, 128–129; tips on vendors to considers during, 131–134; validity and reliability issues of, 109–111. *See also* Staffing assessment methods

Staffing assessment tools: credit reports, 44*t*, 51; criminal record checks, 43*t*, 51; drug screens, 41, 42*t*, 185; electronic recruiting agents, 44*t*, 56, 228; failure to understand or value, 4; knowledge, skill, and ability tests, 48*t*, 49*t*, 65–68, 189–193, 201–202; online assessment, 230; physical ability tests, 41, 42*t*; poor-quality or inappropriate use of, 5; post-hire on-boarding feedback, 231; reference checking, 43*t*, 51; resume screens, 44*t*, 45*t*, 55–56; situational measures, 49*t*–50*t*, 69–72; Social Security verification, 43*t*, 51; sourcing, 228; verification, 231. *See also* Interviews; Self-report measures

Staffing assessment vendors: emotional intelligence fad followed by, some, 129–130; employee profiling technique used by, 131; providing data on validity, 110; tips on selecting, 131–134

Staffing assessments: accuracy of, 94–95; as difference between staffing success and failure, 14–16*fig*; financial value of, 34–36; how job performance is predicted using, 81*fig*–83; impact on job performance over time, 181*fig*–182; online, 230; reducing hiring mistaking through, 237–239; seven basic topics of, 6–7; staffing process using Internet technology and, 16*fig*; staffing process using Internet technology without, 14–15*fig*, 16; tracking and improving performance of, 137–138; two fundamental reasons for disregard of, 4–5; validity of, 27–28, 84; value under different conditions, 32*fig*–33; what is measured?, 20*fig*–25; when are they useful?, 27–36; why do they work?, 25–27, 36. *See also* Hiring decisions

Staffing failure: FEMA, 1–3; story of, 9–11

Staffing Jobs No One Wants, 123–124

Staffing success story, 11–14

Structured interviews: advantages and disadvantages of, 52–53, 185–186; behavioral-based, 186; different approaches to conducting, 55; maximizing time spent with candidates using, 185–186; measurements gained through, 45*t*

Swanson, I., 9–11

T

Tarnehan, R., 12–14

Telephone interviews, 230

Test-retest method, 85

Time issues: "Assessment Length and Assessment Accuracy," 168–169; assessments as taking too much time, 167–168, 169

"Turbo-charging" assessment, 202–206

Typical job performance, 127–128

U

Unfairness issue: "A Brief History of Staffing Assessments," 158–159; as criticism of assessments, 157, 158, 160; "The Cult of Personality and the Realities of Staffing," 157–158

Unstructured interviews, 45*t*, 53

U.S. Federal Emergency Management Association (FEMA), 1–3

V

Validity: case study on estimating, 99–102, 103, 108–109; construct, 96–99; content, 90–91, 98–99, 104*t*–107*t*, 103, 110, 133–134; criteria, 88–90, 91–96, 104*t*–107*t*, 108–109, 110, 132; described, 27–28, 85; determining assessment efficiency through, 86–87; face, 87–90, 102, 104*t*–107*t*, 110; maximizing hiring accuracy through increasing assessment, 175, 176–180; psychometrics and concept of, 84

Validity case study: content validity role in, 103; criteria validity role in, 108–109; Cross-cultural Qualifications Screen, 99–100, 104*t*–105*t*; Cultural Agility Behavioral Interview Guide, 100, 105*t*; Cultural Empathy Personality Measure, 101, 106*t*; face validity role in, 102; operational resources, 104*t*–107*t*; Spanish Language

ABOUT THE AUTHOR

Dr. Steven T. Hunt has helped design and deploy staffing assessment processes that have supported hundreds of thousands of hiring decisions for positions ranging from entry-level staff to senior-level executives. He has worked with a variety of automated staffing tools and methods, including applicant tracking systems, pre-screening questionnaires, personality measures, ability tests, culture fit measures, and interactive job simulations. Although much of his assessment work leverages web-based technology, he has also developed and utilized a variety of in-person assessments for leadership evaluation and coaching using techniques such as structured interviewing, role-play simulations, and group-problem-solving tasks. Emphasizing the alignment of staffing methods with other strategic human resource practices, Dr. Hunt has also assisted companies with performance development, job analysis and design, talent management, leadership coaching, and succession planning. Dr. Hunt has worked with companies in the United States, Europe, and South America, ranging from members of the Fortune 100 to small non-profit organizations. His work experience spans a range of industries, including retail, manufacturing, dining, information technology, health care, hospitality, and public organizations.

Dr. Hunt received a bachelor's degree in applied mathematics and psychology from the University of California at San Diego, and master's and Ph.D. in industrial-organizational psychology from The Ohio State University. He is also certified as a Strategic Professional of Human Resources (SPHR) by the Society of Human Resource Management. Dr. Hunt is an active author and speaker, conducting research, writing, and presenting on a variety of topics related to strategic human resource practices. His work has appeared in both the academic and practitioner press, including *Personnel Psychology,* the *International Journal of Selection and Assessment,* the *Journal of Corporate Recruiting Leadership, Workforce* magazine, the Society of Human Resource Management White Papers, the Electronic Recruiting Exchange (ERE), and *The Wall Street Journal.* Dr. Hunt is a member of the Society for Industrial Organizational Psychology, the Society for Human Resource Management, the Academy of Management, and the American Psychological Association.

Pfeiffer Publications Guide

This guide is designed to familiarize you with the various types of Pfeiffer publications. The formats section describes the various types of products that we publish; the methodologies section describes the many different ways that content might be provided within a product. We also provide a list of the topic areas in which we publish.

FORMATS

In addition to its extensive book-publishing program, Pfeiffer offers content in an array of formats, from fieldbooks for the practitioner to complete, ready-to-use training packages that support group learning.

FIELDBOOK Designed to provide information and guidance to practitioners in the midst of action. Most fieldbooks are companions to another, sometimes earlier, work, from which its ideas are derived; the fieldbook makes practical what was theoretical in the original text. Fieldbooks can certainly be read from cover to cover. More likely, though, you'll find yourself bouncing around following a particular theme, or dipping in as the mood, and the situation, dictate.

HANDBOOK A contributed volume of work on a single topic, comprising an eclectic mix of ideas, case studies, and best practices sourced by practitioners and experts in the field.

An editor or team of editors usually is appointed to seek out contributors and to evaluate content for relevance to the topic. Think of a handbook not as a ready-to-eat meal, but as a cookbook of ingredients that enables you to create the most fitting experience for the occasion.

RESOURCE Materials designed to support group learning. They come in many forms: a complete, ready-to-use exercise (such as a game); a comprehensive resource on one topic (such as conflict management) containing a variety of methods and approaches; or a collection of like-minded activities (such as icebreakers) on multiple subjects and situations.

TRAINING PACKAGE An entire, ready-to-use learning program that focuses on a particular topic or skill. All packages comprise a guide for the facilitator/trainer and a workbook for the participants. Some packages are supported with additional media—such as video—or learning aids, instruments, or other devices to help participants understand concepts or practice and develop skills.

- *Facilitator/trainer's guide* Contains an introduction to the program, advice on how to organize and facilitate the learning event, and step-by-step instructor notes. The guide also contains copies of presentation materials—handouts, presentations, and overhead designs, for example—used in the program.

- *Participant's workbook* Contains exercises and reading materials that support the learning goal and serves as a valuable reference and support guide for participants in the weeks and months that follow the learning event. Typically, each participant will require his or her own workbook.

ELECTRONIC CD-ROMs and web-based products transform static Pfeiffer content into dynamic, interactive experiences. Designed to take advantage of the searchability, automation, and ease-of-use that technology provides, our e-products bring convenience and immediate accessibility to your workspace.

METHODOLOGIES

CASE STUDY A presentation, in narrative form, of an actual event that has occurred inside an organization. Case studies are not prescriptive, nor are they used to prove a point; they are designed to develop critical analysis and decision-making skills. A case study has a specific time frame, specifies a sequence of events, is narrative in structure, and contains a plot structure—an issue (what should be/have been done?). Use case studies when the goal is to enable participants to apply previously learned theories to the circumstances in the case, decide what is pertinent, identify the real issues, decide what should have been done, and develop a plan of action.

ENERGIZER A short activity that develops readiness for the next session or learning event. Energizers are most commonly used after a break or lunch to stimulate or refocus the group. Many involve some form of physical activity, so they are a useful way to counter post-lunch lethargy. Other uses include transitioning from one topic to another, where "mental" distancing is important.

EXPERIENTIAL LEARNING ACTIVITY (ELA) A facilitator-led intervention that moves participants through the learning cycle from experience to application (also known as a Structured Experience). ELAs are carefully thought-out designs in which there is a definite learning purpose and intended outcome. Each step—everything that participants do during the activity—facilitates the accomplishment of the stated goal. Each ELA includes complete instructions for facilitating the intervention and a clear statement of goals, suggested group size and timing, materials required, an explanation of the process, and, where appropriate, possible variations to the activity. (For more detail on Experiential Learning Activities, see the Introduction to the *Reference Guide to Handbooks and Annuals*, 1999 edition, Pfeiffer, San Francisco.)

GAME A group activity that has the purpose of fostering team spirit and togetherness in addition to the achievement of a pre-stated goal. Usually contrived—undertaking a desert expedition, for example—this type of learning method offers an engaging means for participants to demonstrate and practice business and interpersonal skills. Games are effective for team building and personal development mainly because the goal is subordinate to the process—the means through which participants reach decisions, collaborate, communicate, and generate trust and understanding. Games often engage teams in "friendly" competition.

ICEBREAKER A (usually) short activity designed to help participants overcome initial anxiety in a training session and/or to acquaint the participants with one another. An icebreaker can be a fun activity or can be tied to specific topics or training goals. While a useful tool in itself, the icebreaker comes into its own in situations where tension or resistance exists within a group.

INSTRUMENT A device used to assess, appraise, evaluate, describe, classify, and summarize various aspects of human behavior. The term used to describe an instrument depends primarily on its format and purpose. These terms include survey, questionnaire, inventory, diagnostic, survey, and poll. Some uses of instruments include providing instrumental feedback to group members, studying here-and-now processes or functioning within a group, manipulating group composition, and evaluating outcomes of training and other interventions.

Instruments are popular in the training and HR field because, in general, more growth can occur if an individual is provided with a method for focusing specifically on his or her own behavior. Instruments also are used to obtain information that will serve as a basis for change and to assist in workforce planning efforts.

Paper-and-pencil tests still dominate the instrument landscape with a typical package comprising a facilitator's guide, which offers advice on administering the instrument and interpreting the collected data, and an initial set of instruments. Additional instruments are available separately. Pfeiffer, though, is investing heavily in e-instruments. Electronic instrumentation provides effortless distribution and, for larger groups particularly, offers advantages over paper-and-pencil tests in the time it takes to analyze data and provide feedback.

LECTURETTE A short talk that provides an explanation of a principle, model, or process that is pertinent to the participants' current learning needs. A lecturette is intended to establish a common language bond between the trainer and the participants by providing a mutual frame of reference. Use a lecturette as an introduction to a group activity or event, as an interjection during an event, or as a handout.

MODEL A graphic depiction of a system or process and the relationship among its elements. Models provide a frame of reference and something more tangible, and more easily remembered, than a verbal explanation. They also give participants something to "go on," enabling them to track their own progress as they experience the dynamics, processes, and relationships being depicted in the model.

ROLE PLAY A technique in which people assume a role in a situation/scenario: a customer service rep in an angry-customer exchange, for example. The way in which the role is approached is then discussed and feedback is offered. The role play is often repeated using a different approach and/or incorporating changes made based on feedback received. In other words, role playing is a spontaneous interaction involving realistic behavior under artificial (and safe) conditions.

SIMULATION A methodology for understanding the interrelationships among components of a system or process. Simulations differ from games in that they test or use a model that depicts or mirrors some aspect of reality in form, if not necessarily in content. Learning occurs by studying the effects of change on one or more factors of the model. Simulations are commonly used to test hypotheses about what happens in a system—often referred to as "what if?" analysis—or to examine best-case/worst-case scenarios.

THEORY A presentation of an idea from a conjectural perspective. Theories are useful because they encourage us to examine behavior and phenomena through a different lens.

TOPICS

The twin goals of providing effective and practical solutions for workforce training and organization development and meeting the educational needs of training and human resource professionals shape Pfeiffer's publishing program. Core topics include the following:

    Leadership & Management

    Communication & Presentation

    Coaching & Mentoring

    Training & Development

    E-Learning

    Teams & Collaboration

    OD & Strategic Planning

    Human Resources

    Consulting

What will you find on pfeiffer.com?

- The best in workplace performance solutions for training and HR professionals

- Downloadable training tools, exercises, and content

- Web-exclusive offers

- Training tips, articles, and news

- Seamless on-line ordering

- Author guidelines, information on becoming a Pfeiffer Affiliate, and much more

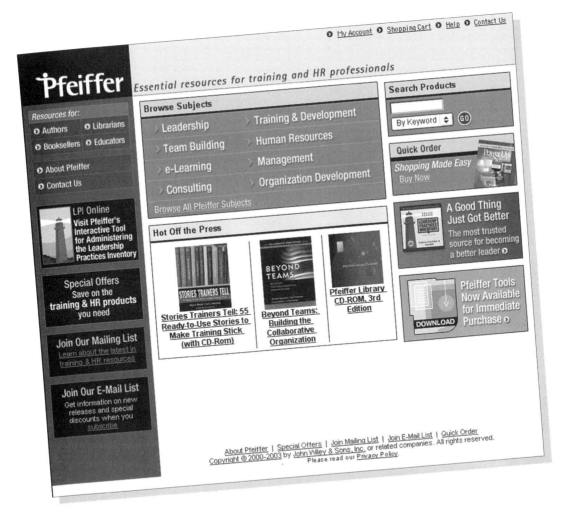

Discover more at www.pfeiffer.com